Tony Hawks is a writer and [illegible] ributions on TV (*Have I Got News Fo* [illegible] on radio (*Just A Minute, I'm Sorry I* [illegible] *iz*). This is his second book. If you ha [illegible] ly urges you to purchase his first – [illegible] – a surreal adventure prompted by a £100 bet.

Unlike most authors, Tony has singularly failed to settle down and live in the country with a wife and four children. This, however, is his ambition.

To Grigore, Dina, Adrian and Elena

PLAYING THE MOLDOVANS AT TENNIS

TONY HAWKS

EBURY PRESS

First published in Great Britain in 2000

1 3 5 7 9 10 8 6 4 2

Ebury Press
Random House, 20 Vauxhall Bridge Road, London SW1V 2SA

Random House Australia Pty Limited
20 Alfred Street, Milsons Point, Sydney, New South Wales 2061, Australia

Random House New Zealand Limited
18 Poland Road, Glenfield, Auckland 10, New Zealand

Random House (Pty) Limited
Endulini, 5A Jubilee Road, Parktown 2193, South Africa

The Random House Group. Limited Reg. No. 954009
www.randomhouse.co.uk

ISBN 0 09 186790 8

Cover design by Push, London

Sky supplied by Telegraph Colour Library

Photography by Tony Hawks and Tim "taffy" Goffe

A CIP catalogue record for this book is available from the British Library

Typeset by SX Composing DTP, Rayleigh, Essex
Printed and bound in Great Britain by Biddles, Guildford

Papers used by Ebury Press are natural, recyclable products made from wood grown in sustainable forests.

Prologue

'You know, your problem is that you're in denial.'

'No I'm not.'

'I rest my case.'

I wish it was always that easy to prove you're right. Sometimes it requires going to enormous lengths.

1

Moldova Beethoven

I'd always played a fair amount of tennis. My father had become fanatical about the game after taking it up at the age of 45. It brought him a great deal of enjoyment over the years, an enjoyment which was only tempered by the fact that other people could play the game much better than him. Millions of people, in fact, and that was just in Sussex. However, like all proud fathers, he decided that what he couldn't achieve himself, he would instruct his children to do on his behalf. And so it was that Ron Burston, a part-time coach at the public courts in Dyke Road Park, Brighton, was entrusted with the task of coaching me and my brother to be the number one and the number two tennis players in the world (with Dad as manager).

Sadly it was beyond the capabilities of all of us, except Dad of course, who clearly had the ability needed to travel the globe, stay in nice hotels, and watch tennis matches from the side of the court. By the time I reached my 35th birthday my father was finally forced to acknowledge that unless the madman who had stabbed Monica Seles was released from prison and ordered to stab every player on the current men's circuit, then the dream was over. He'd simply have to be content with my achievements to date – a runner-up medal in the Sussex Closed Boy's Under 12 event (I'd been robbed – honestly, some of those line calls), and a medal for winning the British Actors' Equity tennis championship. (Most of the entrants hadn't been any good, and hadn't even acted like they were.)

Nevertheless I reckoned I still played a pretty good game, so that's why Arthur's attitude infuriated me so much.

'I don't reckon you're that good at tennis, Hawks,' he said, not lifting his eyes from the footballers on the TV screen, 'Not any more anyway. You've got to be past it.'

Arthur and I were good enough, and old enough friends to

indulge in petty squabbling. We'd met as comedians on London's alternative cabaret circuit and had preserved more than a modicum of the competitive spirit which that world had nurtured. It was manifesting itself right here, before the television.

'Look Arthur,' I replied, relieved to see that a Moldovan player had sliced a shooting chance out for a throw-in, 'I reckon I'm still a pretty capable player – mainly because when I was young I got a good grounding in the basics.'

Quite why the conversation had turned to tennis I cannot remember; perhaps it was because the football was less than captivating now that England were 3-0 up, with the Moldovan team looking unable to trouble our goalkeeper or revive their chances of World Cup qualification.

'That's bollocks,' declared Arthur, pithily.

I'd had quarrels like this with him before. I would put forward a reasonable argument, only to find it countered with abrupt obscenity. He did it to wind me up, I'm sure.

'The thing about tennis,' I continued, a little foolishly, 'is that it doesn't matter how natural a sportsman or sportswoman you are, you still need a certain amount of tuition. You have to have a basic grasp of the techniques required for topspin or slice in order to control the ball.'

'That's more bollocks,' argued Arthur. 'The natural sportsmen in this world can turn their hand to any sport. Take Ian Botham – he played professional football for Scunthorpe. Gary Lineker – brilliant snooker player, Tim Henman – four handicap golfer.' Then he pointed to the TV screen. 'Take those footballers playing now. A lot of them will be natural sportsmen and I bet that you couldn't beat them at tennis.'

'Of course I could, but that's a stupid bet because I'd never be able to prove it.'

'Why not? Just play them.'

'What? All of them? Come off it. I'd never get to play them. For one thing, the English players are virtually royalty. They're constantly surrounded by an entourage of managers and agents. They're hardly going to respond to me ringing up and asking them for a game of tennis.'

'OK then, I bet you that you can't beat the Moldovan players. I shouldn't imagine any of them have got much of an entourage.'

'Arthur, I'm not betting you, but I honestly reckon that I could beat all of them.'

'Bollocks you would, Hawks, you're all talk.'

'*Goal!*' we both shouted, as our petty squabble was interrupted by a fourth England goal.

Four nil to England. A satisfactory result, but to my mind not one that merited a celebratory drink in the pub. Arthur felt differently.

'Come on Hawks, come and have a pint, you lightweight!'

He could be quite persuasive at times.

'Alright, but just one, I've got an early start in the morning.'

Although to this day he denies it, I maintain that Arthur knew exactly what he was doing. He was fully aware that I was a sucker for these kind of things and that in May 1997 I had hitch-hiked around the circumference of Ireland with a fridge to win a one hundred pound bet. So, when the fourth pint was being lifted to my lips, he returned to his mischief.

'I don't reckon you'll take on that bet because the bottom line is that you're not good enough.'

'Well, I happen to think I am good enough.'

'Alright then – I give you this challenge. If you can get those eleven Moldovan footballers who just lost to England, and beat them at tennis, then I'll er . . ., stand in Balham High Road and sing the Moldovan national anthem. Stark bollock naked.'

'And you'd *do* that?'

'Yes. Except that I wouldn't have to, because you'd lose to one of them.'

'I wouldn't.'

'Course you would. One of them is bound to be very good.'

'Maybe. But I still wouldn't lose. I'd be able to draw on all my tournament experience from my junior days, and I'd find one weak shot in their armoury and play on it.'

'Yeah, yeah, don't bore me with all the technical crap. If you're so sure of yourself then why don't you agree to strip naked and sing the national anthem as well, if you lose?'

'Look, I know what's going on here, Arthur. You're just trying to trick me into a bet which will involve an enormous amount of effort on my part while you just sit on your arse. It's not fair.'

Nevertheless, half an hour later over a whisky back at Arthur's, I shook on that bet. I knew I'd been duped, but I didn't really mind. In my heart I knew I was ready to take on another silly adventure.

I didn't even know where Moldova was, but then I suppose that was part of the appeal. As I stood on the chair to take down the atlas from the top shelf I became excited. More excited than anyone had ever been before while in the act of looking up Moldova on a map. I had a strong feeling that this was *it*. Quite suddenly the void in my life, which had resulted from not being faced with a complex and yet ultimately pointless challenge, was to be filled.

I took down the weighty tome used to plan holidays and settle arguments, and leafed my way through to Eastern Europe.

'Ah, here it is,' I said. 'It's on the north-eastern border of Romania.'

'I still don't think you'll beat them all,' replied Arthur. 'Not every single one of them.'

'I *will*. I *will* beat them all.'

There's a scene in the film *Annie Hall* in which Woody Allen gets into an argument with a man standing in front of him in a cinema queue, over the interpretation of certain views expressed by Marshall McLuhan, the famous professor of media studies. Just when the dispute is beginning to get a little heated, McLuhan himself appears from nowhere to interrupt and confirm that Woody Allen is in the right. Woody then turns to the camera, shrugs, and laments:

'If only life was *really* like this.'

Unfortunately, in my case proving that I was right and Arthur was wrong was going to be a wholly more convoluted process. I knew nothing about Moldova, its tennis facilities, its political situation, its visa requirements, its currency, its language, its ethnic make-up or whether its people would take kindly to a decadent bourgeois Westerner swanning around waving a tennis racket in front of its footballers. All I knew about Moldova were the names of eleven men which were printed on the inside back page of my newspaper.

Romanenko
Fistican
Spynu
Testimitanu
Culibaba
Stroenco
Rebeja
Curtianu
Shishkin
Miterev
Rogaciov

'Huh, easy,' I thought.

None of them sounded to me like they were any good at tennis.

Next day in the local reference library, I discovered that Moldova was a small landlocked country wedged between Romania and the Ukraine. It had a population density of 129.1 per sq. km, which seemed acceptable enough provided that the 129 people spread themselves evenly around that kilometre, and I didn't have to spend too much time with the 0.1 of a person. More importantly I learnt that Moldova has two main languages – Romanian and Russian, and so I decided to invest in a copy of *Teach Yourself Romanian*. I felt that I would need a grounding in at least one of the native languages since Moldovans, I assumed, were probably a tad behind the Dutch when it came to a command of English. My reason for choosing Romanian ahead of Russian was not a sophisticated one. It was an easy choice to make – the Russians use the cyrillic alphabet and Romanians use the proper one. I didn't mind the idea of having a pop at a new language, but a new alphabet? Well ьоллокс to that! I'm sorry, but one reaches an age where learning an entirely new alphabet is really not on. (That age, incidentally, is six years old.)

Teach yourself Romanian comes complete with the pleasing anomalies of all language books. In a section marked 'Cuvinte cheie' (Key words), the first word listed is 'Acrobat'. Now, I struggle with the notion that 'acrobat' is a key word. Surely those readers who are not seeking employment with Romanian travelling circuses might manage to get by without using that word at all. It's certainly a word I tend to use infrequently. In fact, I think there was a five-year period in my life when I didn't use it once, and they were happy and fulfilled years too, if I remember rightly. However, I was about to go to Eastern Europe and life there was surely going to be different, and who was I to say what was and what wasn't a *key word*?

I resolved to learn the word 'acrobat' at once. The text before me revealed that this was not going to be a difficult task.

acrobat, acrobaţi (m) – acrobat.

With this under my belt and with confidence very much in the ascendancy, I moved on to some 'Dialog' (dialogue). Two sentences caught my eye. First:

'Mai aveţi timp să reparaţi şi liftul?'

meaning, 'Have you got time to repair the lift as well?' and

'Ai cărui vecin sunt aceşti câini?'

which means 'Which neighbour do these dogs belong to?'

I knew that only a fool would consider any foray into Moldovan territory without a degree of competence in asking both of these questions, so I set about learning them with all speed. By the end of my first hour I had mastered them both and felt comfortable in the knowledge that if I was bothered by any dogs as I stood outside a footballer's flat, it probably wouldn't take me long to ascertain which of his neighbours they belonged to, or to arrange for the neighbour in question to repair any faulty lifts forthwith.

Of course the one key expression that you really want in these books is never there – and that is the equivalent, in the relevant language, for:

'Look, just because I can manage one sentence in your language doesn't give you carte blanche to reply to me at that speed. Slow up or shut up. Got it pal?'

OK, it's a little harsh, but delivered in your totally crap accent it wouldn't be understood anyway.

Buoyed by my recent linguistic advances I was chomping at the bit to book my flight to Moldova and begin my quest. However, there was an immediate obstacle in front of me which needed removing. To travel to Moldova I would need a visa, and according to the *World Travel Guide*, to obtain this I would need to provide the Moldovan Embassy with an invitation from a Moldovan citizen, written on a special Interior Ministry form.

As far as I knew, Moldova hadn't produced a flood of immigrants into the United Kingdom. I certainly didn't know of any. Admittedly, for most British citizens this lack of Moldovans was not a major cause for concern, but for me it was a profound irritation. I needed a Moldovan more urgently than I had ever needed one before, and I simply did not know where to find one – other than in Moldova of course, but I couldn't go there because the bastards wouldn't let me in until one of them had invited me.

One potential solution to this problem involved a plan in which I would hang around outside the Moldovan Embassy with a view to falling into an easy and natural conversation with a departing member of staff. I would then invite this Eastern European civil servant for a drink, and secure the required invitation after the fourteenth vodka – just before we both embarked on gratuitous nudity and mutual expressions of undying love. The only drawback to this brilliant stratagem was that Moldova didn't have an embassy in London, the nearest one being in Brussels. Quite apart from the travel costs and hotel bills, my limited social Flemish would be unlikely to furnish me with the required charm, and my Romanian would founder once the subject veered from tumbling and gymnastics.

All I could do was occasionally mention the subject among friends and work colleagues.

'You don't happen to know anyone from Moldova by any chance, do you?' I ventured at dinner parties, sporting events and at my weekly meetings of Optimists Anonymous. Invariably I got a negative response.

That was until, incredibly, after some months of trying, this tactic finally paid off. I learned from a friend in Liverpool that she was pretty sure there was a guy from Moldova studying at the Liverpool Institute of Performing Arts. A phone call later and the college bursar had confirmed the good news for me.

'Yes, we have a Moldovan,' he said, untroubled by the oddness of my request, 'His name is Andrei, he's a nice guy.'

'Do you think he might be nice enough to invite me to Moldova if I came to see him?' I asked, rather forwardly.

'I don't see why not,' replied the bursar, still failing to recognise anything unusual in the conversation. 'Why don't you come and see his band?'

'His band?'

'Yes, he has a Beatles band from Moldova called The Flying Postmen, and they're playing at next week's Beatles Convention.'

This was a surreal development which felt entirely in keeping with things.

'How wonderful,' I said, 'I wouldn't miss them for the world.'

And thus Liverpool became the starting point for my adventure, just as it had been a century or so before for thousands of emigrants seeking a new life in the New World. My goal was more modest. All I wanted were the Moldovan Fab Four.

I was greeted at Liverpool's Adelphi Hotel by a lobby-full of mop-headed sixties clones ranging from spotty youths to pensioners. Beatles groupies, and lots of them. I should have been expecting it, but I still found it a little bewildering. Dressed as I was, in clothes which did not make me look a bit of a prat, I felt uncomfortably out of place so I quickly checked in and headed for the privacy of my room.

I lay on my bed and perused the programme cover. **'International Beatle Week – with entertainment provided by the world's best Beatle bands'**. I noticed very quickly that one thing seemed to unite the world's best Beatle bands, and that was the inability to come up with a decent name. The Bootleg Beatles having nabbed the only really apposite one, the others had been left to grovel in a creative mire where they had not excelled themselves. Poor efforts included, from Italy, The Apple Scruffs; from the United States, A Hard Night's Day; from Brazil, Clube Big Beatles; and all the way from Japan, a band called Wishing. I studied Wishing's photo. They had splendidly authentic Beatle suits and their hair was terribly good, but there is something in the physiognomy of the Japanese which prevents them from plausibly resembling a scouser. Not necessarily a social disadvantage but in this instance something of a bummer. It would be difficult to suspend disbelief while watching a Fab Four who looked like they had met on the shop floor of Mitsubishi Motors. I decided that their name Wishing was short for Wishing We Looked A Bit More Like The Beatles.

The Flying Postmen was the best name by far because it appeared to have no connection with The Beatles whatsoever. Unfortunately it made no entry in the Convention programme either. Not good news since they were the sole reason for my being here. My mission, which I had already chosen to accept, was to make their acquaintance and somehow get myself an invitation to their country. At the Convention's information desk I learned that their absence in print was due to their late entry to the line up of bands, but there seemed to be a great deal of vagueness about when and where they were actually performing. I would just have to start asking around. I felt rather like a private eye. Or a private dick – unlike the very public ones who were milling about the hotel lobby.

That night's main event was a concert at the Royal Court Theatre by the 'Sensations from Sweden' – Lenny Pane. Ah, yes – *Lenny Pane.* I could see how they'd come up with that name – they'd cleverly switched the first letters of The Beatles' hit 'Penny Lane'. Using the same method, they could so easily have taken the song 'Day Tripper', and arrived at the much better name – Tray Dipper. (Their gigs could have been marked by a crowd pleasing ceremonial 'dipping of trays' towards the climax of the performance.) Disappointed though I was in their failure to have plumped for such an obviously superior name, I elected to go and see their concert anyway and in the process ask around the ersatz Beatles fraternity for clues as to the whereabouts of The Flying Postmen.

Inside the venue, the mob from the hotel lobby and a few extras had gathered in the darkness to welcome their Scandinavian heroes to the stage. The sound was authentic and reluctantly I had to concede that Lenny Pane were surprisingly good. And rather sweet too. Their rapport with the audience was a touch more genteel than I remember Lennon's having been:

'Thank you, we love to come here to this convention in Liverpool,' an overly blond singer effused in a delightfully lilting Scandinavian accent, 'and we would like to pay tribute to all of you, and of course all the other inhabitants of the town.'

Hey, dig that rock 'n' roll attitude. Soon we would be urged to be responsible with our litter on leaving the venue.

I went to bed a little concerned at having no leads on the Moldovans but lifted by the sound of Beatles' tunes ringing in my ears. I began to marvel at just how good the original Beatles had been. Every song seemed to be a classic. Slightly worryingly I began to empathise with the fanatical fans around whom I'd spent the evening. I could think of worse things to immerse yourself in. If you were going to be an anorak, far better to make this your area of anorakdom than hang around Crewe station writing down the numbers of passing trains. And so I fell asleep comforted by the knowledge that if ever I decided to be an obsessive nerd then I was clear as to exactly which kind of obsessive nerd I was going to be.

Strawberry Field is more than just a song. It is, and always has been, a working Salvation Army children's home, the gates of which have become something of a shrine to Beatles devotees. They aren't normally opened for fans, but this year Cavern City Tours had landed something of a coup when it had persuaded the Christian Soldiers to pack the children off for the day so that a huge garden party could be thrown, with Beatles bands playing all afternoon. A rare treat. And, like a lot of rare treats, a major disappointment. To go through the gates into Strawberry Field is to shatter any illusion you may have as to the magical quality of the place. The original buildings, which matched the age of the gates, had long since been demolished and replaced with new ones which had been designed by a man with a slide rule and access to a job lot of cheap and ugly windows.

Lennon's lyrics ('Nothing is real') were no longer relevant. In current-day Strawberry Field *everything* was real, and spending too long here would most likely leave you with quite a lot *to get hung about*. An uninspiring venue at the best of times but when you added to it the temperance of the Salvation Army and their insistence on the concert being an entirely dry affair, you had a really crap place for a party.

The atmosphere wasn't conducive to letting your hair down. I'd been too young to attend the wild rock festivals of the sixties but I can only assume that they didn't have Corporals and Majors from the Salvation Army patrolling around the grounds trumpeting the news that 'Strawberry Tea' was available in the refectory. At Woodstock, this absence of religious militia probably made you more enthusiastic about the idea of removing your clothes, painting your tits and arse green and making love to anyone you happened to stagger into. I looked around me and all I could see were people cross-legged on tartan blankets, sipping from plastic cups of tea. Rather than a 'Love-in', this was more of a 'Feel slightly uncomfortable-in'. Instead of dealers selling a range of illegal drugs, we had fairground stalls raising money for a children's home.

Caught up in the wild frenzy of it all I was severely tempted to try my hand on the stall in which you had to throw hoops over cardboard cut-outs of the Beatles.

'Come on now, four hoops for a pound!' said the wicked tweed-skirted temptress behind the stall.

Just say no, I thought.

'OK, give me four,' I said, in immediate capitulation.

It was all over far too quickly and I missed all four of the Beatles, but I did get quite a high when my last hoop struck a couple who had sat too close to Paul McCartney for their own safety.

I took 'Strawberry Tea' in the refectory and as my cup was being zealously filled by a septagenarian Christian soldier with a blue rinse, I heard the Master of Ceremonies make an announcement of such significance that I left my strawberries and cream unfinished.

'Ladies and Gentlemen, these guys remind me of the Beatles in their early years, the raw hungry years in The Cavern – ladies and gentlemen, from Moldova – The Flying Postmen!'

I rushed around to watch. Four young guys ambled on to the stage and fussed around their instruments and amplifiers, almost oblivious to their audience, in a way that only musicians can. They were in sixties outfits but didn't seem to be trying to resemble the Beatles in any way. The tallest of the four strode proudly to the microphone.

'We are not like the early Beatles – we are like the Flying Postmen *now*!' he announced somewhat arrogantly to a stunned crowd, 'My name is Andrei, I am *not* Paul.'

A remark not without irony given that in one respect he was the most authentic Paul that I had seen since my arrival, being the only one who was left-handed. As he stood centre stage with the neck of his guitar pointing in the other direction to those of the band members flanking him, just for a moment, for me they *were* The Beatles. These boys didn't need to go for the hair, the clothes or the mannerisms. They had the same *design*.

The MC had been right. They had the energy too. The raw energy of youth and a genuine excitement which experience had not yet stripped from them. They began with the song 'Money' which offers us the subtle lyric, 'Give me money – that's what I want', and it occurred to me that this might be the Moldovan National anthem. At the end of their set they were cheered off stage, despite having committed the treacherous act of playing two Kinks songs and one by The Who.

As they relaxed behind the stage area, flanked by some Brazilian Beatles who were preparing to go on next, I nervously sidled up to the four Flying Postmen. I felt awkward, like a child in a playground about to approach some other children and say 'Excuse me, but will you be my friends?' My acquired social skills included occasionally angling for an invite to a party but this was the first time I had ever had a go at getting one to a country.

'Hi guys, great set,' I said, somewhat smarmily, 'Er . . . um . . .

look, I'm going to Moldova soon and I wanted to ask you some questions about your country – how would you feel about that?'

'Great! No problem,' replied Andrei enthusiastically.

And it was really that easy. Two hours later we met in a town centre pub and after a couple of pints I felt brave enough to explain the nature of my prospective business in their country. They laughed. They laughed heartily. When they had finished though, they told me exactly what I wanted to hear. Yes my idea was crazy but no, I would not be made unwelcome in Moldova. In fact Andrei felt that most people there would feel pleased that a foreigner had shown an interest in their relatively unknown country and would do their best to show traditional Moldovan hospitality. No, there were no food shortages and yes, there were tennis courts. Emile, or George Harrison, had played a good deal as a youngster and told me that courts had been built at the side of the Republican Football stadium. He had even seen some footballers playing there. This last piece of news was a little worrying. How much had they played and how good were they? Could Arthur be right – out of eleven players could any of them be good?

I learned that The Flying Postmen were not returning to Moldova after the Convention but had acquired work permits to remain in the UK and would begin a residency at the Cavern Club. I tried to look pleased but I was only too aware that Liverpool's gain was my loss. I had been looking to them to be four potential allies and helpers in a strange country where I spoke none of the language, but it seemed I would have to manage without. However, there was some very good news to come. Andrei told me that he had a friend called Corina who was director of The Independent Journalism Centre in Moldova's capital Chisinau, and that he reckoned that she would issue me with a formal invitation to Moldova. I made sure by producing a mobile phone on which I insisted that we call her right away. I handed Andrei the phone and in seconds he was engaged in a conversation the sound of which confirmed that I would never fully master Romanian. Presently he passed back the small black miracle invention and I lifted the receiver to my ear.

'Hi Tony,' said a faint female voice emanating from this distant and mysterious place, 'I am Corina. You sound mad but it would be nice to have you as our guest at the Journalism Centre. You can use our offices as a base for your project.'

'Wow, thanks,' I managed, still wondrous at the technology that was enabling me to speak to a Moldovan in Moldova outside a Liverpool pub. Corina went on to tell me that if I called again in a week she could sort out accommodation for me, which was fantastic news. I scarcely had a chance to thank her again though, before the line went dead.

But it didn't matter. Things were coming together rather nicely.

'I wish I was coming with you,' said a nostalgic Andrei, who hadn't been in Moldova for over a year.

2

Tupolev 134

'So, do the footballers know that you are coming?'

It was a logical enough question, and one that I had been asked a good deal by concerned friends, but so far the answer had been 'no'.

The fact is I had tried faxing and ringing The Moldovan Football Federation, but the line was either busy or there was no reply. I didn't mind that much though because I liked the idea of arriving in a country and starting completely from scratch. I had decided that this whole project was to be something of an experiment. My intention was to prove that a positive attitude and an optimistic outlook would produce results, provided that belief was sustained. Sure there would be setbacks, sure there would be problems, but just like any of life's problems they would *have* to be overcome. This, the second of my self-inflicted journeys into absurdity was to act as confirmation of a philosophy which I had formulated as a result of my travels with the fridge. Things *can* be done. The people in life who get them done are the ones who *know* that, and the ones who don't are the rest. If I succeeded in tracking down and beating all the Moldovan national football team at tennis, then not only would I have the pleasure of watching Arthur's humiliation, but more importantly I would have proved something to myself. Something which could underpin the rest of my life.

And so I went about my business, having successfully attached enormous gravitas to a manifestly pointless pursuit. But why did there always have to be a point? Why couldn't you just get stuck in and *do* things? What was the point of anything anyway? What was the point in football? What was the point in working, retiring, saving money, raising a family, going to church or standing for election? The only thing I could feel sure had a point was the sharp bit at the very end of a dart, and even that was useless unless it got stuck into things.

So that Sunday afternoon, as I checked in for the Air Moldova direct flight to Chisinau,[1] I felt pretty damn good about the whole thing. One of the world's pioneers. Good old me.

There were some raised eyebrows at the check-in desk when it was noted that I had only a single ticket.

'What is the purpose of your visit?'

'Pleasure.'

Further astonishment.

'How many items of luggage?'

'Two pieces and one piece of hand luggage.'

'Did you pack your bags yourself?'

I was tempted to turn around and point to some bloke in the departures hall and say, 'No, that bloke over there did it. And a shocking job he made of it too. Let me just open my bag and show you – look at that – he calls that folding.'

'Yes,' I said, rather chickening out.

My first item of luggage was conventional enough. A great big hold-all. The next prompted further questioning.

'What's that?'

'It's a plastic round table.'

I was going to be the passenger they talked about at tea break.

'Right. You will have to take that to the outsize luggage section.'

Round tables aren't common items of luggage for international travel, but this was a very important gift. A week earlier I had read in a newspaper that Moldova's gypsy king had recently died and that his son Arthur would be assuming his crown. This was immensely pleasing – Moldova had a King Arthur. I had immediately resolved to pay him a visit and take a Round Table as a gift. It was rather a shame that I had left the purchase of the table until that Sunday morning and had only had time to nip round to Do It All and purchase a poor quality table which the King would have to assemble himself. Still it would be the thought that counted. I hoped it wouldn't count *against* me.

[1]You may find Chisinau, Moldova's capital, spelt 'Kishinev' on old maps. This was its name under the Russian Soviet regime.

'What kind of plane are we flying on?' I enquired of the jaded check-in lady.

'A Tupolev 134.'

Ah yes, the Tupolev 134. I am not normally a nervous flyer but the make of this aircraft was not one which instilled the average Western passenger with oodles of confidence. It sounded old and it sounded knackered.

The waiting area at Gate 36 revealed that only nine passengers other than myself had chosen to put their faith in the plane, but as I viewed it from the window I decided I liked what I saw. It did look very Russian, but it was sleek and it was very pointy, and frankly that was good enough for me. Anyway I figured that if the pilot and crew were happy to gad about in it all week then it had to have some things going for it.

Inside, the plane was surprisingly plush, and since there were only nine of us it was comfortably spacious. There were no overhead lockers, just shelves, and there was no music, no welcoming announcements or anyone telling you where to sit. I rather liked this. An airline that didn't treat you like a baby. Before take-off none of the hostesses made that headmistress-like patrol of the cabin to check which one of us naughty passengers hadn't put our seat belts on or lifted our seat-backs into the upright position. What *is* that obsession with 'ensuring that your seat-backs are in the upright position'? What difference is the angle of your seat going to make? Only recently above Heathrow there had been a near miss between a BA 737 and a Virgin Jumbo, averting collision by a mere 200 feet. If they had collided, I feel it unlikely that there would have been survivors nursing light bruises in a casualty department saying 'Well, thank God we had our seat-backs in the upright position.'

We took off. It was the clearest of days. Soon I looked down and saw the port of Dover, and on the horizon beyond it, France. I was struck by just how narrow this strip of water was, but also how historically significant it had been in protecting Britain from the great conquerors and Empire builders of Europe.

Moldova had not been so lucky. Like many parts of Eastern Europe it seemed to have been one of those territories whose people had been easily subjugated by the particular prevalent power of the day. Prior to its emergence as the independent Republic of Moldova in 1991, political control over this land seemed to shift after each major European conflict, the main players being the Ottoman and Russian Empires. After the First World War, the territory which was then known as Bessarabia voted to become part of Romania but it was grabbed back again by the Russians after the Second World War, becoming 'The Soviet Socialist Republic of Moldavia'.[2] During this period, the ethnic majority of Romanian speaking Moldovans saw a huge influx of Russians and Ukrainians who arrived to industrialise the cities, enforce communism as a way of life, and generally make everybody miserable. Theirs had been a harsh regime, the results of which would soon become apparent to me.

I knew from appearance alone that there were three other Brits on the flight. They were identifiable primarily because they were the only passengers who didn't resemble baddies from a 1980s Cold War thriller. One of them was sat across the aisle from me. He seemed a benign fellow, slightly greying and with open features. I lent over and made an invasion of his personal air space.

'Why are you going to Moldova?' I asked, assuming that he wasn't on a two-week Thomson package holiday.

'Both Esther and I,' he said gesturing to the young woman sat alongside him, 'are going to work in a home for handicapped children in Chisinau.'

David turned out to be a vicar from an Anglican church in East London who knew as little about our destination as I did. When he asked for the reason for my trip I felt a little sheepish. My cause, after all, lacked the nobility of his, but when I explained it to him he laughed and promised to say a prayer for me.

'I'm not sure if I can influence Him on that one, but I'll give it a go,' he joked.

'Any help gratefully received,' I replied. 'Who knows, I may need a little looking after.'

I wondered whether God, whoever or whatever He was, would approve of what I was undertaking. I decided that He probably

[2]Moldavia is the Russian language name for this area, and Moldova the Romanian one.

would. After all wasn't He suppose to move in mysterious ways? My way, once explained to people, mystified them immediately – so maybe God and I had an affinity on the mystery front.

The other British passenger was sitting two rows in front of me, and my not knowing why he was Moldova-bound was making me peevish. I tried to guess but it wasn't easy, only having the back of his head to go on. After studying it for some twenty minutes I felt pretty sure that this was the back of the head of a diplomat. It bore all the hallmarks – ears sticking out each side, and hair on the top going right the way down to the nape of the neck. Eventually I plucked up the courage to go and check on the validity of my prognosis.

'Sorry to bother you,' I said, climbing into the vacant seat beside him, 'but I've been trying to guess why you're making this trip. Are you on official business?'

'Kind of. I'm going to get married,' came the reply.

'Blimey.'

Kevin explained that he had met a Moldovan girl on the Internet, as you do, and after an eighteen-month courtship in which they had exchanged hundreds of messages he had finally proposed marriage. This was to be the journey in which he married her and brought her back to live with him in England. I was a little concerned that their relationship might not work so well when it had to move into the physical world where primitive methods of communication such as using words and touching are still favoured. Perhaps they would be OK if they just passed notes to each other for the first two months, or set up computers in each room so they could send each other e-mails.

To: Cutiekins@upstairsbathroom.co.uk
From: Kevin@kitchen.co.uk
Message: How long are you going to be in there?

'What do you do Kevin?' I asked, still secretly hoping he might be in the diplomatic corps.

'I work in computers.'

Well of course. How could I have misread the back of his head so badly?

As we touched down I felt an adrenaline rush. I was excited to be in Eastern Europe for the first time. I simply did not know what to expect. Would it be stark, unwelcoming and primitive as most of my friends had predicted, or would I find a justification for Andrei's words. 'I wish I was coming with you'? The thrill was in not knowing.

I had my first contact with a Moldovan on home soil when a stern-looking man in oil-stained blue overalls stopped me from filming the plane as I left it. He was scary. With one fiery look and a demonstrative gesture with his hands he ordered me to put my video camera away, making me feel like an enemy of the state who was about to pass on secrets to Whitehall. This plane had been clearly visible to hundreds of people at Gatwick airport so I couldn't fathom why filming it posed a security risk, but this guy didn't seem to be the type to start niggling with. Neither did the bloke in customs who searched my bag with an unswerving vigour that suggested he had been tipped off about me by the bloke in the overalls. He viewed my pristine white plastic round table with suspicion but said nothing. He must have had a long day.

I followed the instructions that Corina had given me over the phone and took a taxi straight to the Hotel National where she had booked me in for one night only. She had asked me whether I had wanted luxury, cheap or middle of the range and I had plumped for the latter. Largely ignored by the driver, I slid the round table into the back seat, got in the front, and started to put my seat belt on. The taxi driver immediately turned and physically restrained me from so doing. I sat back suitably chastised. Clearly wearing a seat belt over here was not a safety precaution but an insult meaning; 'Look mate, I'm putting this on because you're a crap driver and I don't want to die just yet.'

Darkness had fallen so I couldn't see much as we bounced our way along uneven roads to my hotel, but to my right I could make out some shabby-looking high-rise blocks of flats. I looked across to the left over the shoulder of the taciturn driver and saw shabby-looking high-rise blocks of flats. Finally, we arrived at the Hotel National which was situated alongside some shabby-looking high-rise blocks of flats. I paid the driver, got out and surveyed my hotel. How should I describe it? Well, it was shabby-looking, and it bore an uncanny resemblance to a high-rise block of flats. Yes, that does it nicely.

The hotel reception was huge, empty, dimly lit and spartan. For the owners of this place, whether state or private, 'redecorate' was not a word in their working vocabulary. Flaking paint covered the walls on which an occasional faded drab painting hung apologetically. A grey linoleum scarred by decades of discarded cigarette butts spread itself over the wantonly ample floor space. The words 'Mmmm, this is nice' were an awfully long way from the tip of my tongue.

Behind the reception desk a middle-aged woman sat in an overcoat staring at the floor. Far from giving me a warm welcome she appeared to be profoundly irritated that I had interrupted a session of splendidly gloomy soul-searching. Begrudgingly, she looked up at me. She didn't make a sound but made a gesture with her head which seemed to mean 'Yes, and what do *you* want?' I offered the necessary information and she dispensed me to the lifts as quickly as the confiscation of my passport and issuing of a key allowed.

'Would you like someone to help you with your bags, sir?'

Yeah, right. In your dreams Tony.

I struggled up to my room and let myself in. I had never visited a prison before but now I had some feeling for what the cells were like. My disappointment was tempered by a relief that I hadn't plumped for the cheap hotel option. I set the round table down in the corner of the room where it looked uncannily at home and slumped on to the bed.

My God. What had I taken on?

3

Almost Impossible

I woke up feeling surprisingly sanguine.

I walked to the hotel window and surveyed the city for the first time in daylight. From here on the eleventh floor I had a fine view of the city of Chisinau. Immediately below me was a square, at the centre of which stood the statue of a heroic soldier in triumphant pose; square jawed and fighting fit, an anachronistic symbol of disciplined strength. Over-crowded trolley buses and under-powered Ladas struggled past noisily. At the far side of the square there was some kind of government building or seat of learning behind which rose the azure dome of an Orthodox basilica, the golden cross at its apex drawing the eye away from the grey panorama of drab and soulless apartment blocks which sprawled beyond it. The early morning sun lit the autumnal trees of the city parks with an incisive crispness and looked set to burn away the distant haze on the horizon. It was going to be a lovely day and I had a good feeling about things. Clearly it had been the tiredness of a long journey which had caused me to exaggerate the bleakness of the previous night's arrival. I felt sure that any lack of warmth in those I had encountered up to now was either imagined or a passing aberration.

After a satisfactory breakfast involving a yoghurt drink called '*chefir*', a coffee, one sausage and some unusual bread, I was in a state of readiness for the task ahead. This morning I was to be met by Iulian, an interpreter arranged for me by Corina. I was to pay him thirty dollars a day, apparently excellent money by Moldovan standards, but a wage which would barely cover your rent in London. As I waited for him in reception I realised that he was to be crucial to my chances of success. I wondered if he had been briefed by Corina and was fully aware of the unusual nature of my business here which left me in need of his services. I was also wondering how we were going to recognise each other, when a voice came from over my left shoulder:

'Are you Tony Hawks?'

'Yes.'

'I am Iulian. I recognised you by the table.'

Of course, it was leaning up against my bags. I had mentioned to Corina on the telephone that I was bringing it. She had laughed, possibly nervously. I wondered what kind of mental picture she had created for me – the man who was arriving here to challenge the Moldovan national football team one by one to a game of tennis, bringing a plastic round table with him as a gift for the King of the Gypsies. She was unlikely to be thinking, 'He'll be the fifth one this month, and I expect he'll just look like all the others.'

I shook Iulian's hand, the man who would be working with me on a daily basis. The one charged with making things happen. He was thin, bordering on gaunt, but with a self-assured manner and a pleasant face when he was smiling, as he was now.

'So Iulian,' I asked. 'You know about my bet, I trust?'

'Yes I do.'

'So this is hardly the normal job for you, how do you feel about it?'

'Okay,' he returned, with a reticence I would soon begin to recognise as a national characteristic.

In the taxi on the way to the Independent Journalism Centre we made small talk about my flight and the weather, both of us wishing to defer for as long as possible the discussion about how on earth we were going to tackle the problem that lay ahead of us. Iulian seemed a nice chap and I felt sure I was going to like him. Then it dawned on me that he was my employee. I'd never had an employee before. All right, I'd hired the likes of builders, window cleaners and mechanics to do things which I didn't know how or couldn't be arsed to do, but this was different. I was employing someone to work closely with me on a project of my own. Like a secretary or a personal assistant. I hoped that Iulian didn't expect me to take him to Paris at the weekends.

Corina greeted us outside the fine old building which housed the Independent Journalism Centre. She was elegant and beautiful and someone with whom I would have gladly made the Chisinau-Paris trip if it hadn't been for the fact that I knew she was happily married with a little baby boy.

'Tony, I think that you are mad,' she announced, 'but even so, you are free to use this centre as a base for your impossible task.'

'Thank you, you are very kind.'

And I was very lucky. Less than a month previously I hadn't even known one Moldovan, let alone had the use of an office to use as my base.

'Do you really think that it will be impossible?' I asked.

'Well, I suppose that nothing is impossible,' said Corina, 'but you will see that it is difficult to make things happen in this country. Let us say – your task is *almost* impossible.'

Almost impossible. Two words which didn't do a great deal to lift the spirits. I elected for a change of subject.

'So tell me a little more about the Independent Journalism Centre.'

Corina told me the full story. The centre was a non-governmental organisation which had been set up to promote young journalists and to encourage the development of an open society through creating a quality and objective media. It was largely funded by the American billionaire George Soros, a man who has made unthinkably large sums of money trading in the world's financial markets. Born a Hungarian Jew, his childhood experiences fleeing Nazi SS death squads and then an oppressive communist regime led him to formulate a passionate belief in the importance of an open society.

At the age of 49, and having acquired a personal fortune of roughly 25 million dollars, he decided that it was time to embark on some healthy philanthropy. Now, each year he gives millions of dollars to Eastern Europe, and Corina was just one of many grateful recipients. In September 1992 a good deal of this money came from the British taxpayer when George Soros bet heavily against the value of the pound. He had been a brave man indeed to have taken on such a formidable figure as the British Chancellor, Norman Lamont, but after a week of hectic trading the British taxpayer emerged £15 billion worse off, and Soros emerged beaming rather broadly.

I've always been impressed by the way Lamont, who had effectively overseen the removal of five pounds from the pocket of every taxpayer in the United Kingdom, appeared to be genuinely aggrieved when John Major eventually sacked him. I'd always imagined that the exchange between them went roughly along these lines:

JOHN MAJOR: I'm afraid Norman, that as a result of small businesses closing at the rate of three a day and vast numbers of the population suffering negative equity on their properties, added to which you managed to lose this country billions of pounds in a single day, I have decided to replace you as Chancellor of the Exchequer.

NORMAN LAMONT: But why? What have I done wrong?

To this day, it is still Norman Lamont's opinion on the major political issues of the day which helps me decide which stance I should adopt. Indeed, my main reason for being in favour of further British integration in Europe is because Norman Lamont is vehemently against it. My thinking is that if I can live my life taking an opposing view to Norman Lamont on everything, then I can't go too far wrong.

Corina led me up the stairs and into the room which was the hub of the centre where five or six people sat tapping away at computer keyboards. I was introduced to her staff:

'This is Tony from London, who I told you about.'

The workforce spun round on their chairs, nodded politely and then went straight back to work. Oh. That was it then, was it? For some reason I had imagined that much more of a fuss would have been made of me. I had envisaged that I might have been the focus of attention for longer than 0.1 of a second. Corina had told them about me, so where were the exclamations of wonder? 'Oh, so *you're* the madman . . . Ah, *this* is what he looks like . . . Well, well, here he is, the great adventurer is upon us . . .'

The received greeting fell well short of expectations. I decided that either these people were astonishingly good at suppressing their emotions, or none of them gave a toss. My robust ego had taken its first knock.

The silence created by this wholesale lack of interest in me was filled by the noisy arrival of a tall, thin man who appeared to be in need of a healthy meal. He then began addressing Corina at a totally unwarranted volume, seemingly failing to realise that she was in the same room as him. Everyone winced slightly, especially poor Corina who was directly in the line of fire.

'This is Marcel,' said Corina, taking advantage of a temporary respite in his exclamatory delivery, 'the brother of Andrei from the Flying Postmen.'

'Ah yes, Marcel – hello,' I said, shaking him by the hand. 'You're going to sing the Moldovan national anthem for me at some time, I believe.'

This was what I had arranged with Andrei back in England. The slightly odd figure now standing before me was his opera-singer brother, and it had been decided that his should be the rendition of the anthem which either Arthur or I should attempt to emulate, when the result of the bet was known.

'He doesn't speak English,' said Corina, 'but he says that he wants to take you to the opera while you are here and that he will be in touch through this office in the next few days to arrange it.'

'Tell him I shall look forward to this and thank him for his kindness.'

Corina passed on the message and Marcel made a few more preposterously loud remarks before leaving the office, much to everyone's aural relief.

Corina returned to her desk leaving Iulian and me on a long sofa at the end of the room to discuss the inevitable – how we were going to go about doing this. Yes. How *were* we going to go about doing this? I hadn't really given it much thought. I had figured that it was best to wait until I got on the ground and started to discover how things worked. I began by making a short speech to Iulian stressing how the most important thing about what I was trying to achieve was that we had fun doing it.

'We may need to be like private detectives too sometimes,' I added.

'No problem,' said Iulian confidently.

I then read him the names of the eleven players that I would have to play.

'Have you heard of any of those?' I enquired, expecting the answer 'yes'.

'No.'

'But they're the national team, you must have heard of *some* of them.'

'I haven't. I'm not interested in football.'

'Oh right. How about tennis?'

'I don't know anything about tennis. I don't like sport really.'

Monday morning, ten minutes in, first setback.

'Never mind, I don't think it makes much difference for this,' I said, with feigned insouciance.

Who was I kidding? If he knew all the footballers and had all their home numbers, then things would obviously be much easier. His comprehensive ignorance of all things related to the project was not a boon.

'Do you have to play all eleven of them?' asked Iulian, lovechild of Alan Hansen and Sue Barker.

'Yes.'

'And you have to win?'

'Yes.'

'Wow, that's a tough one.'

It was getting tougher by the minute.

'Right Iulian,' I continued. 'Any ideas where to start?'

'No, I don't know.'

Christ, he'd done as much homework on this as me. Then his eyes lit up.

'Ah, Corina mentioned that there is a sports journalist who may be able to help. I need to get his mobile phone number from his wife who works at the American Embassy.'

'That would be a great start – to talk with him.'

'This shouldn't be a problem, I will arrange for us to meet with him later.'

There was nothing in Iulian's confident tone of voice to suggest that I wouldn't actually speak to this journalist until Friday afternoon. In fact, the whole of this first morning served to show me how getting things done here was not straightforward. We wanted to call this sports journalist as well as the country's Tennis Centre and Football Federation, but with each phone call we either got no reply or the engaged signal. Either people here made phone calls and then just went out immediately or the phone system was powered by the batteries from a Sony Walkman.

Just before we were about to adjourn for lunch, Karen, an American volunteer who was working at the centre, broke with the general office trend and asked how I was getting on.

I explained how things were proceeding and she offered a bleak prognosis, predicting that I would only have three matches. Corina, overhearing in passing, was more optimistic and forecast that I would manage six. Neither prediction did much to lift the spirits.

'I must admit,' I added rather plaintively, 'I thought I might have achieved more from a full mornings work.'

'Welcome to Moldova,' came Karen's ominious response.

After lunch we set off for the Moldovan Football Federation and spent two and a half hours getting lost. It seemed that Iulian had a propensity for confidently heading off in the wrong direction, a confidence which didn't seem to wane in the face of repeated failure. It was impressive and somehow noble, but quite tiring on the legs. I didn't really mind though. Wandering around any city is always the best way to get to know it.

Much of Chisinau was destroyed in the Second World War and as a consequence it is a city with a muddled and eclectic architecture. Charming nineteenth-century two-storey buildings adorned with ornate porticos were flanked by Sixties boxlike structures, and many new buildings were under construction, a sure sign that Western companies were moving in to exploit a new market. The area of 'old Chisinau' around which we were walking had a pleasant feel. The roads were wide and tree-lined, and the traffic, though constant, circulated freely. How long before these streets would be grid-locked I wondered? In the new capitalist system which this fledgling country was now openly embracing, owning a car was surely going to be the way individuals signalled to the rest of society that they were doing all right thanks.

The hub of life in the capital centred around a main street called

Boulevard Stefan cel Mare. One end of it was home to all the government buildings and the other formed the main shopping area. The people went about their business looking uncompromisingly stern, and the atmosphere, though not hostile, was hardly one of geniality. A privileged few sat outside cafes sipping coffee and basking in the winter sun, but laughter and frivolity was not the order of the day. I guessed that the years spent living under an oppressive regime with its institutionalised system of secret police and informers had left the population favouring a cautious approach to any public display of emotion. Not here the heated street-corner debates of southern Europe with raised voices and animated gesticulations, but instead a measured, deadpan exchange of the required information. No frills.

Suddenly I noticed that all the tables in the cafes and bars were round and made of plastic. For some reason the expression 'Carrying coals to Newcastle' popped into my head. Everywhere I looked, there were plastic round tables. And thanks to me – and Do It All of course – now Moldova had one more. King Arthur wasn't going to be that impressed.

I needed to change the dollars which I had brought with me, and Iulian took me to one of the many roadside bureaux de change which dotted the main street. When I began my transaction the small kiosk was empty, but by the time I had completed it I turned round to see that a large queue of people had formed behind me.

'Where did they come from?' I asked Iulian.

'People must have noticed you come in.'

'What do you mean?'

'Well, you don't look typically Moldovan. They realised that you must be changing foreign currency and people want to buy it.'

'Why?'

'That is how they save. No-one trusts our currency – or the banks.'

With a pocket stuffed full of Moldovan money, I left behind the line of locals who were desperate to get their hands on the dollars which had been in my pocket only moments before. It seemed odd, but on an infinitesimally small scale these people were playing exactly the same game that George Soros played. Some would be winners and some would be losers. Welcome to capitalism, folks.

'What have I got here?' I asked Iulian as I sifted through my wad of new notes.

'You have about 700 lei. Our currency is the *leu*. It means "lion".'

Lion, eh? Well, judging by the scene I had just left behind, the *leu* wasn't exactly a lion which was King of the World's Financial Jungle.

Our perambulatory and unintentional exploration of Chisinau's backstreets continued until finally we stood outside a building with 'Federatia Moldoveasca de Fotbal' emblazoned above its door. This was a good sign, literally, as it surely meant this was the Moldovan Football Federation, unlike the four previous buildings that we had been to. I could see that Iulian looked a little uncomfortable. The morning's failures on the phone had driven me to opt for this policy of just turning up, and it wasn't really Iulian's style, or given his sense of direction, his forte.

'What shall I say?' he asked me as we hesitated on the steps outside.

'Not too much at first. Just say that I'm a journalist from England who would like to find some of the national footballers for an interview.'

'OK.'

Inside Iulian spoke rapidly to the man behind the desk who bore as little resemblance to a pretty receptionist as I could remember ever having noted. He shuffled off and returned with a delightfully gentle-looking young man who spoke excellent English. He politely introduced himself as Andrei, the team's translator.

'How may I help you?' he asked.

I explained. I gave him the truth, the whole truth and nothing but the truth. He laughed, especially at the bit about stripping naked and singing the Moldovan National Anthem.

'So how may I help you?' he said again.

'Er, well . . . here's a list of the players I have to play – it would be very helpful if you could tell me which clubs they play for, where they train, and offer any ideas on how best to contact them.'

Andrei looked a little taken aback and a little short on ideas. To be fair to him, an Englishman turning up wanting to play tennis against the footballers for whom he translated may not have been what he was expecting of his Monday afternoon. Nevertheless he promised to help and returned ten minutes later with all the relevant details nicely typed out for me in English. What a splendid fellow.

He went through it with me. Some of the news was good. Five of the players played for one club – Zimbru Chisinau, and two other players also played for clubs based in the capital. A further two, Stroenco and Rogaciov, played for clubs in Transnistria. This I knew could be a problem.

When Gorbachev began *perestroika* during the later 1980s there had been an upsurge in Moldovan nationalism which favoured the adoption of Romanian as the national language. However there was also much opposition to this from the Russians who formed the majority in the region east of the River Dniestr known as Transnistria. These Russians supported a political movement called *Yedinstvo* ('Unity') and when Moldova became a republic in September 1991 they refused to recognise the new government and suspended application of Moldovan law in their jurisdiction. Unilaterally they gave themselves the snappy title 'The Transnistrian Moldavian Soviet Socialist Republic', and embarked on a full-scale civil war with the Moldovan government in Chisinau. All this had gone largely unnoticed by Western observers and particularly by me. I'd been too busy practising my serve.

The lingering problem was that although the fighting had ceased, none of the disputes had been resolved. The region had its own police force, currency and army, and it operated strict border controls even though it was not recognised by the International Community. 'Not being recognised' by the International Community meant that apart from the International Community walking straight past you without nodding, they didn't bother to invite you to enter the Eurovision Song Contest, or allow you to have a national football team which could compete on the international stage. And so it was that Stroenco and Rogaciov played for 'Moldova' even though they came from the 'Transnistrian Moldavian Soviet Socialist Republic', a territory described to me as bandit country and a place which I should consider unsafe to visit.

The other bit of bad news was that two recent transfers meant that Alexandru Curtianu was now playing his football for Zenit St Petersburg in Russia, and Marin Spynu was with a club in Israel.

'This might take longer than I thought,' I said with a wry smile.

'Yes,' said Andrei.

Iulian remained silent.

'I'll meet you tomorrow at ten at the Journalism Centre,' I said as we stood outside the bar, 'and the plan will be just to turn up at the headquarters of the football clubs.'

Iulian nodded obediently and headed off into the Chisinau evening, his first day over with his new boss. I wondered what he had made of it all. He didn't look in the least bewildered. Perhaps he was good at dissembling.

I couldn't really have chosen a more downmarket bar, but it was close by and it suited my purposes. I wanted to ruminate on the day's events over a beer before wandering back to the Journalism Centre where in an hour Corina and her husband Aurel would meet and drive me to the lodgings they'd arranged for me. The bar was grim and stark. Apart from two posters advertising Coke and Orbit chewing gum, there were no decorations anywhere. Totally incongruous House music blared from a radio which wasn't quite tuned in correctly. Behind the bar there was one shelf with a dozen or so bottles standing on it, a calendar and a big woman who would have struggled to meet the criteria for entry into Stringfellows.

I ordered an Arc beer using a combination of vague Romanian and accurate pointing, and went and sat down at one of the four empty tables. The other customer, an old man crouched over a vodka at the end of the bar, looked up and viewed me suspiciously. Then he gathered himself, threw back the vodka in one swift action and marched out of the bar without ever breaking eye contact with the floor just in front of his shoes. I looked up at the barmaid and smiled. She immediately averted her eyes and went back to washing up some glasses. I took a sip of my beer and sat back pensively.

A few minutes later another man ambled in. There was a short exchange at the bar and a vodka was poured. He took hold of the glass, threw the drink down his neck, turned around and walked straight out of the bar again. The whole transaction had taken no more than thirty seconds. Other imbibers followed at regular intervals. The fastest time was set by a big bloke in a leather jacket who managed to order, down his drink and be out of the bar in seventeen seconds flat. I had been there fifteen minutes and was still only half way through my beer. No wonder I was getting funny looks. Theirs was not social drinking. There was no joy in this. People came into this bar to demolish drinks. No passing of the time of day, not even a nod which acknowledged the presence of anyone else; simply a quick fix and then out again. Nurse, give me something to deaden the pain.

Presently a man with a ruddy complexion which divulged the nature of his favourite pastime, staggered over to me and muttered something. I shrugged and gave him my apologetic Romanian for 'I am from England':

'*Sunt din Anglia.*'

Then he did something odd. He smiled.

'*Sunt Moldovan,*' he said, before wobbling out into the night.

I looked up to see the barmaid smiling too. I felt good. Two smiles. As Corina had said that very morning, 'Nothing is impossible.'

Darkness had fallen during the period of revelry in the bar. I started to walk back to the Journalism Centre, confused by something. This was odd. It seemed that the darkness was darker here in Moldova. It was, it was definitely darker here. How could that be? I looked up and around me to discover I was enveloped by an inky blackness. I could see nothing except for the reason why this was so. No streetlights. Not a light on anywhere. Behind me I heard breathing and, startled, I stopped and turned, only to feel a body brush past me. In the murky dimness I could just make out a woman carrying a shopping bag. I fumbled around in search of the pavement, which I was only able to do by taking advantage of the occasional moments of illumination provided by cars' headlights. Nervously I negotiated the two blocks back to the centre.

'Is there a power cut?' I asked Corina from the back seat of the car, as we headed towards the home of the family where I was to stay.

'No, it has been like this for four years now,' came the reply. 'The government is trying to save power by having no lighting in the streets.'

'Wow.'

'Yes, I suppose that you are surprised. We are used to it now. The worst thing about it is the manholes.'

'The manholes?'

'Yes, they have no covers, they are made of metal so organised gangs steal them and melt them down for profit.'

'I see. Nice mix – pitch darkness and random holes in the ground.'

'Yes, we have many injuries.'

Corina registered my look of disbelief before continuing, 'You are lucky to be staying with Grigore and Dina, they have hot water – most of the flats in Chisinau don't have this or heating because of problems with the boilers and this power shortage.'

I had become used to power always being available at the flick of a switch. I was yet to discover that much of my journey was to be taken up with learning how to cope without it.

4

Forty-three Ears

At once, I liked them both very much. Grigore was in his early forties, dark, plumpish and with a neatly trimmed wispy moustache running along his top lip. His wife Dina had an elegant beauty which I guessed would have made her quite a catch in years gone by. Kindness was in their faces. They greeted me warmly, and though evidently weary, their eyes shone with a sense of being alive which had been so absent from many of the faces I had seen throughout the day. These were my landlords. 'Two doctors – you will like them. Typical Moldovan,' Corina had said. Their children stood proudly at their sides; 17-year-old Adrian, and just the sweetest little 11-year-old girl Elena. This was to be my family while I was here. Good, I liked the idea of this.

Adrian and Elena went off to do their homework and I was left in the hallway with Dina, Grigore, and a huge communication problem. Grigore's linguistic skills covered Romanian, Russian and a little German while Dina spoke Romanian, Russian and knew a few French words. I spoke English and French. So, from our vast collective vocabularies we were reduced to scrabbling about in Dina's sparse lexicon of French in order to hobble towards any semblance of understanding.

Things moved discouragingly slowly. Grigore said something to me in rapid fire Romanian and looked at me expecting a response as if I had understood him completely. I shook my head. Dina repeated the same sentence more slowly and this time I shook my head in such a way as to suggest that I was getting closer to understanding, even though I plainly wasn't. Then I took a guess and picked up my bag, thinking that they wanted to show me to my room. They waved at me to put it down, saying '*Nu, nu, nu, nu.*' (From my extensive studies I knew that 'nu' meant 'no'.) Then Dina struggled with some French. It served no purpose other than making me feel very good about mine.

Eventually the miming began. I took to this with ease as I already felt like a man walking into the wind. Grigore made frantic gestures with his fingers near his mouth.

'Ah!' I gushed in excited realisation. 'Do I want to *eat*?'

'*Da da!*' exclaimed a relieved Grigore.

From my extensive studies I knew that Dada was either an early twentieth-century international movement in art and literature repudiating conventions and intended to shock, or Romanian for 'Yes, yes'. I took an intelligent guess that the latter had been intended, and offered my very own '*Da*' in authentic Romanian, adding in English,

'I *am* hungry.'

Grigore immediately responded at enormous speed in his native tongue. It was as if he felt that now we'd cleared the blockage caused by not knowing whether I was hungry or not, there was nothing to prevent a free-flowing dialogue from here on in. At the end of his long sentence I was too weary to try and communicate that I hadn't understood a bloody word of it, so I took a chance.

'*Da*,' I said, in confident bluff.

Grigore and Dina said nothing; in fact they looked a little shocked. I decided to change tack.

'*Nu*,' I said, correcting myself.

The two faces looked instantly relieved and Grigore laughed, picked up my bag, and lead me to my bedroom. To this day I do not know what he'd asked me. For all I know he could have said:

'Are you intending to introduce my children to Western pornography, sleep with my wife and steal vintage brandy from my collection beneath the stairs?'

'*Nu*' was the right answer to this one every time, even if you didn't really mean it.

At dinner, for which Grigore opened a bottle of Moldovan white wine in honour of his new house guest, communication was a little easier because Elena was eating with us and she spoke incredibly good English for her age, picked up largely from watching American cartoons on television. The poor girl was under enormous pressure since all dialogue was relayed through her. The delay caused by waiting for the translations brought a weighty formality to proceedings. It was like we were delegates at a meeting of the United Nations. I suddenly became aware of the power of the interpreter, a power which could easily be abused. One had no choice but to trust that they were giving an accurate representation of your views. I wondered how many of the world's troubles had been caused by interpreters simply deciding to give their own spin on things:

'The senator is saying that the US Government has decided to halt further food aid to Russia because Mr Primakov smells.'

'Well, that's interesting because Mr Primakov says he will not support sanctions against Iraq because your President has girly hair and his eyes are too close together.'

Adrian joined us at the table and ate with zeal, no doubt with a view to being back in his room as soon as possible. He looked more stern than the rest of his family and clearly had the potential to be a sulky incommunicative adolescent. His English was very good but he was a less effective translator than Elena simply because he really couldn't be bothered. On one occasion, in order to rest his increasingly tired young sister, I looked to Adrian for elucidation on something his father had said, but he just shook his head as if to say 'Honestly, that really wasn't worthy of translation.' Grigore shrugged and pulled a face which crossed language barriers. 'He's at *that* age.'

A few minutes later the inevitable question was asked.

'My farver wants to know,' said the bubbly and enchanting Elena, 'what you are doing here in Moldova.'

Ah yes, that little question. I suppose it had been bound to come up sooner or later. How I longed for a simple answer – 'I'm working at the UN' or 'I'm teaching English in a school.' Instead I had to explain, via an 11-year-old girl with an English vocabulary gleaned from animated cats and dogs, something which even fellow English speakers had struggled to comprehend. Elena did her best but was severely hampered by not knowing what the word 'bet' meant. This proved to be an insurmountable problem, and after blank looks and many a furrowed eyebrow, Adrian had the decency to step in and offer his services. In manageable chunks, I told him the nature of my task which he relayed to his expectant parents. With each piece of information their faces filled with bewilderment and by the end of the explanation Grigore's jaw was hanging open in disbelief.

'*Tu es optimist*', said Dina in her best French.

'Yes. What I am doing is kind of like a scientific experiment to prove that optimism produces results.'

On receipt of this last sentiment the entire family regarded me as if I was some kind of circus freak. Grigore filled my wine glass, said something which got a big laugh, and proposed a toast. I was oblivious to its nature, it was probably something like:

'To the nutcase we've let into our house. May we not live to regret it.'

I raised my glass.

'*Prost!*' I said, not actually knowing if this was the Romanian for 'cheers' but guessing that '*prost*' was widely used everywhere east of Strasbourg.

A sudden silence descended over the table.

'We say "*Naroc*",' said Adrian coldly, '*Prost* means stupid.'

'Oh, right, sorry.'

I immediately logged this away as 'Useful Information', reckoning that not calling the host 'stupid' had to be a distinct social advantage in any country. Fortunately, the initial astonishment around the table softened into smiles and laughter.

The wine was good. Moldova's climate and soil provides excellent conditions for vine growing, and it used to be the biggest wine producer in the former Soviet Union. In fact, in its Cricova cellars which remain state-owned, it can still boast the largest wine cellar in the world, with 64 kilometres of underground tunnels storing about 3.5 million decalitres of wine at a depth of 60 metres. It seems that when the Soviets did things, they did things big. Moldova was *the* winery of the former communist state and Cricova was *the* wine cellar. Apparently, Yuri Gagarin, the legendary first man in space, wrote in the visitors book when he visited Cricova in 1966:

'It is easier to overcome the power of gravitation than the attraction of these wine cellars.'

Gagarin clearly meant what he said since he spent a full two days in the place before venturing back out into daylight. Well, if you liked a drink, as Yuri clearly did, then you could see his point of view.

It became apparent that Grigore liked drink, if not as much as Yuri Gagarin, then certainly as much as I did, since most of the bottle served to replenish our two glasses only. The rest of the family, the abstemious ones, retired to bed early and Grigore and I were left alone. He offered me a Moldovan cognac and I judged that it would have been rude to refuse. Besides, here was an opportunity to bond man to man with a nice easy chat. Grigore poured the brandy proudly and raised his glass.

'*Naroc!*' I said, keeping my fingers crossed that my poor pronunciation hadn't meant that I'd just called him an arsehole.

'*Naroc!*' he replied, beaming playfully.

Things had got off to a good start.

It was to be downhill from here. I was bombarded with another torrent of strange guttural sounds which meant that Grigore was asking me another question. His eyes twinkled expectantly awaiting my reply. You had to admire his complete refusal to accept that I had a vocabulary of only four words in his language. One of them, '*Prost*', was going to become relevant soon if he carried on like this. I smiled vacuously in recognition of not having recognised a word. Grigore took a sip from his brandy and it somehow gave him the inspiration to attempt some English.

'What iz you? Ears?'

'What?'

'What iz you ears?'

'Ears?'

'*Da* – ears. *Uno, doi, tre* – ears! What iz your ears?'

'I'm not sure I know what you mean.'

Yes I was. I was damn sure I didn't have a clue what he meant.

'Me,' continued Grigore bravely. 'Me – *patruzeci trei* ears.'

Ah, I recognised some numbers in there. I'd learned a bit of counting.

'*Patruzeci* – that's forty.'

'*Da.*'

'And *trei* is three.'

'*Da.*'

'Right. So you're saying you have forty-three ears?'

'*Da! Da!*' he cried with immense relief.

I looked at him in disbelief. He appeared to be exaggerating by forty-one.

'Oh!' I said, the penny finally dropping. 'You're saying you have forty-three *years*.'

'*Da. Da*. What iz *your* ears?'

'I'm thirty-eight.'

He looked blank. No surprise that he had failed to understand. Five minutes later after much laborious holding up of fingers he had a rough idea of how old I was, which would have been something he could have divined simply by looking at me. I took a sip of brandy. This male bonding thing was rather hard work. I wasn't looking forward to the part where we moved on to politics. However, by manufacturing three consecutive yawns I was able to signal that bedtime was upon us and thankfully our struggle was over. We exchanged goodnights and shook hands cordially. The little chat, though hardly a flowing one, had confirmed one thing at least. We liked each other.

As I lay on the single bed in my colourless, uncomplicated bedroom I felt strangely at home. The family had set me at ease. They'd brought to me a warmth. This was something I would come to rely on in the coming weeks. In Moldova you looked to relationships for warmth. The radiators were useless.

We were lost again, just as we had been the previous day.

'Is it a national characteristic of Moldovans not to number things correctly?' I asked Iulian cheekily.

'People do number their addresses correctly,' he replied, 'but I'm trying to convince the driver that he's not where he thinks he is.'

I would need less convincing. I already felt as if I was in some kind of suspended reality. I had spent the morning in the back of a Lada which was driving us around the drab suburbs of the city in a search for Zimbru Chisinau's training ground. At ten-minute intervals we had pulled over the side of the road so that Iulian and the taxi driver Alexandru could argue over the map before setting off to a number of locations which had only one thing in common – that of not being Zimbru Chisinau's training ground.

At one point I had been hopeful. We were outside some gates with 'Zimbru Chisinau' written on them. For me, this was promising. Surely worth getting out and asking. But no, Iulian insisted that this was the wrong address and he instructed the driver to take us off in search of the right one.

An hour later we pulled up outside the same gates.

'This is not it, but I will go and ask,' said Iulian without enthusiasm.

I watched from the back seat as he ambled up to two men who were sharing an animated conversation. He did not interrupt but stood patiently by for them to finish. Iulian was confident and self-assured but he certainly wasn't pushy. Ten minutes later, when the men had finished their conversation and exchanged protracted goodbyes Iulian seized his moment. The discussion which followed did not seem to be taking the form of Iulian receiving directions to another location. When he returned to the car I sought enlightenment.

'Well?' I asked.

'This is the place, the players are training in there,' he said without a hint of an apology.

'Good.'

'Wait. It's not all good. That man was the club's president Nicolae Ciornii. I told him what you wanted to do and he said that they are operating a closed regime at the moment. No-one is allowed into the grounds. They are practising every day because they have a full programme with matches every other day. He says that right now they will not have any time to help you but they do have a short break between the 1st and 7th November when it might be possible.'

I sat numb in the back seat of the car. This wasn't how it was supposed to be. Closed regime? Players practising every day? I had expected the Moldovan footballers to be amateurs who I could meet at the factory gates after work and lead jovially off to the tennis courts. I wasn't at all happy with this revelation. The facts that Iulian had just related to me swirled in my head. Today was 20th October. The players might be able to help between the 1st and the 7th. But that was two weeks away. I looked up at Iulian with a wry smile.

'This is disastrous news,' I said.

'Yes,' he smiled back, 'but we can try the others.'

And try the others we did. At the offices of FC Constructorul a man told us that the players were training but that he didn't know where, and anyway he doubted if they would have time to play any tennis because they too were playing matches every other day. At the club called Moldova Gaz the man pretty much told Iulian to get lost. I'd had better mornings. Lunch would need to be damn good.

We ate at a *cantina* which was a favourite among the staff of the Journalism Centre. It was called La Fertilitata, meaning 'fertility', somewhat ironic given the barren nature of our morning. The food was good here, although you would not have guessed it from its shabby decor. It was dimly lit with its too few windows swathed in thick net curtains deadening any natural light. This place was still state run and a fairly good yardstick for what all restaurants would have been like seven years ago before independence and the move towards capitalism. I was beginning to discover that 'taking the trouble to make it look nice' had not been high up on the communist regime's list of priorities. Give them what they need, not what they want.

Most of the tables were full, with people eating in virtual silence. This environment wasn't proving to be the great spirit lifter which I badly needed; however, I was enjoying my *prajita*, a kind of pastry stuffed with cheese, and Glen was proving to be good company.

Glen was another American volunteer from the peace corps who knew Iulian and had come over to join us at our table. He was affable and seemed to have a good sense of humour. It wasn't long before he asked the inevitable.

'So Tony, what are you doing here in Moldova?'

'Take a guess.'

He took lots of guesses, most of which involved my being from some business, government-backed organisation or Aid programme. Twenty minutes later and after several determined utterances of 'Now wait up, I'm gonna get this', he still wasn't even close. Finally the staggering truth was revealed to him.

'That is the weirdest bet I have ever heard,' he stated emphatically. 'Tony, you're cool.'

'Thanks.'

I wished I felt it.

'What did you put on your visa form for "Purpose of visit"?'

'Pleasure.'

'Wow. You know you must be the only Western guy in this country who has come here for pleasure. If I had a hat on I'd take it off to you.'

Momentarily I pictured a Moldovan civil servant in the Interior Ministry logging details of his country's visitors:

Businessmen	*Aid workers*	*Nutters*
34	76	1

'How's it going so far?' asked Glen.

'Not too well at the moment.'

'And how long have you been going?'

'This is my second day.'

'Oh well you've only just begun. Things take a little while longer here.'

I explained about the unsuccessful morning and how my next idea was to send personal faxes via the clubs to all the players, explaining about the bet.

'I've brought some Wimbledon Tennis T-shirts as well,' I added. 'I'm going to send one of them to each player in a grovelling attempt to make them think more favourably of me.'

'You're quite something Tony,' said Glen before turning and addressing Iulian. 'That's the thing I love about travelling – you always get to meet some of the weirdest characters.'

When I had travelled extensively as a younger man I had always thought the same, but I'd never imagined that I would become someone else's 'weirdest character'. I felt uneasy about whether this was a sign of progress in my life.

'Oh I don't think I'm so weird,' I began in my defence. 'I'm just trying to prove that I'm right and someone else is wrong. People do that all the time.'

'Not in Moldova they don't.'

'I promise you, I'm not weird.'

'Oh, I think you are. It's a positive weird, but you're weird.'

'I honestly don't think I am.'

Iulian stepped in just before the discussion rose to the intellectual heights of 'Are!' 'Am not!' 'Are!' 'Am not!' by announcing that we should get back to the Journalism Centre and begin work on the faxes.

'There you are,' I said to Glen. 'I can't be weird. I've finished lunch and I've got to go back to the office. You can't get more normal than that.'

For a moment Glen looked beaten, but I let myself down badly when Iulian asked what we would do in the next couple of days while we waited for a response to the faxes.

'Deliver the Round Table to King Arthur,' I said.

Game, set and match to Glen.

Thank goodness he wasn't a Moldovan footballer.

5

'Don't Play Spynu'

The round table fitted quite neatly under the back seat of the dilapidated bus. My carrying it on board had not caused much interest among the rest of the passengers, my guess being that in this country it wasn't unusual to be travelling with something unusual. However, when I began speaking English with Iulian, heads turned to stare. A foreigner. Moldovans didn't see many of them, especially travelling on their buses. Most Westerners avoided the discomfort and spent twenty dollars on the hire of a car and a driver. Since I was planning on staying over in Soroca it hadn't really been an option. No, the passengers would have to endure our English for the three and half hours it would take us to reach our destination.

Well, they would have done if the driver hadn't turned the radio on. Loud. God no! Truly excruciating Russian pop. Now there are some things the Russians do very well, (nurture young gymnasts, produce hirsute and scarcely female shot-putters, and encourage visits to Siberia with compulsory labour and comfortless accommodation thrown in) but in the sphere of pop music they do not excel. Their pop songs are catchy, but much in the same way as infectious diseases. Their songwriters understand the need to provide a melodious hook, but its endless repetition means that by the end of the song it is a hook you feel like hanging yourself from. Russian pop music does for the soul what . . . no, let's just leave it there – Russian pop music does for the soul. No wonder the bloke in front of me looked like he wanted to kill himself. Three and a half hours of this and he'd want to kill everyone around him too. (I figured I'd be in no danger provided he did the suicide part of things first.)

Soroca, the mountain village where King Arthur resided, sounded good to me. Apparently it possessed an ancient fortress built by Stefan cel Mare. Stefan cel Mare (Stephen the Great) was the big

Moldovan hero. He'd been King of the Moldovans in the fifteenth century and scored significant victories (though short-lived) over his assailants the Slavs and the Ottomans. After independence from the Soviet Union in 1991 all the statues of Lenin had been removed and replaced by this chap, and now the main streets in all the towns were named after him instead of Communism's great architect. It was just as well that Leningrad wasn't in Moldova. Stefancelmaregrad would be as easy on the ear as a Russian pop song.

The journey was hardly through breathtaking scenery. There were occasional gentle rolling hills which were pleasant enough but mostly it was flat expanses of dull brown farmland. Villages were set back from the road, their names emblazoned in garish blue and yellow on large columns by the roadside. From time to time the bus would pull out to overtake a farmer riding in a horse and cart, untouched by any of this century's technology. Then we would splutter to a halt at a bus-stop to exchange one set of life-weary passengers for another. No-one needed to tell you that village life was hard. The faces said it all. No plumbing, no hot water and in many cases no electricity. Bearable in the summer maybe, but during the Moldovan winter? No thanks.

'They are worse off now than they were under communism,' said Iulian.

'In what way?'

'Well, under the old system everyone could afford a family holiday by the Black Sea, and if you saved hard you could buy a car after ten years. There was not much choice of goods though. Under the *new* system, everything is available but no-one can afford it.'

'So they regret the change then?'

'Some do. The old ones. But at least they can move about freely now.'

'What do you mean?'

'Well, under the Soviets they had to carry internal passports and they could not leave the village without a reason which had to be approved by a party official.'

My God. They couldn't even move about their own country without creeping to some sycophantic bureaucrat. I realised how I had taken freedom for granted. I looked out of the window, and as the trees and houses sped past me as if on rewind, I let my mind spool back to my childhood in England, and the number of times I'd said, 'I can do that, this is a free country.' I'd used those words without any comprehension of what not being in a free country meant.

The conversation with Iulian brought other explanations as to why the average Moldovan face when in relaxed mode looked sullen. His grandparents had saved hard all their lives and finally had enough money to buy a small house of their own when independence came and private ownership was permitted. Then the Moldovan currency collapsed overnight and in the morning their savings were enough to buy them a joint of meat.

'My God. They must have felt terrible,' I said, rather regretting the crass obviousness of the comment.

'It killed them. Within two years they were both dead.'

It was another ten miles before I could resume any conversation.

I was the last one off the bus when we reached Soroca, struggling with my royal gift.

'I suppose we should head for the centre now,' I said, looking at the deserted streets around me.

'This is the centre,' said Iulian.

'Are you sure? You said you hadn't been here before.'

'I'm ninety-five per cent sure. This is the main street.'

'But there's nothing here.'

'I know. Chisinau is dull but it is nothing compared to the rest of Moldova.'

Iulian, I took it, had never applied for a job at The Moldovan Tourist Office. I looked around me and all I could see were decaying concrete buildings. No shops, no cafes, no people.

'I can't believe,' I said, 'that we've spent three and half hours on a bus to come here. *And* we're going to spend the night.'

'We could get last bus back,' quipped a chuckling Iulian, 'Anita will know when it leaves.'

Anita was Glen's friend. Like all the Americans I had met so far she was another volunteer from the Peace Corps. This was an entirely philanthropic organisation set up by President Kennedy in 1961 for the purpose of fighting tyranny, disease, poverty and war. That's what JFK said anyway – others might feel that one significant bi-product of its work was to make Third World countries think more kindly of the Americans and therefore facilitate the insidious invasion of their economies by incoming US companies. So, was the Peace Corps benevolent or cynical? As far as I was concerned the jury was out. But not in Soroca. No-one was out in Soroca, the place was dead.

Over lunch I asked Anita why she had signed up to this organisation.

'Well,' came her reply, 'that depends who you ask. If you ask me, I'll tell you that my life back home had gotten into a rut and that I wanted to do something new and I reckoned I could live with the hardship, especially if I was helping others. If you ask my brother he'll tell you it's because I'm a fucking idiot.'

Two perfectly sound arguments. From Iulian's face I could tell which one he favoured. The irony was that he would have loved the chance to make a go of it in America, the land of opportunity, and yet here was someone who had voluntarily turned her back on that playground of plenty to come and struggle along with the Moldovans. I could see both his point of view and also Anita's, but I wasn't sure whether either of them could see mine.

'And you're doing all this just to win a lousy bet?' crowed Anita between sips of soup.

'Is it so lousy? I think it's rather a good bet.'

Her face told me that she shared the same feelings towards my reason for being here as her brother did about hers.

'What do you know of the gypsy community here?' I asked her.

'Well, they were forced to settle under the Soviet regime and they've prospered living that way. They're a wealthy community and they live in these great big houses on the hill but I've never been up there. The Moldovans in the town say that it isn't safe.'

'We'll be alright, we come bearing gifts. Well, one gift anyway.'

I pointed to the round table which was leaning against the wall still neatly wrapped and dotted with Air Moldova stickers and an entirely inappropriate 'Fragile' sign.

'Glen said you were bringing that,' said Anita with a chuckle. 'You do know that Moldova is absolutely full of plastic round tables.'

'Yes, but this is a special one though, it's from Do it All,' I replied to an increasingly bemused Anita.

'Why do you want to meet this King so much?'

'Well, when I last took on a bet of this nature I went to Ireland and I met a king there – the King of Tory island – so meeting royalty is a tradition.'

'Makes sense. Can I come with you guys? I could do with an adventure.'

There probably weren't that many adventures to be had here in Soroca so it was probably a good idea to grab them when they came along.

'Of course you can come with us Anita. The more the merrier, and it'll be one more person to take turns in carrying the table,' I said, gallantly.

The fortress, like almost everything else I had experienced in Moldova so far, was a disappointment. It was just an old round fortification and what's more it was closed. Anita, who had brought us there as part of a short sightseeing tour, said that it was quite interesting inside but to obtain admission you had to go round to some bloke's house who had the key and hope that he was in and not too soaked in vodka to conduct a guided tour. Moldovan tourism.

Anita, who had previously been lucky enough to have done the tour, explained that the original builder of the fortress, Stefan cel Mare, had been the cousin of Vlad the Devil who himself was the father of Vlad the Impaler. Interesting family. I wondered whether they'd all been vicious sadistic killers or if there had been a rather more gentle brother called Vlad the Librarian. I liked to think so. I could picture the scene at dinner.

VLAD THE DEVIL: (Munching on the dismembered arm of a victim)
Well Vlad, what kind of day have you had?

VLAD THE IMPALER: It was a good one today Dad – six eviscerations.

VLAD THE DEVIL: No impalings?

VLAD THE IMPALER: No, but I've got two booked in for tomorrow.

VLAD THE DEVIL: Excellent. And how about you Vlad?

VLAD THE LIBRARIAN: Well, I've had quite a day too, Father. We fined Vlad the Tardy for returning two books which were three weeks overdue and I had to say 'Ssssh' eight times to Vlad the Bellower in the reference section.

VLAD THE DEVIL: (Under his breath)
Where did Vlad the Mother and I go wrong with that boy?

We continued walking along the banks of the Nistru river looking over to the Ukraine on the opposite bank. Not far up from the fortress there were deserted looking international checkpoints on each side of the river. There was no bridge linking them. Movement between the two countries was such that a ferry sufficed.

'We could nip over to the Ukraine for a cup of tea,' I suggested.

'No you couldn't,' replied Iulian, 'not unless you have a visa.'

'Couldn't they issue me one there?'

Iulian laughed.

'You don't understand how things work here,' he said. 'You would have to apply for one in Chisinau and it could take up to two weeks before it was issued – and it would cost you one hundred dollars.'

'It's crazy,' I moaned. 'These countries desperately need foreign money injected into their economies and yet they make it so hard for people to go there.'

'I know, but most of the former Soviet bloc countries are being run by guys who came up through the Party system and they are still suspicious of the West.'

And so the Ukraine was to remain unvisited. It was a case of so near and yet so far.

'What would be the first big town we hit if we kept walking in that direction?' I asked, pointing into the far distance.

'Chernobyl, I think.'

Okay. Maybe not going to the Ukraine wasn't such a great loss.

Chernobyl; a place where Grigore's first sentence to me in English would have made complete sense.

'Me, I have forty-three ears.'

'Yes I can see that. Nice to meet you.'

We left the river bank and wandered up to Soroca's hotel where Iulian and I were intending to stay. It was unusual for a small Moldovan town to have such a hostelry but this one had been built to cater for Communist Party officials who visited Soroca and its fortress as part of a tour which they took as one of their many perks. The drab grey crumbling structure before us resembled a closed-down factory. I reached the large glass double doors and pushed. To my surprise they opened. Inside there was no sign of life. Iulian called out and presently a grumpy unhelpful looking woman appeared. (She must have pipped hundreds of other grumpy unhelpfuls to the post.) She explained that a double room with two single beds would cost the equivalent of $20.

'That's expensive,' said Iulian.

'Well, we're not exactly spoiled for choice here,' I replied. 'Tell her we'll take it.'

The woman then asked me for something and held out her hand.

'She wants your passport,' explained Iulian.

'But I haven't brought it,' I said, recognising yet another reason why the Ukraine was off limits, 'I thought since we weren't leaving the country . . . look, tell her we'll pay her in advance and she can have a credit card as further security if she wants it.'

The grumpy unhelpful one was having none of it. Forms needed to be filled out which required my passport number. She was adamant – no passport, no bed for the night. The thought of a cold night sleeping rough did not appeal, but pleading fell on deaf ears.

'Ask her,' I said to Iulian, 'if she is going to turn away two paying customers from an hotel which is clearly empty, simply because of some minor administrative detail.'

Iulian did so, and got shouted at for his trouble. This was a state-run hotel and the notion of profit meant nothing. This lady moved in a world where rules, regulations and looking grumpy were what mattered, and she was good at her job. She would have earned promotion had such a concept existed.

'You're both welcome to my floor,' said Anita generously.

'Thanks. It'll be nicer than this place anyway.' I said.

I thanked the woman with a grace intended to provoke a modicum of shame (it didn't) and left her to punch the air in celebration at having turned two more people away.

Huge houses, some as big as palaces, dominated the skyline at the top of the hill.

'Quite something isn't it?' said Anita.

'It certainly is,' I replied, shaking my head in wonder. 'They must be so rich – they're the opposite of gypsies everywhere else in the world.'

I clung on tight to my video camera remembering what Anita had been told by the villagers about it not being safe but I did not feel worried. I felt that this was probably a paranoid fear which had been nurtured over centuries of prejudice against the Romani peoples of the world. Theirs has not been a happy history. Persecution mostly. Their social organisation probably hasn't helped them much in acquiring a general acceptance wherever they end up, since gypsies are largely encouraged not to socialise with non-Romani, whom they call *gadje*. Keeping yourself separate in this way is always going to result in your being pretty high in the International Scapegoat chart. But with wealth comes power and here in Moldova, in an extraordinary twist on our expectations, the gypsies had it better than everyone else.

'Do gypsies build houses like this in England?' asked a gypsy man as he proudly stood outside his palace. Of course, he already knew the answer.

We had asked him if he knew where King Arthur lived and he promised that he would tell us, but not until he and his wife had taken us on a guided tour of their house. It was built on a lavish scale with an oriental and Moorish design and with an extraordinarily shiny metal roof. Inside it was commodious and ostentatious with exotic chandeliers and frescos of biblical scenes covering the walls. The husband who appeared to be in his late fifties explained that he had built the house with the money that he had earned from working in Russia for one year. It was fairly apparent to all of us that in a year you simply couldn't make that amount of money legally. He must have been involved in drug smuggling or some such illicit activity. It was odd to be accepting the hospitality of someone who we were sure was a criminal. Quite possibly this whole community was built on criminal activity. Theirs was a lopsided culture in which breaking the law was the norm, and boy did it pay. For them it was not indecent, and it wasn't wrong. Those who followed the rule of law were mugs. Like the Moldovans struggling down in the village.

I felt nervous as Iulian listened to the directions to King Arthur's place. As expected, a long period of aimless wandering followed. At almost every turn we stumbled on a house which was fit for a king, but sadly not King Arthur's. Iulian looked decidedly pissed off. Since I was filming with my video camera it had fallen upon him to lug the Do It All round table and he was not enjoying the experience.

Eventually, by taking the opposite direction to the one proposed by Iulian, we met a little old lady in a black headscarf who was sitting on a seat in front of some big, black wrought-iron gates. She told us we were standing directly outside King Arthur's house. We asked if she was sure and she replied that she was, and we felt confident of this when she went on to explain that she was his mother. She told us that King Arthur had gone to Chisinau and wouldn't be back until tomorrow.

Great, I thought. He was in exactly the place from which I'd just spent three and a half hours travelling on an uncomfortable bus. However, once the mother learned that I had travelled all the way from England with a gift for her son, she immediately invited us inside and gave us the now standard tour of the property.

It was capacious and gaudy with frescos of the family on all the walls. Justifiable I suppose since they were a royal family. The gypsies governed themselves according to an intricate pattern of family relationships with a group of related families forming the *vista* (clan) which was headed by a leader called the *baro* (king). King Arthur's mother, Anushka, babbled in a mixture of Russian and the gypsy language *Roma* which Iulian struggled to translate. She had been recently widowed when her husband Mircea, the former King, had died. She may have all these riches, she said pointing around her, but she was nothing without a husband and so she no longer went out. Anita let out a little yelp. These were hardly the feminist views which she had learnt on America's West Coast.

'Is it true,' I asked, 'that according to gypsy tradition, the belongings of the deceased are buried along with them?'

I had read about this and thought it a rather noble custom since it encouraged people to distribute wealth while they were still alive rather than hoard it and then pass it on to some spoilt child for subsequent squandering. It seemed that Mircea's death may have been rather sudden and precluded a satisfactory distribution of his assets, since according to Anushka he had been buried along with a computer laptop and a mobile phone. The spiritualists and psychics in the gypsy community must have felt under threat. No need for a seance to contact the dead any more. Just ring the mobile. (Assuming that Mircea had gone to heaven of course – one of the major drawbacks of hell is that you can't get a signal down there.)

After we had toured the huge bedroom which was almost like a dancehall, Anushka showed us a smaller room which contained some of Mircea's other possessions which for some reason had not been buried. One was a gun. A large rifle.

'What did he use it for?' I asked.

'Shooting at night – just shooting at night,' came Iulian's translation.

'Shooting at what?'

Anushka spoke for some time.

'Anything – he'd just go out and shoot,' was Iulian's abridgement.

Fair enough. A man needs hobbies.

Back in the living room we met two new old ladies; one was Anushka's mother, Dunea, and the other a cousin named Natasha. I announced that I wanted to make a formal presentation of my gift. On learning this, Anushka scuttled off to bring drinks. I don't know what kind of gift she felt that I had brought for her son, but the impressive array of champagnes and cognacs which were laid before us suggested that she was expecting it to be rather better than a Do It All round table. I became a little nervous as to what response its eventual offering might elicit.

We were asked if we wanted Moldovan brandy with champagne chasers and we said 'Yes, thank you'. Well, it would have been rude not to. Dunea and Natasha didn't put up much of a fight either. An easy half an hour passed with regular replenishment of all of our glasses and I marvelled at how quickly we had gone from being strangers outside the gates to being treated like old family friends. These people either prided themselves on being excellent hosts or would settle for any old excuse to sit around and get pissed.

Then the moment arrived. I stood up on slightly wobbly feet and made a slurred speech to three old gypsy ladies in a remote outpost of northern Moldova explaining the historical significance of King Arthur and his round table. (An inevitable event in my life – in fact I couldn't understand why it had taken so long to come about.) My now drunk translator did his best, but frankly I don't think he had a clue what I was rambling on about.

I made a formal presentation of the table to Anushka and she accepted it with good grace. She showed neither pleasure nor disenchantment. She had every right to be insulted, it was after all a shabby present, but she remained unmoved, her years as a royal probably having required her to develop an expression which disclosed no emotion, even in the light of disappointing furniture. She left the room and I felt a tad nervous that she might have been fetching her late husband's gun with a view to demonstrating how it was still in full working order, but she returned bearing gifts. She proudly presented Iulian and Anita with a pair of socks each, and I was given some underpants with 'Made in Romania' stamped on them. A fair exchange. A plastic round table for a slightly dodgy pair of pants. (I only wished I'd suggested a similar barter in Do It All instead of parting with cash.)

I enquired whether my new lady friends knew of anyone who could read my fortune, and Natasha was quick to put herself forward as something of an expert in reading the cards. I was whisked into another room where I was promptly asked to part with 50 lei (around ten dollars). I began bargaining, believing that not to do so would be an insult. I waved twenty lei back at Natasha and she shook her head dismissively. I was just about to produce another ten when I heard

Anushka's voice and turned around to see her at the door sternly castigating her cousin. Natasha meekly nodded to her, took my twenty lei and began the reading. My, Anushka really must have been taken with that table.

I had never been to any kind of fortune-teller before, my thinking being that doing so puts you in a no-win situation. If they're right then you know what is going to happen and the fun goes out of finding out (*Yeah, yeah, I knew I was going to get that promotion)* and if they're wrong you might not find out till you'd already followed their advice and gone out and made yourself a Lloyds Name. However on this occasion I decided that it was entirely the right thing to do, a decision in no small way linked to the amount of brandy and champagne chasers I had drunk.

Natasha set three cards down before her and launched into the usual clichés.

'You will have a trip,' she declared, via the patient Iulian.

Not a difficult prediction to make since I was in Moldova and she knew I didn't live here. It was a fair assumption that getting home without making a trip would be tricky. I wasn't impressed. It was a bit like beginning a fortune-telling with the words, 'You will go to the toilet soon.' We all know that. We want something more specific like, 'You will go to the toilet some time in March.'

She continued.

'Watch out during the night – there is some danger.'

What danger? Which night? But before I could ask she had placed more cards down on the table and was offering further divinations.

'You are planning some work and you will manage it.'

Excellent, did this mean that I would beat the entire Moldovan national football team at tennis? Or did it simply mean that one day I would successfully creosote the shed in my back garden? Natasha needed to be more precise.

'Can you ask her,' I whispered to Iulian, 'if she can tell me what's going to happen to me in the next three weeks?'

'She says she will get to that,' said Iulian.

First I had to sit through more excruciating nonsense.

'There are two women in your future,' she went on. 'A dark one and a blonde one. Pick the dark one.'

I see, it was as simple as that. Pick the dark one. That might not be such an easy decision if I found myself involved in a love triangle with Denise Van Outen and Anne Widdecombe. 'Sorry, Denise, but you've got the wrong colour hair.'

There was more drivel to follow including the extraordinary information that there would be 'some white man in my fate'. Who would have thought that living as I did in a country with a population in the region of 25 million white men, there would be one who would manage to become involved in my fate? I should certainly be keeping a close eye on all the white men in my life from here on in.

Finally growing tired, I lent over with my notebook and showed her the names of the footballers and asked her to tell me which ones I should play first and which ones were going to be good at tennis. Something in her expression told me that this was a question she hadn't been asked before. This did not fall within her usual domain. Normally for twenty lei she didn't actually tell you anything that might be of use to you but on this occasion she had Anushka standing over her, and Anushka loved me because I'd given her son a plastic round table.

Natasha took my notebook and looked at the names for some time before turning to Iulian and declaring that she couldn't read. I wondered what had caused the delay. She should have been party to that information immediately. It was almost as if she had looked at the notebook in the hope that she *could* read and then discovered that for some reason today it just wasn't happening. 'I'm sorry but I can't read today. Sore throat.'

Iulian read the footballers names to her and instead of telling me in which order to challenge them she told me which ones I should play and which ones should be avoided. Romanenco and Fistican met her approval but the moment she heard the name Spynu, she shook her head forcefully and uttered disapprovingly,

'Don't play Spynu!'

She went on to damn Culibaba, Sishkin and Miterev with the same dismissive air. These four, she said, should be avoided at all costs, and I should not play them. Furthermore she maintained that I should not drink with these characters as they would try to poison me.

This was dramatic stuff and not at all what I had been expecting. I had thought that maybe one or two of the footballers might be unwilling to play me but I had never imagined that any of them would harbour any desire to have me poisoned. Surely they didn't take their tennis that seriously?

I thanked Natasha but decided to ignore her advice, for two reasons. First, because to have followed it would have meant that the bet was lost, and secondly because she was clearly talking complete bollocks.

That night, as I lay awake cursing the hardness of Anita's floor I imagined the exchange which might have taken place between King Arthur and his mother when he arrived back later that evening.

'Mother, I don't believe it – you're pissed again.'

'Only a little.'

'And what's this crappy table?'

'Well, apparently there were these English knights who all sat—'

'And where are my new socks and boxer shorts?'

'Ah. *Yours* were they?'

6
Independence Day

I was ready to break out on my own.

'Are you sure you'll be all right?' enquired Iulian like an over-protective parent.

'I'll be fine,' I replied like an over-confident teenager.

It was Thursday afternoon and we were at Chisinau bus station having left Anita, Soroca and my three gypsy girlfriends three and a half hours behind us. Up until this point I had always been chaperoned around the capital but now I felt I had acquired enough basic Romanian and city experience to be able to get home alone. Iulian had given incredibly detailed instructions, right down to the last lamp post. I couldn't blow it.

The maxi taxis, as they were called, seemed to be a very good idea and the city swarmed with them. These were minibuses which could be flagged down at any point and would drop you anywhere on demand, and they were my favoured travel option. The city trams looked no fun at all, jam packed as they were with contorted passengers, but always willing to stop for the indecorous stuffing of yet one more human inside, just like one might try and force a shirt into an already overflowing linen basket. There was no such thing as a 'TRAM FULL' sign in this town.

With the directions memorised down to the last detail I hauled myself on to the maxi taxi. I attempted to offer money to the driver, but he was having none of it and waved me away impatiently. This was strange. I thought these things were privately run – surely they couldn't be free? I sat down near a window and began looking for the landmarks by which I would chart my course and felt a tap on my shoulder. I turned to see a woman handing me a one lei note. Stranger still. It appeared I was being *paid* to travel on the capital's transport system. No wonder the economy was in trouble – these Moldovans really hadn't grasped this free-market business at all. I smiled at the woman and declined her kind offer, but she frowned, muttered something and forced it upon me. Baffled, I sat holding the note in front of me like an infected needle until she pointed to the man in front and urged me to give it to him. Ah, she must have owed it to him, I thought, so I timidly tapped him on the shoulder and passed it on, happy to have fulfilled my intermediary debt-collecting role. Instead of thanking me, the man simply took the money and gave it to the woman in front of him. Crikey, how many passengers owed other people money on this bus? It wasn't until the money had arrived at the driver and he had turned and shouted something angrily at me that I finally understood the system. You get on, sit down and pass one lei forward to the driver. In a slight panic I apologised, quite possibly in Italian instead of Romanian, and passed my money forward while my fellow passengers demonstrated their well-rehearsed dirty looks. This hurdle over, the rest of the journey should be fine, I thought.

I hadn't reckoned on the diversion. Just around the corner from the bus station the road was blocked and the police waved their batons frantically re-directing us on to a route devoid of any hospital, basilica, or roundabout mentioned by Iulian. Within a mere five minutes of leaving him I had become completely lost in a strange city with a hostile crowd and a suspicious driver for company. Twice before I had been driven from the Journalism Centre to my lodgings; but on both occasions it had been pitch dark and I'd learnt nothing from the journeys of an orienteering nature which could be useful to me now. All I knew was what Grigore had shown me on my first night when he'd led me out of his back door, walked me through his garden and shown me a shop called 'Avida' which was in the main road where all the buses, trams and maxi taxis stopped.

Desperately I scanned the street ahead in the hope that the shop might appear like a saviour before me, but it didn't. I took a moment to assess my immediate prospects. Having no map, hardly any language, and no idea in which direction we were heading, they probably weren't that good. After the ten minutes had elapsed which Iulian had estimated for the journey I felt I should take some action before I ended up somewhere in some remote backwater of the city's suburbs. The maxi taxi had now become rather full with bodies filling what little standing space had become available. I grabbed my bag struggled forward to ask my chum the driver for assistance.

As I reached him he stopped the van to let a passenger off, much to my relief. It was too crowded on here, and now that I was standing I needed enough room to be able to bend down so that I could look out of the window for a glimpse of the elusive 'Avida'. A lady got off but the driver wanted to let three more on. What was he thinking of? There simply wasn't room. Two men forced themselves through the door but the third guy couldn't manage it. The driver turned to me, pointed to my bag which I was clutching to my chest, and signalled to me to put it on the floor by his gear stick. Reluctantly, and under a barrage of clamorous and ill-tempered Romanian, I obliged. This enabled the cramming in of one more body.

Excellent, what fun I was having. It was now difficult for me to bend down to see out of the window without forcing my bottom into the face of the elderly woman sitting immediately to my left. She looked a little shaken, probably never having been subjected to a British arse at such close proximity before. If things carried on like this, in ten minutes she would be able to select mine as her specialist subject on Mastermind.

When the driver made his next stop two people squeezed past me to get off but astonishingly another four were admitted. This had the alarming result of forcing me down the minibus and away from my bag and, given that I couldn't see beyond the back of the head of the man in front of me whose neck my nose was being plunged into, anyone could take my bag and I could do nothing about it. Inside it there was a camera worth the equivalent of three years' salary for the average Moldovan. It might be someone's lucky day. So far, it hadn't been mine.

Just when I had finished an exhaustive mental search of the 'What on earth should I do?' section of my brain and decided that the only real option was to start crying and shout '*I want my mummy!*' at the top of my voice, quite miraculously we drew up alongside a shop with the letters 'AVIDA' spelt out above its window.

'Stop!' I bellowed, fighting my way forward towards the door.

Grudgingly, passengers made what little space they could and I forced my way through this black hole of Calcutta to the front of the mini-bus. To my immense relief, the bag with its valuable contents remained untouched at the very front of the vehicle. It seemed that the years spent under a disciplinarian communist regime with its harsh penalties for offenders meant that opportunist thieves were still thin on the ground. Never mind, a few more years of capitalism would sort that out. For now though, I thanked my lucky stars, grabbed my bag and hopped on to the pavement a relieved man.

With surprising ease I found the back gate to my lodgings and made my way through Grigore's small but nonetheless overgrown garden and headed round the side of the house to its back door. On reaching it, I realised that I had a problem. I had in my hand the front door key and I was standing in front of the back door. No problem you'd think – simply walk round the path to the correct door. Easy, but for the large Alsatian dog which was barring that particular route, chained to its kennel and staring me out with eyes which suggested that it was the dog equivalent of a fanatical terrorist. The dog looked mean. The dog looked hungry. The dog looked like it might be very good indeed at taking hold of my leg in its teeth and never letting it go.

I had a problem. No-one in the family would be back for three or four hours and, given recent experiences, I wasn't overly keen on taking a maxi-taxi back to the Journalism Centre. I weighed up the situation and decided that it might be possible to run past the dog. If I took a run up, I could be travelling at a sufficient speed to prevent it being able to get enough purchase on my leg to hang on. However, I knew there was a risk of injury and my fitness was of paramount importance, given that I was in this country on purely sporting business. I wasn't aware of any tennis player on the professional circuit who prepared for matches by running past savage-looking Alsation dogs – other than maybe Goran Ivanisevic. It was a risk, but eventually I concluded that it was a risk worth taking. Furthermore, I had the brilliant but perhaps in hindsight somewhat foolish idea to film the event so that my heroic encounter with a savage dog might be on record for posterity.

Dumbly, I began setting up the camera tripod, just beyond reach of the dog's chain. For some reason, this seemed to provoke the dog and it began barking furiously. With the sound of each extension of the tripod's legs my canine friend became more agitated, for as far as the poor dog could make out, not only was I an unwanted trespasser but now I was an unwanted trespasser setting up a piece of equipment specifically designed for dog torture. It didn't make for a relaxed atmosphere. The deafening sound of the barking was augmented by the rattling of the chain as the now terrified dog made successive charges at the man who was about to commence its ritual torture. The combination of sounds was louder than any house alarm I had ever heard. I tried to quieten the dog down but my pleas of 'There, there, it's only a camera tripod' fell on deaf ears.

By the time the tripod was fully erected a neighbour had appeared on the scene. An old man who shouted at me in Romanian, doing his utmost to be heard above the already tumultuous hubbub which I had brought to this otherwise peaceful neighbourhood. The old man was convinced he had caught a man red-handed in the act of robbery. To the dog my camera tripod looked like an instrument of torture but to the neighbour it was quite evidently the apparatus and house-breaking equipment of an experienced burglar. He began screaming at me and waving his arms. I had every reason to suspect that he was threatening to call the police. I needed to try and calm him down but I did not know the Romanian for 'I am not a burglar, I am simply setting up camera equipment so that I may film this angry dog.' Those Teach Yourself language books just don't give you the useful phrases you need for everyday life. I shouted back at him in English, just to add further to the general clamorous cacophony.

'It's all right, I live here!' I cried, as unthreateningly as is possible while bellowing.

A woman appeared now, anxious to see the cause of all this unexpected brouhaha. I continued my high-volume pointless exchange of ideas with the old man, the dog continued to try and break free from its chains in order to tear me apart limb by limb, and the woman continued to look on, dumbstruck. Iulian would have been proud of me.

Presently, the old man concluded that I wasn't a burglar, presumably because most criminals don't tend to hang around and argue their case, even though in this instance my argument must have been as incomprehensible as it was incoherent. In a rare moment of calm when the dog must have been pausing for breath, he was able to make a series of sounds and pointing gestures which suggested to me that there was another way around the house to the front door. I set off and discovered that a lengthy circuitous route did exist which eventually brought me out into the road by the entrance. The old man viewed me with suspicion.

'Thank you for your help,' I offered meekly, and made my way to the door.

He made some remark or another which could have meant anything from 'Glad to have been of assistance' to 'Sod you!'. I didn't care. I had made it home, and I had made it into the house. All on my own. Was there no limit to what I could achieve in this country?

Further forays into the world of independence were considerably more successful in the latter half of the day. The first of these took the form of my walking to Moldova's National Tennis Centre, which I found with ease, unhampered as I was by Iulian's idiosyncratic sense of direction. I walked through the gates and there on my left was a large statue in the style of socialist realist art – a huge, Greek godlike, semi-naked man clasping a tennis racket, and doing so in such a way as to suggest that this particular item was going to provide the solution to all of Man's problems. An image which resonated with this particular beholder who was only too aware that the tennis racket would have to provide the solution to one of his. My growing worry was that the tennis racket was never going to have the opportunity.

Without Iulian by my side I had assumed that any form of communication with those who ran the centre would be impossible, or at best unsatisfactory. Not for the first time on this extraordinary day, I'd got things quite wrong. Jan spoke no English, but we were still able to understand each other perfectly.

Jan was the short, stocky man who had called me over, having for some minutes watched me with interest wandering aimlessly around his tennis courts. Our initial verbal exchanges furnished neither of us with any answers as to who we were or what either of us wanted. But then came an unusual twist.

'*Est-ce que vous parlez français?*' asked Jan.

'Oui, je parle français,' I replied, instantly launching us into an unexpected new world of communication.

Jan's French was considerably more adequate than Dina's and he was able to alert me to the fact that he was the director of the tennis centre, before going on to outline the many problems facing Moldovan tennis. I learned that in Uri Gorban, Moldova had once boasted the number one player in the whole of the USSR, but now he couldn't even make the lower reaches of the world rankings because he didn't have the funds to travel to the tournaments. The sad truth was that a government which couldn't afford to power the street lights in its capital was never going to prioritise the overseas travel of budding tennis players.

When I told Jan what I was doing in his country he managed a brief smile before his face returned to its 'business as usual' expression. I was getting used to this now. This was not a country where they made a fuss. Asking if it would be OK for me to play the pick of the nation's footballers on his tennis courts provoked no raising of the eyebrows, but instead just the deadpan reply that it would be no problem provided it did not coincide with a junior training session, when all the courts were used. When I suggested that I would telephone ahead to ensure this didn't happen, Jan alerted me to a problem.

'Le téléphone ne marche pas,' he said, shrugging resignedly. *'Nous n'avons pas payé donc ils ont coupé la ligne.'*

The phone had been cut off. The bill hadn't been paid, and so it was that the telephone of the country's National Tennis Centre had been disconnected. I don't recall this ever having happened to The All England Club in Wimbledon.

My visit to Bar Victor represented another example of my now-growing confidence. I'd seen the little red neon sign a couple of times before on the way back to my lodgings but never before had I descended the steps into the basement bar in order to partake of a local beer. Today was different. Today I was making things happen. Today I had the measure of Moldova. Nevertheless, as I drew closer to the hostelry's thick wooden door I became concerned that it had been placed there to shield the innocent from the depraved world of

Moldovan low-life. I hesitated before pushing open the door, fearing that behind it may well lurk Mafia figures, drug dealers, pimps and prostitutes, all with their own motives for preying on the naive Englishman who had voluntarily walked into their clutches.

I was greeted by a sharp-suited man holding a violin who could have been a gangster out of a Thirties movie if it hadn't been for a face which was too warm, too open and too generous to be that of a baddy. The goody in question was a proudly moustached man called Marin who was to become the leading protagonist in an evening which would be completely at odds with my experience of Moldovan social life thus far.

Marin was excited to discover that I was from London because this meant he could speak what he believed to be English. I smiled politely as he addressed me, and tried hard not to display the blank look which his unfathomability warranted. The one thing I did understand was an introduction to Gallina, the lady behind the bar whose beautiful features were only tarnished by her smile. She appeared to have wooden teeth, and unvarnished ones at that. She would be no friend to plaudits of Moldovan dentists, if indeed either group existed. I had seen little evidence to suggest that the upkeep of a good set of teeth was a priority in this society. Indeed, why should it be? There had been no precedent for it to be so. The Soviet masters of this country had done nothing to encourage any interest in dental hygiene. No Five Year Plan had included any mention of orthodontistry. Lenin, Trotsky and Stalin had managed without braces and so could everyone else. Besides there was no reason to believe that slapping a piece of metal across a worker's mowlers did anything to increase his productivity.

Marin communicated more to me in the one hour in which he played the violin than he would have done in a lifetime of speaking to me in his hybrid English. He was part of a duo in which he was incontrovertibly the talented half. His partner sat looking bored behind a rack of keyboards which produced an irritating electronic accompaniment to the beautiful tone of Marin's skilful bowing. I felt the accompanist should go solo and make an album called 'Bored Bloke – Unplugged', and I wanted to begin the journey down this road by unplugging him right now.

When I took out my video camera to film Marin, my status in the bar changed completely. Henceforth I was perceived to be the Western talent scout who would make their 'discovery' and set them up with fame and fortune in the West. Marin produced a smile which was so cheesy you could almost smell it, and the keyboard player even managed an expression which suggested that he might not be as bored as all that. Gallina underwent an immediate transformation from barmaid to nightclub singer and grabbed the microphone to produce second-rate renditions of third-rate pop songs, regularly peppered with flashing smiles of gleaming mahogany. I felt unsure whether there was a career in the West awaiting her. That smile would only really secure one gig a year – at the Society of Carpenters and Joiners Christmas party – and I'd be looking for a more steady income from my 'discovery'. Marin certainly had the talent but he probably wasn't going to measure up against Vanessa Mae as a box-office draw. Never mind, I'd let them down as gently as I could and until then I'd sit back, sip my beer and soak up the rare moment of 'feeling special'.

At one point I was invited to join a table of robust-looking male drinkers whom I might normally have been nervous of joining had my status not been that of 'King of the Bar'. They too performed for my camera, providing it with beaming smiles, raised glasses and even their own rendition of a traditional Russian folk song which left me feeling relieved that I was not a traditional Russian. One of them, the least tuneful singer, flashed his ID card in front of the lens of my now constantly filming camera and to my astonishment I saw that he was Chisinau's Chief of Police. It was incredible, but it was true. I was drinking with the Chief of Police. I really was managing rather well on my own.

The songs, merriment and general bonhomie continued until around midnight when there were general goodbyes and a plethora of drink-induced embraces, and I stumbled back to my lodgings oblivious to the dangers of the night and supremely confident that any would-be assailant would surely know better than to tangle with a good friend of Maior Viorel Vieru.

I went to bed greatly encouraged by what I had achieved since I had left Iulian's protective wing. After a couple of crash landings I had managed a few yards of unassisted solo flight. Soon I would be soaring above the clouds. At last I had proved that it *was* possible to make things happen here. Finally I had some fledgling evidence to support my theory that in life you are rewarded if you make the effort. I knew now that my task here was eminently possible. I had taken the bull by the horns, and what's more, if necessary, the Chief of Police was on hand to kick it up the arse.

7

Three Shepherds

'He's not the Chief of Police,' scoffed Iulian, spinning round from his desk at the Journalism Centre, after I had shown him the footage I had shot the night before.

'All right – Mayor of Police then. What's the difference?'

'He's not Mayor. Maior means Major and that is quite lowly rank in our police force – possibly like your sergeant.'

'Oh. Well, he still could be of help if needed.'

'Not really. If you want help in this country you need to be in with the Mafia – not the police. The Mafia controls everything.'

'Oh. Right.'

Iulian was a master of deflation. It was almost like he felt it was his duty to haul the romantic idealist back to reality. Iulian dealt in facts. I dealt in notions. We were quite a team, and we had a track record to prove it. So far we had achieved nothing.

That was, until 11.15am when Iulian received a phone call, and I some stunningly uplifting news.

'That was Grigorii Corzun,' said Iulian, with the beginnings of a smile forming on his lips.

'Who's he?'

'He is the President of Tiligul Tiraspol, the club for whom Sergei Stroenco plays.'

'Of course,' I replied, pretending to be on top of who my footballing opposition were. 'What did he say?'

'He says that you can go there – to Transnistria – any time you like. You will be his guest and you can stay in a hotel which has a tennis court, and he will arrange for you to play Stroenco.'

'You're joking!' I said, not knowing which was the more unlikely – this piece of news – or Iulian making a joke.

'No, this is what he says.'

The confirmation was music to my ears.

'*Yes!*' I shouted, jumping to my feet and punching the air.

This particularly un-Moldovan open display of emotions caused a few heads to turn from nearby computer screens, some in surprise, some in disapproval. But no questions were asked. I was beginning to understand the thought process at work here:

'The Englishman Tony has received some exciting news, but that is his business and not ours. We will not allow his loud exclamation and physical gesticulation to distract us unduly from our morning's tasks. Perhaps there will be a time when we will enquire into the nature of his news but for the moment this brief turning of the head has been an adequate reaction.'

'Corina!' I said, bursting into her office unannounced. 'Something amazing has just happened!'

I needed to share this news with someone and I felt that Corina would somehow understand. Her husband Aurel worked for Rank Xerox and they had both enjoyed the privilege of foreign travel in the West. She had seen people get excited before.

'This is wonderful news,' she said, after listening patiently to my flurried babbling. 'I hope that he means what he says.'

'Of course he means what he says,' I blurted, 'Why else would he say it?'

'I do not know, but if he means it, then this is good news.'

Corina may have travelled extensively in the West but in outlook she remained unequivocally Moldovan. Cautious, circumspect, and in control. All the things I was not. How I longed for a brief respite from this ordered, disciplined environment. I wanted a glimpse of some passion, I wanted occasionally to have to tiptoe around a fiery temperament, or witness some genuine *joie de vivre*. Even the Americans in the office, Karen and Tom, on learning of my good news, only managed a meek smile and a half hearted 'That's good, isn't it?' Before their induction into Moldovan life surely they would have been the first to stand up, give me a 'High Five' and scream 'Way to go!' at unreasonable volume. They had been in Moldova too long. Theirs had been a slow but steady inculcation into a pattern of behaviour which had left them as conspicuously dispassionate as everyone else.

*

Lunch with Leonid provided what felt like yet another positive wave in a tide that was inexorably turning my way. Leonid was the sports journalist whom five days previously Iulian had promised to arrange for me to meet 'right away'. Leonid seemed to have an encyclopaedic knowledge of Moldovan football and I fired questions at him for a full hour and a half. He showed me a list of Saturday's games and one fixture immediately caught my eye.

FC Agro v Dynamo Bender

The mind boggled. What an extraordinary spectacle this might be. In a moment of disgraceful political incorrectness I imagined Dynamo Bender being represented by eleven men who minced about the pitch shouting 'chase me' to a load of bewildered thugs from FC Agro who all got sent off for fighting.

On a less frivolous note I discovered that local team Zimbru Chisinau were playing at home to Olimpia Belţi the following day, and it was generally agreed that I should turn up to this match and try and meet some of the players after the game. They should be pleasantly disposed towards me, I thought, since by now they would all have been grateful recipients of the Wimbledon Tennis T-shirts which I had sent them.

They just had to be dying to meet me.

'Are you not going to have dinner with us tonight?' asked a disappointed Elena in the hallway, 'You have not eaten with us since Tuesday.'

She had grown rather fond of me in the course of this first week, and I of her. Her cheeky, bright little face lit up my mornings, and during the course of my days I found myself looking forward to seeing her in the evenings when she would run towards me with some question or other, more often than not connected with her English homework. In exchange for the help I gave her, she valiantly taught me a Romanian sentence which I believed may come in useful on my trip.

'Mā numesc Tony. Sînt din Anglia. Am fàcut un pariu, cà-i voi bate la tenis pe toţi din echipa naţionala de fotbal. Vreţi sà jucati cu mine?'

('My name is Tony. I am from England. I have made a bet that I can beat the entire national football team at tennis. Will you play with me?')

That, I felt, ought to do the trick.

My reason for having chosen not to eat with the family was that it was Friday night, and I wanted to dine out, and thus experience the Chisinau weekend night-life. Just as I was on the way out of the house, Adrian emerged from his bedroom and intercepted me on the stairs.

'I am meeting some friends. I will travel with you to Chisinau centre if you wish,' he said.

'That would be nice.'

I also thought it would save me another embarrassing solo journey on a Maxi-taxi, although as it turned out, Adrian had a simpler method of transport in mind.

'I prefer to walk,' he said, as we reached the bus stop.

'But isn't it too far?'

'It's only forty minutes. I enjoy to walk'

'But there are no street lights – won't it be too dark?'

'Only if you don't know where you are going.'

'And you know where you're going?'

Adrian stopped and eyed me cannily.

'That is a difficult question to answer. Do any of us know where we are going?'

There was more to this lad than met the eye.

'That's a fair point Adrian, but I was talking physically rather than philosophically. There are manholes out there with no covers on them. That's not how I want to die.'

I don't actually know how I *do* want to die but in the top ten of my least favourite ways, falling down a manhole in the pitch dark in a strange Eastern European capital would probably come in at about number seven.

'I know where the manholes are. No-one is going to die.'

No-one is going to die. Always comforting words to hear before any Friday night out.

The long walk provided me with an opportunity to get to know

Adrian better, whose agenda up until this point had apparently been one of keeping himself to himself and not showing a great deal of interest in what I was doing in Moldova. (Lord alone knows how he could have acquired these characteristics in this country of all countries.) However during the course of the next three-quarters of an hour I was to discover that he had allowed time for contemplation of why this Englishman had come into his family's house.

'I am interested by what you are doing in our country,' he said at one point, grabbing my arm and leading me in a wide arc, presumably to lessen the chances of my falling down a manhole, 'but I do not see how you will succeed.'

'Why not?'

'I do not think that the players will agree to play you.'

'Oh I think that they will.'

'How can you be sure?'

'I can't be sure. We can't be sure of anything,' I averred, immediately adding, 'And I'm not even sure of that.'

'So, why are you doing this? It is a big risk.'

'Because I want to win my bet and I want to prove my point. The risk doesn't bother me. I'm a risk taker.'

'This is bad – to take risks.'

'Oh I don't agree Adrian. Not to risk anything is to risk everything.'

'And what does that mean?'

I'd hoped he wouldn't ask that. Profound remarks carry so much more weight when left unchallenged.

Twenty minutes into our walk we reached Boulevard Stefan cel Mare which has the privilege of being the only street in Moldova to be lit at night. Once again I was able to enjoy the luxury of illumination which previously I had taken for granted, and I could now see the buildings which surrounded us. One such edifice was the country's main Parliament building in front of which independence from the USSR was declared in 1991. How I would have loved to have been there to witness that historical moment, if for no other reason than to have been able to stand back and utter the words:

"They think it's Moldova . . . *it is now!*"

I gleaned from Adrian that the present ruling party was made up largely of ex-communists who now had flourishing businesses and used their positions in government to assure that they flourished still further.

'They are corrupt,' he said with an unswerving certainty.

'What about the opposition party? Are they any better?' I asked.

'The one is the other. There is no difference.'

'Does anyone fight the corruption?'

'Some journalists publish stories in the newspapers exposing embezzlement but no-one does anything about it. We Moldovans are very good at shrugging our shoulders. There is an old Moldovan folk song about three shepherds . . .'

Adrian was really warming to his subject. I hadn't seen him like this before.

'. . . one was Hungarian, one was Wallachian and one was Moldovan. The Hungarian and the Wallachian were jealous of the number of sheep which the Moldovan shepherd had in his flock and so they made a plot to murder him and share his sheep, but a magical fairy lamb told him of this plan and warned him that he must defend himself. But instead of trying to avoid death, the Moldovan shepherd instructed the lamb to tell his family that he was married to a beautiful girl, who symbolised death, and that they should organise the funeral and careful distribution of his remaining riches.'

'That's a very negative story,' I remarked to a jaded-looking Adrian, weary from the concentration of relating the tale in English.

'Not really,' he countered. 'His Orthodox faith has taught him to accept his fate.'

'Maybe you're right,' I replied, taking care not to say what I was really thinking.

What I was really thinking is that it's a fine line between accepting your fate, and losing your spirit.

Adrian left me just by the concourse of the bland manifestation of Sixties Soviet architecture which was the country's Opera House and trudged off into the darkness to meet his friends. My plan was to head for a restaurant called Barricuda which had been recommended to me by Corina. Although I'm normally not keen on dining alone, on this occasion I was looking forward to watching and studying the people who ate in one of the capital's few upmarket restaurants. As directed by Adrian, I turned off Boulevard Stefan cel Mare at Pushkin Street and found myself once again plunged into pitch darkness. This time it was different. This time I was alone. And this time I didn't know where the manholes were.

In the dark, one is so much more conscious of sound. The footsteps, the rustling of nearby coats and the sudden sharpness of voices seem somehow amplified. In this suddenly spooky and threatening atmosphere, it felt like everyone was closing in on me. I became aware that I was enormously vulnerable. I was easy picking for anyone with even the slightest criminal bent. The only thing I had going for me was that no-one could see how shit-scared I was, and there was a good chance that I might be just as terrifying a prospect to the others in the street with my suspiciously slow gait and fear-induced heavy breathing.

I heard a loud voice from a doorway to my right, the intonation of which suggested that a question was being asked of me. All I could understand was that I should keep on walking and pray that a rogue arm was not extended, yanking me into the doorway for some swift and violent wealth redistribution. Fortunately, I was left untouched and as the yards began to develop between me and my potential assailant, I began to wonder whether it had been entirely my imagination that had invited in this sense of the sinister. The question I had been asked may well have been completely innocuous – 'Have you got any spare change?' or 'Do you have the time?' or 'I'm having some trouble with 4 down, I don't suppose you happen to know what's the capital of Poland?'

I was turned away rather unceremoniously by the man on the door at the Barricuda because I had not made a reservation. I could see by looking through the windows into the basement restaurant below that the establishment was completely empty, but this fact seemed to have no bearing on the executive decision taken by the arse-hole at street level. I did not bother to argue, my life experience up to this point having taught me that arguing with doormen is as likely to be as successful as a Mancunian Olympic bid.

Undeterred, I stumbled back through the darkness to Stefan cel

Mare where I continued my night on the town, only to find that the few bars and restaurants I passed were completely empty. It was Friday night for God's sake – what was going on? I recalled the pop song written in celebration of this particular day of the week – 'Friday on My Mind', and that there was an entire restaurant chain called 'Thank God It's Friday!' It was clear that in the West, Friday night has come to represent the end of the week's toil and drudgery and is in itself a mini festival heralding in the freedom of the weekend. From the evidence I was assimilating on the ground, Friday night appeared to have acquired no such status in Moldova. So, having shunned at least four establishments which barely passed as restaurants, on the grounds of being empty, horrid-looking, or both; I took a beer in a quiet bar and resolved to dine in the next restaurant I happened upon. Regardless.

'I'll have a Big Mac and fries please,' I said to the uniformed girl behind the till.

Yes, I'm afraid it had come to that. My search for night-life and culture had led me to McDonald's. I pray for the people of Moldova that this is not an omen for their cultural future.

'*O zi buna*,' said the girl, this neatly turned out servant to multinational profit.

This, I took it, meant 'Have nice day'. What else? That anodyne platitude which has come to so irritate me. I have nothing against common courtesy and manners, but surely 'Thank you' and 'Goodbye' suffice. Whenever someone in a fast food restaurant says 'Have a nice day' to me, I want to go back to that establishment the next day and tell them exactly what kind of a day I had – in great detail – when they're really busy.

I made my way over to a characterless synthetic table and planted myself on the standard McDonald's plastic seat, designed in such a way as to provide adequate comfort for the consumption of a meal but not to nurture any desire to sit back and relax after its completion. You can imagine some ambitious American go-getter standing up to speak at the 'Profit Maximisation' meeting: 'Every second that a table is occupied by a non-eater costs us dollars and cents. Remember – time is money.'

I walked home, as unsatisfied with my meal as by what it had come to signify for me. I found it upsetting that however hideously wrong their previous economic system had been, countries like Moldova were so eager to replace it with one which was also so manifestly flawed. They wanted to be capitalists, and they wanted to be capitalists fast. This was to be the answer. Now all they had to do was work out what the question was.

That night I became ill. My stomach erupted like a mini-volcano and my bowels were evacuated as thoroughly as wartime London. I had begun to feel the nascent rumblings earlier in the day but had chosen to ignore them in the hope that they would go away. This very rarely works (not just with regard to ailments but in other areas too – mortgage lenders, stalkers and occupying foreign troops), but somehow I feel it's always worth giving it a go. The tactic had once again failed. The stomach was having its say – finally revolting against the melange of Eastern European food-stuffs to which it had been submitted in recent days. The irony was that the meal which appeared to have triggered the releasing of the sluice gates was as Western as they come. A Big Mac and fries. That bloody gherkin.

Up until now my stomach had stood up pretty well to the rigours of world travel, certainly having performed considerably better than the intestines of an erstwhile travelling companion of mine Tim, whose stomach would flush out the entire contents of his body as soon as the ferry docked in Calais. Of course being such a sufferer, the contents of his baggage always included an entire medicine cabinet containing potions which could regulate the speed at which he bad farewell to his food intake. My problem was that I was hopelessly unprepared. I didn't want to disturb the two sleeping doctors in the house so I had a quick rummage through my bag in search of medication, but was only able to produce some Strepsils. Damn. Oh well, I took one anyway, thinking that not to take anything at all would have been negligent.

It was a miserable night. For eight interminable hours I lay in my bed shivering, knowing that it was only a matter of minutes before the house's dubious plumbing system was subjected to another deposit from mine. I tried to convince myself that this experience wasn't entirely negative.

It's OK. It's character building, I thought to myself.

But did I really need any more character built? And even if I did, hadn't I reached a point in my life where I could get character builders in? A reputable firm of character builders, with references and everything, who'd do a good job and not let me down?

At 4 am, in a weakened state close to delirium, my mind began to run further out of control. I imagined a beer-bellied foreman standing before me, from just such a company.

FOREMAN: And you say you want us to do something with your pain threshold?

TONY: Yes, it definitely needs building up. Perhaps you could add an extension?

FOREMAN: Could do, but an extension's a big job. It'd take us at least four weeks.

TONY: Oh, I was hoping you could do it quicker.

FOREMAN: Not a chance. They're tricky numbers – your pain thresholds. You look like you've got some cracks appearing in your resilience.

TONY: Really? Is that expensive to put right?

FOREMAN: Not really. We can just concrete over them.

TONY: Good. Talking of concrete . . . and cracks – you couldn't concrete over my arse could you?

FOREMAN: We could, but not until Tuesday week.

TONY: That's no good, I need it done now. Can't you see that it's urgent?

FOREMAN: Oh dear. Your patience is in a terrible state. Who put that in for you? Cowboy character builders, I bet. They give us lot a bad name.

*

Morning finally arrived. I could confidently state that, other than my vital organs, there wasn't a single solid left in my body. The only consolation was that my throat wasn't sore, and that throughout the long and hellish night, I hadn't coughed once. Those Strepsils really are terribly good.

Still feeling shaky, I made my way down to join the family at breakfast. At last here was an opportunity to take advantage of the fact that I was in the house of two doctors whose counsel I could seek on the subject of my ailing stomach. Even in a country like Moldova, which isn't known for its stockpile of the world's latest drugs, surely they would be able to offer a more effective treatment than Strepsils. The problem, as ever, was communication. Adrian was still asleep and Elena had absolutely no idea what the word 'diarrhoea' meant. (She had obviously not paid attention in the English class which had covered bottom disorders.)

While I struggled to make myself understood, Grigore went about the business of offering me food. My polite refusal only served to make him re-double his efforts to find me something I wanted. And so here was the scene: an Englishman trying to describe the nature of diarrhoea in simple words for the comprehension of an 11-year-old Moldovan girl, while her father ransacked a fridge in order to hold a range of dairy products in front of the said Englishman's nose for his immediate rejection. All my life had been building to this. Finally I nodded to a yoghurt, thinking that not to do so might have serious consequences for Grigore's health. There was no point in two of us being ill. The Status Quo thus prevailed, which involved my being ill and nobody else knowing about it.

At one point I excused myself and went to my room to see if my *Teach Yourself Romanian* book could be of any assistance. Of course it couldn't. According to its authors, 'Acrobat' is a far more important word than 'Diarrhoea'. Not a lot of use unless I wanted to be prescribed a cure for cartwheels. And so I returned to the breakfast table with only one option open to me. Unfortunately that option was mime.

I looked at Elena, a little girl desperate to know what it was I was trying to tell her. I shook my head at Grigore for a final time as he waved what looked like a pig's head in front of me. Then I did something that I didn't want to do, especially to a host family happily engaged with breakfast, but my hand had been forced. I stood up, walked to the middle of the room, pointed to my bottom and then ran out of the room in the direction of the toilet. It was brief, it was unsubtle, but it was successful – because seconds later, when I returned to a room full of people desperately suppressing laughter, there was a small bottle of medicine waiting for me at my place setting.

'Thank you so much,' I sighed, immensely relieved at the sight of the drugs.

The junky had finally got his fix.

8
The Television

The plan was uncomplicated. Go to the match and make friends with Testimitanu, Miterev, Rebeja, Romanenko and Fistican. Easy. Provided Zimbru had the big home win which was expected of them, I could see no reason why the players wouldn't be absolutely delighted to meet the man responsible for giving them the T-shirt which had so enhanced their wardrobe.

'At home', for FC Zimbru Chisinau, meant playing at a stadium in a small village thirty miles out of the capital. Quite why they did this, the football expert Leonid had failed to explain, but I had accepted it as just another of this country's many anomalies. Like Moldova's night-time streets, I was to remain in the dark.

I had hired a car (well, to be more precise a Lada) and a driver, and as I climbed into the back seat I prayed that Grigore's magic potion would ensure that the yoghurt I had eaten at breakfast would remain inside me. I did not wish my first meeting with a Moldovan footballer to coincide with a small accident in my trousers which left them thinking:

'My goodness, he *is* nervous.'

We were looking for a small village called Speia and, naturally enough, we got lost. Iulian was involved in the now standard map reading quarrel with the driver, a pasty fellow called Iura. I resisted the strong urge to point out that we would get there quicker if we worked from the assumption that Iulian was always wrong. When Iura realised this for himself, he got us on to the right road and finally to Speia which was no more than an ugly spread of a few small apartment blocks with all the community atmosphere of Croydon. We drove around in search of the ground but found the streets to be deserted but for the occasional stray dog. Where were the hordes of fans making their way to the game? After all this was Moldova's premier football club we were attempting to find – there ought to be a fan or two on show.

Twenty minutes later, after having visited a school, a doctor's surgery, and the Moldovan equivalent of an industrial estate (a lock-up garage), quite by chance we found ourselves driving towards the stands of a surprisingly big ground. All around it were fields and gently rolling hills. It was bizarre to see such a big stadium in so emphatically a rural setting. No doubt it had been one of the absurd decisions taken during the years of communism by the People's Committee for Absurd Decisions:

COMRADE 1: Comrades, the Proletariat must have recreation, and the Workers must be rewarded for attaining the levels of production specified in Comrade Brezhnev's last Five Year Plan – therefore it is proposed that we reward them by building a stadium with a capacity of 22,500 in the middle of sodding nowhere.

COMRADE 2: Excellent idea Comrade.

COMRADE 3: Nice one.

COMRADE 4: (Aside) He talks a lot of sense, but he will spoil it by swearing.

There was no admission fee to enter the ground. It was unclear whether this was because of a continued adherence to the philosophy that this was a stadium which belonged to the People, or because nobody could be arsed to build a wall around it. Maybe turnstiles were considered to be a bourgeois Western idea – or maybe they were just bloody difficult to get hold of. Either way, it didn't matter given that no-one turned up anyway. Zimbru Chisinau may have won the domestic Championship five years out of the last six, but they appeared to have acquired only three loyal followers for each of the years that they had done so. It was only down to our last-minute arrival, which bolstered the attendance by three, that the crowd outnumbered the 22 footballers who were warming up down on the pitch.

In my view, not charging an admission fee, however nominal, is always a mistake. It's a psychological thing. If the punter parts with some money then he *commits*. He's more likely to have a good time because he'll work harder to try and get his money's worth. Even if he hates what he has come to see, he has the satisfaction of being genuinely aggrieved *because* he has paid to see it. Had it been something free which had irked him so, then the punter would be forced to accept that the blame lay with him for having been mug enough to have used his time so wantonly. Therefore I conclude that the old adage 'The best things in life are free' is erroneous, and should be replaced by 'The best things in life are £12.50, £10.50, £8.50, and £6.00 for concessions.'

Whatever the best things in life are, and whatever they cost, I was not experiencing any of them on this particular Saturday. My stomach still threatened treachery and my entire body felt weakened by the exertions of, to put it poetically, 'The night of a thousand poos'. Furthermore, the dire football which I was watching was rendered even more tiresome by my translator's spectacular ignorance.

'That was a good kick . . . Oh. What did he blow the whistle for?'

'Because he was off-side.'

'Oh . . . what is off-side?'

It wasn't as bad as explaining the rules of cricket to an American, but bringing Iulian up to speed with the nature of the off-side laws wasn't a breeze. My initial attempt at keeping it simple left him utterly confused, and in my next effort I made the mistake of providing far too much detail. This still left him utterly confused, but somehow feeling obliged to give the impression of comprehension. This took the form of him asking pointless follow up questions throughout the afternoon, beginning with:

'Do you think they are going to use the off-side trap?'

'I don't know Iulian.'

And then, twenty minutes later:

'Did you say that you cannot be off-side from a throw-in?'

'Yes Iulian.'

Concluding with:

'Shouldn't the defence be pushing out now?'

I didn't reply to this one. I felt this was a better option than saying what I was thinking.

*

To our right, behind one of the goals, a group of some fifteen youths were gathered in a huddle chanting enthusiastic support for their team.

'*FC Zimbru! FC Zimbru!*' they shouted, somehow believing this to be a worthwhile activity.

It said something for the drabness of their lives that what was unfolding before them appeared exciting. It was one of the worst football matches I had ever seen.

At half time the score remained 0-0 with neither goalkeeper having been troubled by anything other than wayward backpasses. As the players traipsed off the pitch for their half time team talks ('Look, for God's sake – be better!'), I noticed that the president of Zimbru with whom we had spoken earlier in the week, didn't follow his players into the dressing room.

'Let's go and talk to him,' I suggested to Iulian.

'You think we should? I imagine that he does not want to talk right now.'

'Well, there's only one way of finding out.'

'I don't know – he looks anxious.'

'Come on Iulian. I'm never going to win this bet if I do things by half measures.'

Iulian, who even on a good day was only a quarter measure man, followed me reluctantly down to the touchline where we cornered Nicolae Ciornii and asked if I could meet the players after the game. He told us that this would not be a problem, news which lifted my spirits for the second half.

According to Iulian, Zimbru meant Zebra. Of course it did, and no doubt that was why the team played in those well-known zebra colours of yellow and green. The highlight of the second half was when an Olympia Belţi defender went to clear a ball and his boot flew off. I might have found this funny if I hadn't felt so ill, bored, and pissed off that Zimbru couldn't score. A nil-nil draw would be a disaster for me since the players, who had been expected to win easily, would be depressed and in no mood for socialising.

The referee blew the whistle for full time. A nil-nil draw. Iulian and I wandered down to the touchline and were told by Nicolae Ciornii that the players, having been expected to win easily, were depressed and in no mood for socialising. It seemed that tonight, Testimitanu, Miterev, Rebeja, Romanenko or Fistican would not be my drinking partners in one of the hostelries in fun-packed Chisinau.

On my insistence, we hung around by the Zimbru coach in the hope of falling into a conversation with one of the players after they had showered, changed and been given a thorough dressing down by their manager. I hovered over Iulian urging him to stop players and introduce me to them. His face told the story of a man who was in the employ of someone who had lost his mind, but who was paying him and therefore needed to be gratified. We managed to intercept one footballer with a shaven head who turned out to be one of the players I needed – Ion Testimitanu. Iulian addressed him in Romanian and pointed to me in a way which I took to be an introduction. Of course he may have been saying 'Look I'm sorry about this, but this bloke pays me thirty dollars a day to bother footballers. Just shake his hand and I promise I'll get him out of your hair straight away.'

I moved forward and shook Testimitanu's hand. He looked like he was going to cry. The after-match team talk must have been severe. Football managers are evidently the same the world over. After their players have failed, they motivate them for the next game by telling them that they are lazy, talentless shits. It says something about footballers that they respond to this.

'Did you receive my Wimbledon T-shirt?' I said to an exhausted looking Testimitanu.

The fatigued footballer launched into a long speech which appeared not to be entirely positive in nature. What could the problem be? Was he not happy with an Extra Large? When he finally ran out of words, he turned and got on to the coach without even so much as a goodbye.

'What did he say?' I asked Iulian.

'He said he was tired.'

How could that have been? I knew that I was no expert in Romanian but how could Testimitanu have spoken for such an extensive period only to have articulated a feeling of tiredness? Either Testimitanu was a master in circumlocution, or Iulian was knackered. He just couldn't be bothered. Or, was he saving me from the savage truth of Testimitanu's words so that my increasingly fragile optimism wouldn't have to take a further knock?

'Let's go home,' I said, skilfully gauging the general humour.

Testimitanu was in a bad mood. Iulian was in a bad mood. I was in a bad mood. There was nothing else for it. As the Zimbru coach roared off, we piled back into Iura's car for the hour's drive back to Chisinau. What fun.

The entrance to Moldova's capital is marked by what locals call 'The Gates of Chisinau'. Disappointingly these aren't ancient gates but rather two vast triangular apartment blocks on either side of the main highway into the city. Pretty they may not be, but they are striking. I asked Iura to slow the car down so I could film them for posterity and he happily obliged, although I noticed that he did so while remaining in the fast lane. Moments later there was a blaring of a horn behind us. Seeing that I was still filming Iura maintained his slow speed despite the noisy protest from the car behind.

'It's OK Iura I've finished filming,' I said, eager not to witness an incidence of Moldovan road rage.

I was too late. A spanking brand new navy-blue Mercedes drew up alongside us and the man in the passenger seat began shouting obscenities at Iura. At least I assumed they were obscenities – it did not look like he was enquiring as to the nature of the time.

'Oh no, this is not good,' said a nervous-looking Iulian.

'Why?'

'That guy is well known – a very powerful man. He is known as "The Television".'

'Why do they call him that?'

'Because he is famous for having crashed his car while watching television in it.'

Evidently Moldovan soap operas make compulsive viewing. I suppose his one consolation would have been that after the accident he could have watched himself on the traffic news – 'Look, there's me! Being cut free from that car!'

Whatever he was watching at the moment wasn't calming his nerves. I wondered whether his behaviour was governed by his viewing subject matter. I just prayed that he wasn't presently engrossed in a movie involving a high-speed car chase which ended with a roadside shooting.

'He is mad,' whimpered Iulian. 'He is trying to force us off the road.'

He was too. The blue Mercedes kept cutting in front of us while The Television waved his arms frantically, gesturing towards the side of the road.

'I think, Iulian, that he wants us to stop,' I said, as calmly as I could.

'I agree that this is what he wants,' replied an ashen-faced Iulian. 'And I think we should stop.'

Iulian instructed Iura to pull over, and the blue Mercedes drew to a halt in front of us, enabling The Television and another man in a suit to get out and walk back to our car like traffic cops. My mind raced with the possibilities of what the next few minutes might hold for us. None of them involved all of us being invited back to their place for tea and scones.

An anxious Iura was ordered out of the car, and he wisely obeyed. He was then given a five-minute lecture by The Television, the subject matter of which I could only assume involved a list of negative consequences should he not produce an apology for his foolish driving. Iura nodded meekly to each point which was being made to him. Precisely the right course of action, I thought. No point in getting involved in a protracted argument over the finer points of the Highway Code with this man – broad-shouldered, mean-looking, as he was. The problem with this Television was that if you didn't like what you saw you couldn't just switch channels – 'I've had enough of all this violent gangster stuff, what I'd like now is a nice gentle wildlife documentary.'

Iura's apologies must have been accepted because the two men who'd been so concerned for our road safety returned to their car and drove off without demanding any further redress.

'Iura says that this guy wasn't The Television after all,' said Iulian, as Iura climbed back into the driver's seat.

'Really?'

'Yes, I made a mistake.'

'Easily done,' I quipped. 'The Television all looks the same these days.'

Iulian didn't smile. Either because he was still thinking about what had just happened, or because he had spotted that I hadn't said anything funny. The look of relief on both his and Iura's face suggested that we may have been in more danger than I'd actually realised. It was comforting to know that we could now continue our journey into Chisinau without recourse to stopping at any hospitals on the way.

Our car joined the traffic again, its passengers all a little shaken but greatly relieved to see that the danger had been averted. Iura had performed the meek stuff very well. In fact his meekness had been something of a triumph. It certainly would have won the admiration of Jesus, who had always rated the meek highly.

'Blessed are the meek for they shall inherit the earth,' he once said, in all earnestness.

The only problem is that the meek would then reply:

'Ooh, I couldn't possibly. You have it.'

That evening I was able to eat lentils, bread and feta cheese without seeing any of them again in the night. Grigore urged me to wash it all down with a Moldovan brandy which he maintained would be good for the stomach. My kind of doctor.

'My farver wants to know if you will come with us to church in the morning?' said Elena.

'Yes, that would be nice. Thank you,' I replied.

I needed some help, and I was prepared to try anything. Turning to the Moldovan Orthodox Church for succour seemed as logical a next step as any alternative on offer.

I apologised profusely for holding everyone up. Not long before, I'd been summoned from my room by Adrian and told that the church party was leaving.

'But I thought we said eleven o'clock,' I protested, still in my pyjamas.

'It is eleven o'clock. The clocks went back one hour last night.'

'Oh right. Sorry.'

So, winter was upon us. Darker nights from here on in. How I hate this artificial shortening of the afternoon hours of daylight. I've never understood why it is necessary but I'm told that it's something to do with the wishes of Scottish farmers. It did seem a shame that they had surrendered to their demands here in Moldova too.

Grigore wore a suit and Elena a splendid blue dress with matching cape and bonnet. She looked exactly like any father would want his 11-year-old daughter to look on a visit to church. Grigore must have felt proud, I thought. It was just the three of us making the trip since Dina was going to visit a sick relative and Adrian was going to practise sitting in his bedroom with the door closed. He was already good at this but I suppose there's always room for improvement.

'After church,' said Elena, as we found ourselves seats on the maxi taxi. 'My farver says that he wants to show you his hospital.'

Grigore's choice of worship turned out to be the basilica which I had observed from my hotel bedroom on my first morning in this alien country. It had struck me then as being something of an anachronism, a throwback to the days when religion had a powerful stronghold in society before the dogma of Communism had stripped it from people's souls. The people, it seemed, had long memories. The paved area in front of the entrance to the basilica was so crowded that it resembled a busy station concourse at rush hour. We forced our way through the throng and into the basilica itself. Inside, it appeared even busier, with worshippers pacing around, crossing themselves and occasionally dropping to their hands and knees to kiss the floor. Such devotion. Such fervour. No similarity here to the conservative sedentary churchgoers of middle England. Here, I was witnessing an event. Something was *happening*. Evidently it takes more than a fifty-year totalitarian regime ruthlessly enforcing atheism to remove from the people the belief that there is a greater, higher force worthy of their worship.

I was surrounded by beauty. OK it was lavish and ostentatious; colourful frescos, ornate golden chandeliers and a magnificent altar surrounded by colourful bouquets of flowers; but it was beauty nonetheless. I think I prefer this to the dour modesty of Protestant churches which seem to be designed to remind you that life is tough and drudgery is pretty much all you can hope for. Could that be why the pews are increasingly unoccupied every Sunday? God knows.

A choir, positioned on a balcony above the door through which we had entered, began singing. An enchanting and mellifluous sound which echoed around the building and heralded the beginning of the formal service led by Father Theodor. This man, Grigore had been at pains to tell me on the way here, was his good friend. I had been promised that I could meet him after the ceremony but I had been warned that he spoke no English and that once again Elena would have to be my vessel to understanding.

Father Theodor enlightened me as to the role the Church had played during the years of Communism. Apparently religion had not been totally outlawed, but the State had made it its business to oversee the organised persecution of those who still frequented the churches. Churchgoers were ridiculed in school or at the workplace and were effectively barred from most areas of employment. Little wonder that during this period the only worshippers were old folk who had little or nothing to lose.

The Father then handed me a leaflet giving details about his basilica, which included a delightfully hopeless English translation of the text. It was riddled with mistakes, my favourite being the constant use of the word 'warship' instead of 'worship'. It seemed a fitting error, somehow acknowledging the role that religion had played in the fostering of warfare down the years.

We left that 'place of warship' and headed to one where a real battle was taking place. Grigore's hospital. Its dilapidated exterior was mirrored by what lay within. Dark, dank corridors flanked by flaky walls lead to wards displaying diverse antiquated medical equipment which looked like it had been plundered from the set of *Carry On Doctor*.

'My farver asks you to tell the doctors back in England what the conditions are like here,' said Elena.

'Right, OK,' I replied, aware that I didn't have any pals who were doctors in England and wondering how I could broach this subject in the course of a routine visit to my GP. 'Elena, can you ask your father if the government here is going to provide any more money?'

The little girl relayed this information and quickly returned her father's answer.

'My farver says the government makes many promises, but he thinks they will spend the money on fast cars and big houses.'

'This is sad,' I said.

'Yes, this is sad,' said Grigore.

Poignantly, the only accurate English I ever heard him speak.

As we watched Grigore waiting by the kerbside to flag down the maxi taxi which would take us home, Elena turned and looked up at me.

'So do you like my farver's hospital?' she asked.

This was a difficult one. Elena was clearly so proud of her father, and why not? He was an able man who was Head of Paediatrics with his own office in this massive edifice. To Elena, who had never seen another hospital, this was a mightily impressive place. I looked down at her inspiring face eagerly awaiting my response. Did I like her father's hospital?

'Yes, I like it,' I said, with some difficulty. 'But it needs more money.'

Just as I had enunciated these words, a large Mercedes sped past, splashing Grigore with the muddy water from a roadside puddle. $50,000 worth of car had just sprayed shit over the Head of Paediatrics outside his decrepit hospital as he waited patiently to avail himself of public transport. Grigore brushed himself down with all the dignity he could muster.

It looked like he'd done this a hundred times before.

9

Arsehole of the Universe

Iulian had decided it would be a good idea if we took a packed lunch with us on the bus and so he took us to a state-run shop to purchase what was required. The shop resembled a large arcade with separate sections, all with predominantly bare shelves, manned by members of staff dressed in white overalls. They all shared a common lack of interest as to whether anyone bought anything, coupled with an expertise in presenting an exquisitely morose expression to the customer. It seems that when you remove the word 'profit' from the vocabulary of the shopkeeper, this is what you get.

The oversized woman in the cheese section handed over our portion. I smiled at her, but this only provoked a hardening of her already stony countenance.

'Do you have a Reward Card, sir?' she enquired.

Not really – this line was provided by my active imagination. This was a shop where they were more likely to offer you a Punishment Card. You hand it in at the bread section and they clobber you with a rolling pin.

In terms of distance it wasn't far to Transnistria, only a hundred miles or so, but for me it was a big journey. This was a place I had been told it would be unwise to visit. On leaving the Journalism Centre, Corina's last words had been 'Be careful.'

'OK. I'll try not to knock any drinks over,' I'd said, in an attempt to make light of things.

The truth was that this was an absurd risk I was taking. Iulian had told me about an American journalist, Patrick Cox, who had spent time in Transnistria and whose candid summary of the place had been that it was 'without doubt one of the world's hell-holes'. A dangerous hell-hole. In the 1992 war for independence, the whole Transnistrian nation had fought against Moldova and all the men had carried guns, most of which were still at large today. Furthermore Transnistria has a reputation among Russia's criminal class as a lawless place perfect for laundering money. Then you can add the fact that the Transnistrian authorities have to this day retained a powerful KGB who imprison political opponents, close down private media outlets and have set up road blocks at the so-called 'border' with the rest of Moldova, manned by guards decked out in Soviet uniforms. All in all it probably wouldn't be your number one choice for a spring weekend break.

Iulian, who had been to Transnistria once before and experienced only minor difficulties over paperwork at the border, displayed a surprising confidence.

'I believe that we will be OK,' he suggested, 'because we are the guests of an important figure. I just advise you not to do any filming on the streets there. Crime is rife. Someone will see that thing and then just grab it. I actually believe that you should not bring it with you.'

'But I have to. How else will I prove to Arthur that I have played Stroenco and Rogaciov?'

'OK, but in that case you must hide it in the bottom of your bag. The police or army on the border may just choose to confiscate it if they see it.'

'What – for no reason?'

'They can do what they like. In some respects it is close to anarchy there.'

It was for this reason that we had chosen to take the bus and not hire a car and driver. Cars were searched at the border and lots of awkward questions asked. Foreigners, particularly ones from the West, were often refused entry with no reason given. However on the bus, the border guards usually only made cursory checks and Iulian felt it was unlikely I would even be asked to produce my passport.

Given the nature of my destination, I ought to have felt trepidation, but in fact I was in ebullient mood. For me, today wasn't just Monday and the beginning of a new week, but it marked a change in fortunes and the heralding in of a new era. At last things were going to start to happen. In Grigorii Corzun, the President of Tiligul Tiraspol FC, I had finally discovered a man who had displayed some enthusiasm for my task.

'Come to see us,' he had said. 'You can stay in our hotel which has a tennis court and you can play our players as you wish.'

It seemed bizarre that the only positive noises I'd heard so far had emanated from a place they called 'bandit country', which I'd been urged to omit from my travel itinerary. Maybe it wasn't such a bad place. Maybe the stories I was hearing were the product of prejudice. I was going to keep an open mind. And a closed bag. I wanted to have a camera when I came back.

Although it felt heartening to know that the tennis rackets I was carrying looked like they were going to be used in anger at long last, I also felt a pang of nerves. Was I ready for tennis? I hadn't played for a week and my recent stomach problems must have weakened me physically. It would be just too humiliating if I lost to the first footballer I took on. I banished the thought from my mind. Don't go there Tony, I thought, get stuck into your half of the cheese dominated packed lunch instead. As I did so, Iulian looked up from the sheets of paper he'd been studying.

'Oh dear,' he said.

Sounded ominous.

'What?'

'I made a mistake. I thought that both Stroenco and Rogaciov played for the same club – Tiligul Tiraspol – but according to this information which Andrei gave us from the Moldovan Football Federation, he plays for the other team in Transnistria – FC Sheriff.'

'Right. So that means opening another line of enquiry once we get there.'

'Yes'

'Never mind'

This was a blow and was certainly going to make things more complicated, but I convinced myself that Stroenco and Rogaciov were probably mates and a simple phone call from one to the other would be all that was required. I was determined to stay positive.

The bus approached the border.

'Good luck,' said Iulian. 'Try not to look conspicuous.'

'OK,' I replied, not entirely sure how to go about this task.

I looked around me and saw that only about ten of us had chosen

Tiraspol as our destination, and most of the others were young mothers. If only I'd borrowed a baby for the day, I would have blended in perfectly. I resolved to try and look as Moldovan as I could and so adopted the sourest facial expression in my repertoire. The one I save for those blokes who try to clean your windscreen at traffic lights. We drew up alongside an army-border checkpoint and a soldier carrying a gun climbed on to the bus and began talking with the driver. Not for the first time on this trip I felt genuine fear. Soon he would be walking down the central aisle on the look out for anyone conspicuous. If I didn't look Moldovan enough I could be singled out for questions, removed from the bus and ultimately refused entry to the country. Should that happen then the bet would be pretty much lost, with two of the required footballers beyond reach. I thought of Arthur back home in England. He was probably still in bed. How had I got myself into a bet which involved my subjection to daily peril when all he had to do was go down the pub, sit on his arse and wait for me to fail? I would have to be more circumspect with regard to the bets I took on in the future.

The soldier's conversation with the driver looked to be reaching its conclusion. I felt like an escaped POW on the run from Colditz – if I was challenged I was lost, if I was left unchallenged then freedom would be mine. All it needed was a tired, lacklustre soldier with other things on his mind. All it needed was for things to go to plan for once. What it definitely didn't need was a tap on the shoulder from the lady seated behind me.

'You are American, no?' she asked boldly.

Oh no. What was going on? What was she doing? And why was she doing it now? I looked ahead and noted with relief that the soldier was still talking and had not heard. I turned around with the intention of immediately severing all communication with this woman.

'I am not American, I am sorry,' I replied coldly, and with a definite full stop.

I turned to face the front again, praying that would be an end to things. But no.

'But I have been hearing you speak English,' she said, 'Where you from?'

Shit. Just my luck. The first chatty Moldovan I had met, and this had to be the moment.

'I am from England,' I turned and whispered, again trying to give the impression that this should mark an end to this exchange.

'Ah, this is better!' she announced, at a most alarming volume.

I looked across to Iulian who was shaking his head.

'You must quieten her,' he muttered.

Easier said than done because now she had got to her feet and was standing in the aisle waving a piece of paper at me.

'Will you read this essay?' she requested. 'I am studying English in classes in the evening and this is my homework. Could you see that there are no too many mistake?'

'Please – I will help – but when the soldier has gone,' I said, looking at her imploringly. 'Please?'

Mercifully she nodded and sat down.

I'm not sure whether the soldier heard nothing or whether I'd lucked out and got the lazy guy who just didn't care, but amazingly he ignored me completely, checked a couple of bags in the overhead shelves and then buggered off. Hurrah. Three cheers for sloppy work. Without it how would we ever get things done?

As it happened the lady's essay was pretty good. Grammatically bang on. It was all about how she hoped one day to visit her friends in England who lived in Slough. She was sure it would be a beautiful place. This was her only mistake, but I didn't bother to correct it. I didn't have the heart.

We arrived at Tiraspol's deserted bus station, which was effectively just five bus stops in close proximity to each other, and I stepped on to Transnistrian soil for the first time. This place was almost a museum piece. While the rest of the Soviet Union had embraced Perestroika and introduced reforms, this relatively tiny land had hung on doggedly to pre-1991 Communism. Economically it wasn't strong. Spiralling inflation now meant that one lunch would cost you a million roubles. Today you'd get 360,000 roubles for one dollar. Tomorrow's exchange rate would be anybody's guess. This place was still the home of collective farms, state-owned businesses and crazy Five Year Plans.

'Tony, if you think that life is tough in Moldova, you should spend more time here,' said Iulian, as we gathered our bags together, 'This place is backward. It is crazy.'

'Is there nothing at all to recommend it?'

'For me, no. The only thing that is better here is that they have street lights at night.'

'How come?'

'Because all of Moldova's power stations are here and the Chisinau government has to buy electricity from them. This is why our streets are dark – they control the price.'

'How inconvenient.'

Another inconvenience was that there appeared to be no Grigorii Corzun there to meet us as arranged, although we weren't too concerned since we had said four o'clock and it was only five past now. Grigorii, we decided, was probably a busy man and there was no need to commence any major anxiety until around four thirty.

At four thirty I promptly kicked off that process by dispatching Iulian to a call box to find out what was happening.

'Do you need some change?' I asked.

'No, it is free to make calls here.'

'Really?'

'Yes, look at the phones,' he said, pointing to one that was mounted on a wall near us which looked like the next model up from a can with a piece of string attached. 'They were made so long ago and no-one has the money to convert them to ones which take coins.'

'Ah well that's another advantage of this place,' I said, gently teasing Iulian. 'Phone calls are free.'

'Yes, but nobody has anything good to say to each other.'

While Iulian was making the call I sat on a cold step and did my best to maintain the confident spirit which I had nurtured on the bus. I tried not to think about the consequences of a Grigorii no show. Like my present surroundings they were just too bleak. Iulian returned to say that he had spoken to the club's secretary who believed that Mr Corzun had gone to watch his team training, and knew nothing of any collection of any Englishmen from any bus stations. Silence was my chosen response to this new information.

There was nothing to say. All there was now was to wait. Wait and hope.

The step on which I had been sitting had made my bottom colder than it had ever been before, and colder than any bottom ought to be, leaving it almost completely numb. I have a sensitive bottom. It tends to go numb in the face of defeat. Just at this moment I wanted my entire body to become numb in order to deaden the pain of the constant blows which this country was dealing me.

'This looks hopeful,' said Iulian, momentarily lifting me from an inexorable slide into gloom.

I looked up and saw a shiny Mercedes turn a nearby corner and then draw up before us. Could this be our man? A smartly dressed, middle-aged man signalled to us from the car window. Iulian called out to him and the man shouted back.

'This is him,' said Iulian, turning towards me, as close to excited as I'd seen him. 'You are in luck – although he doesn't seem in a very good mood.'

It didn't matter. He had turned up and all was not lost, as my bottom had begun to think it might be. It was feeling positively vibrant as the car door opened and it was lowered on to the plush leather seats of this luxurious car. It was a happy bottom now.

Grigorii Corzun both drove and talked at speed. His conversation with Iulian was so intense that it was a full ten minutes before there was a lull in proceedings which enabled me to catch up with what was happening.

'What's he been saying?' I asked of a slightly fraught-looking Iulian.

'It's not good,' came the now alarmingly familiar reply. 'He says that his player Stroenco was robbed last night and that he did not come to training today. He also says that the team are playing on Wednesday and you cannot play any tennis with the players before then – he does not want them distracted.'

My heart sank. Surely not. Not now. Not another disappointment.

'So I cannot play Stroenco until at least Thursday?'

'This is correct.'

'Well, maybe I could try and get Rogaciov before then.'

'I don't think so, because their match on Wednesday is against FC

Sheriff, and since this is Rogaciov's team, he will be in training for this game too.'

Oh dear.

'So where is he taking us?' I asked.

'To the hotel.'

'And we're supposed to stay there until Thursday?'

'Yes, but there is more bad news.'

I braced myself.

'What is it?'

'Well, it is his hotel and he says that you must pay to stay there, and he says that it will cost you $200 a night.'

This was outrageous. Iulian had reckoned that the State run hotel in Soroca had been expensive at $20 a night.

'$200? He's taking the piss, isn't he?'

'Yes, I think so. But at the moment I cannot think what we can do. We are in his car and he is driving it.'

Iulian had stated the obvious, but had correctly identified the quintessence of our predicament. We were in this man's car and he was driving it. We knew nothing about him, where he was taking us and what he planned on doing with us. Short of grabbing the wheel and forcing him over to the side of the road, we were powerless. My bottom went numb again.

As Grigorii Corzun drove us further and further into the countryside, Iulian and I fell silent. Occasionally there'd be a short conversation in Russian between Iulian and our host but I didn't even bother to ask for a translation. I'd decided that for the moment I would rather not know what was going on. Presently, we turned down a narrow lane and drew up in front of a huge house which resembled a Transylvanian castle; gothic style complete with turrets and the odd gargoyle. As if events weren't unfolding unkindly enough, just to compound things, the place to which we'd been brought looked like it belonged in the opening shot of a horror movie. This was the kind of place Scooby Doo would have refused to have entered, regardless of how many 'Scooby Snacks' he'd been offered.

Grigorii eased himself from the car and headed towards the house's big wooden door beckoning us to join him. Reluctantly I emerged from the back of the car immediately stepping in some horse shit as I did so. This wasn't turning out to be my day. Grigorii, seeing where I'd stepped, turned and said something.

'Does he want me to take my shoes off before I go in?' I asked Iulian.

'No, he says that this is good luck.'

Good luck eh? If horse shit brought good luck, then the way things were going at the moment I would need to do more than step in some. I'd need to immerse myself in an entire vat of the stuff.

Grigorii went inside expecting us to follow but I wanted a quick *time out* with Iulian.

'Before we go in there,' I said, 'let's just confirm what's going on here.'

'OK.'

'We've been collected at a bus station in a hostile territory by a strange man who neither of us have met before, and we've been driven miles into the countryside and invited to stay at what looks like Vincent Price's house in *Bloodbath at the House of Death*.'

'Yes, this is not what we were expecting.'

'Not exactly, no.'

I sighed. The moment clearly warranted it.

'The thing is,' said Iulian, 'he insists that we stay here. He says that if we go to a hotel in Tiraspol it still won't be any cheaper than fifty dollars a night and there will be no heating, no hot water and you will have to register with the police.'

'Hmm. I don't fancy registering with the police that much,' I replied thoughtfully. 'They might just take a shine to my video camera and opt for a bit of confiscation. Oh, what the hell, let's just go in, if I die here I'm sure my loved ones will understand.'

'I don't think we have a lot of choice.'

We went in. Behind the door was a short corridor which led us through to a large courtyard around which there were many buildings. This wasn't an hotel but instead a huge and somewhat opulent complex – a holiday camp for horror movie extras. Grigorii took us on a guided tour. Through the landscaped gardens, past a large wishing well complete with decorative hand-carved gnomes, and then on to the tennis court. He was very proud of this, even though it was the smallest tennis court in the world. OK, it was marked out in regulation size but the fencing hugged the exact dimensions of the court, so there was no luxury of standing behind the base line, and running for any balls which were hit out wide would result in a premature collision with a perimeter fence. Grigorii then proudly pointed above us to some overhead netting about twenty feet up. On this court it seemed that no wild shots were going to lead to any balls getting lost, but then not many winning lobs would be hit either. Grigorii looked at me expectantly, no doubt seeking approbation for this absurd netting. It was difficult, but I managed a benign smile.

'Mr Corzun asks you,' said Iulian, 'if the houses in England have tennis courts like this.'

I wanted to tell him that there were no houses in the world which had tennis courts like this, but instead instructed Iulian to inform him that not many private houses in England had enough land for tennis courts.

'Maybe in America, but not in England,' I added.

Grigorii maintained that in the past he had shown Americans the tennis court and they had said that they didn't have courts in their gardens but that the British did. This deluded man clearly appeared to be of the belief that all Westerners were millionaires and, just as he thought I was doing, they had lied to conceal the fact. I resisted the temptation to say, 'Look mate, if I was a millionaire, which I'm not, then I certainly wouldn't have done what you've done and built myself a castle – such a vulgar and ostentatious shrine to wealth – especially if most of my fellow countrymen were living in abject poverty, you prat.'

I didn't think it would help somehow.

As the guided tour continued I tried to fathom exactly why it was that this rather strange and disagreeable man had brought me here as his guest. His motivation didn't appear to be drawn from any altruistic desire to assist me in my quest, since he had made it plain that his footballer was unavailable for any tennis activities until at least Thursday. My initial presumption that the whole thing had been a stunt to relieve me of my dollars was still plausible, although the palatial surroundings suggested that he was not a man who was short of a bob or two. Perhaps he just wanted to show off to a Westerner how despite the communist system it was still possible for an individual to amass a huge fortune. For a moment I considered the absurd possibility that he made his money from kidnapping Westerners and that I was soon to be the subject of a huge ransom demand.

This couldn't have been further from the truth. The real reason for my invitation was as unexpected as it was bizarre. It became clear as we were led through the gym and past the indoor swimming pool and down into the basement to view a collection of vintage brandies.

'Mr Corzun is suggesting that you bring people here from England,' said Iulian, 'and they stay in his luxurious hotel, and he says that you can take a cut.'

Oh no, surely not. He wanted to go into business with me?

I worked hard to suppress my initial impulse which was to laugh back in his face, and tried to formulate a polite refusal which would not offend. This was a tough call and one which threatened to be beyond me.

'This is a very interesting proposition,' I began my response, still with no idea where it was leading, 'and were I more of a businessman I should definitely be interested, but this is such a lovely place and I should certainly like to help in some way.'

Not bad given that what was really going through my head. 'Look mate, you must be joking, no-one in their right mind would want to come here.'

After a few further exchanges on the subject, in which my would-be partner drew my attention to what an excellent area this was for hunting, and in which I promised to write favourably about his leisure complex on my return (a promise which I am now absolutely delighted to be breaking), we were led to the basement. Grigorii had said that this was to view his enormous collection of over three thousand bottles of brandy, but there was a part of me which flirted with the notion that because I had not shown enough enthusiasm for a partnership in 'Transnistria Tours' I was being led here for ritual execution.

We descended the marble stairs, beneath exotic chandeliers and beside mirrors adorned with decorative wood carvings, and entered a small room brimming over with bottles of spirit, covering every inch of wall space. If it was true that Yuri Gagarin had spent two full days holed up in the Cricova wine cellars, then he would have needed at least a fortnight in here. Seemingly all sizes, shapes and colours of bottles were represented. It was explained that as well as 3,000 bottles of brandy, Grigorii also had over 750 bottles of vodka, and that he had just recently started to collect whisky and rum too.

He pointed to a big barrel on the floor and boasted that this was 40-year-old Cognac. He filled a glass and forced it into my hand, instructing Iulian to film me drinking. No doubt this was intended to be a nice little touch for the insert on *The Holiday Programme* which he so eagerly sought. I took a sip and announced for the camera how delightfully smooth it was, slightly irritated by the fact that I hadn't had to lie. It *was* delightfully smooth, but I had wanted to dislike it as much as I was beginning to dislike its purveyor. His taste buds didn't deserve to be caressed by such an exquisite flavour. When Grigorii stood over me and insisted that I knocked back all the brandy in one big swig, I obeyed. For three reasons it was a good idea; it would taste good, it would please Grigorii, and best of all it would get me slightly pissed. I was happy to lose some of my grip on reality, since reality didn't feel that good just at the moment.

When we finally left this alcoholic's paradise and began to climb the stairs, Grigorii turned and said something to me which appeared to be of some import; however, before Iulian could furnish me with the translation, I cracked my head on a low beam above my head. An almost inevitable consequence of the recent infusion of brandy. After a few moments taken by those present to ensure that I was OK and that no blood had been drawn, we continued on our way.

'What was he saying to me before that happened?' I asked Iulian. 'It seemed to be quite important.'

'It was,' came the swift reply. 'He was telling you to mind your head.'

Oh.

'I must have a word with you about how quickly you provide your translations.'

Apart from the crack on the head, another consequence of the liquor now coursing my veins was diminished fear. Just like the small bloke in the pub who's had a skinful, I wasn't going to be afraid of looking up at the hulk along the bar and saying 'Yeah? Come and have a go if you think you're hard.' The problem with this course of action is that nine times out of ten the hulk *is* hard and the small man usually suffers a dent to his pride, as well as one to his skull. I have always felt that it is for this reason that alcohol should carry a health warning as well as cigarettes:

WARNING: THIS LAGER MIGHT CAUSE YOU TO PICK ON SOMEONE MUCH BIGGER THAN YOU.

Temporarily emboldened by the alcohol as I was, the next time Grigorii asked me to do a piece to camera for *The Holiday Programme* I was somewhat mischievous. I had been ushered into a large boardroom and deposited before a fireplace with 'Tiligul Tiraspol FC' carved in stone across it, and urged to embark on another reverential tribute to the wonderful world of Grigorii.

'Here I am in the boardroom of Grigorii Corzun,' I began, smiling for the camera and adopting my most artificial TV presenter pose. 'A man whose greatest asset is the fact that he doesn't speak English and therefore cannot understand what I am saying now. So, although I am presently gesturing to things around this room and pretending to talk about how beautiful they are, in fact I am taking this opportunity to put on record that this man is in fact the 'Arsehole of the Universe'.

Grigorii applauded. A great moment for me. I looked over to Iulian who was choking back a laugh. A minor victory had been achieved. True, we were still technically the prisoners of this man with no coherent policy for escape, but the thinking was – if you're going to get kidnapped then you may as well enjoy it.

I suppose that as unpleasant, opinionated, unwanted hosts go, Grigorii wasn't a bad one. At least he offered food, and the brandy kept flowing too. We found ourselves in a kind of dining-room area on one wall of which hung a vast wood-carved plaque depicting hunting scenes and, on another, three guns arranged in a rising diagonal just like the three birds of the stereotypical English working-class home – the key difference being that those birds very rarely get used in anger. ('Choose your weapon.' 'All right – sparrows at dawn.') Grigorii began recounting a story of how he'd been on a trip to England with the national football team and he'd ended up in a hotel bar in Manchester. One beer and a sandwich, he claimed, had cost him £25.

'You were robbed,' I said.

When Iulian duly translated, the mood in the room changed dramatically. Grigorii was not happy. His face became contorted with wrath and he suddenly turned on me with an angry tirade of words, and with an unexpected venom. I had clearly touched a nerve.

'Mr Corzun says that you have made a mistake,' said Iulian, clearly toning down the language, 'and that people in your country earn big salaries and that twenty-five pounds is what they pay for what he had.'

Twenty five pounds for a beer and a sandwich? In Manchester? This bloke was mad.

'I really don't want to stay here Iulian,' I said, while Grigorii shouted at a member of his staff in an adjoining room. 'When he gets back let's see if we can persuade him that we're dead keen to return here but that we can't afford to lose three days out of our schedule just relaxing here – beautiful though it is.'

'OK, I'll try, but up to now he has been really insistent that we stay.'

'Yes, but I want you to go really over the top. Say that I have fallen in love with the place and that I want to start talking to some contacts back in the UK about it. Also tell him that most of my dollars are back in Chisinau and I want to be able to pay him properly for his hospitality and I can't do that until I've been back there to pick them up.'

'I will try.'

Poor Iulian, he'd never been over the top in his life. It didn't appear to be a particularly Moldovan trait.

When Grigorii returned, Iulian gave it his best shot. My feeling was that we had a chance, especially since I'd mentioned that my money was somewhere else. I had this hunch that Grigorii was going to be more keen on having me around the place if my pockets were stuffed full of dollars. Another factor in our favour was that Grigorii's mood seemed to have softened since he had poured himself a soothing brandy, and for the moment I appeared to have been forgiven for slandering him over the price of beer in Manchester.

Iulian and Grigorii conversed for some minutes and I could only look on, powerless to influence events. Eventually Iulian turned to me and I braced myself for what was to come.

'Surprisingly,' said Iulian, 'Mr Corzun says that we can go back to Chisinau tonight. He says that two of his footballers will drive us to the bus station in a few minutes.'

'Unbelievable – what do you think made him change his mind?'

'I told him that you are really sincere about wanting to go into business with him.'

'Right. This could be a problem when we come back here.'

'Yes. But at least we are free to go now.'

I thanked Grigorii and promised to return with a detailed business plan, omitting to mention that I didn't know what a detailed business plan looked like. We shook hands and he produced a slightly disarming smile, and Iulian and I made our way out to the awaiting car, doing our best not to break into a sprint.

In the car, the two footballers ignored us and instead shared an animated conversation in Russian. When we arrived at the bus station Iulian told me that they had been discussing how Stroenco could make back some of the money he had lost as a result of being robbed, by charging to play me at tennis. This was a potentially expensive development. A fee for each game from the millionaire Englishman.

Our only stroke of luck in the entire day was that we made the last bus back to Chisinau by five minutes. Missing it would have meant hiring a taxi and running the risk of extensive questioning at the border. As it happened, I was questioned by a Transnistrian border guard but I felt no fear. My feelings had been numbed by the brandy, and the events of the day had left me very close to the point of *just not caring any more*.

The soldier asked what I had in my bag and he looked a little bemused when he was told it contained tennis rackets. For someone who'd been trained to be on the alert for cigarette smugglers and stolen cars, this was an unusual development. After a confused frown he insisted that I open up the bag and sure enough, there they were.

Two tennis rackets. He shrugged and moved on. Underneath them had been a video camera which would have interested him greatly and no doubt have led to further questioning, but the tennis rackets had confused him too much and he'd simply chosen to resume his search for the conventional offender. Lucky old me.

Yes, lucky old me. At every turn things were falling nicely into place. Surely only a pessimist would have viewed the day as having been wasted. I'd had the privilege of travelling to Transnistria and back on a clapped out old bus, and even if I hadn't played any footballers at tennis and Grigorii Corzun hadn't turned out to be the dream host, at least I'd had the pleasure of traipsing horse shit into his hallway. Yes, there's always an upside to everything – you've just got to look for it.

Looking for the upside in Moldova was becoming an exhausting business. It was proving to be hidden in ever more obscure places. I looked out of the bus window and into the pitch darkness of the unlit streets and shivered for the first time. There was a nip in the air which no doubt marked the onset of Moldovan winter. I began to worry that I was going to run out of spirit. In this part of the world there wasn't enough to go round.

Some selfish bastards stockpile it all in their basements.

10
The Green One

That night was a cold one. It felt like a new kind of cold to me. A drier, more penetrative one, which chilled the bones rather than the flesh. My night's sleep hadn't been made any more comfortable by the fact that the house's central heating system appeared to be in permanent rest mode. A few days previously, Grigore had taken me round the back of the house and shown me the boiler. It was unclear whether he had been attempting to explain plans for its imminent repair or whether he was simply proud to have a boiler and was keen to show it off, working or not. Warmth, I was learning, was a luxury commodity in Moldova.

As I lay in bed shivering I remembered that Anita in Soroca had told me that the school where she taught had once been closed for three months because they had no heating, and temperatures had dropped so low that it had been deemed unwise to hold lessons in classrooms no warmer than butchers' cold stores. For me, just like freedom and not being hungry, warmth had been one of life's givens. It was something you regulated with a switch or a dial and not, as I was discovering in my bed now, by the number of jumpers you wore or blankets piled on top of you.

I didn't want to get out of bed. It was cold out there. I didn't want to see Elena's sprightly, expectant face at breakfast looking up at me and asking if I'd beaten the Transnistrian footballers. I wasn't ready to explain that all I'd done was to go there and come straight back. I wasn't ready to admit that I'd failed. Failed *again*. I didn't want to get out of bed. It was cold out there. Getting out of bed meant undoing what felt like my only noteworthy achievement of the trip so far, which had been to get myself warm under the covers.

My other problem was that I didn't really know what to do with my day. I'd said I'd meet Iulian at the Journalism Centre but the truth was that I had absolutely no idea what we were going to do when we got there. I was running out of ideas, and bed seemed a much better option than trying to think of any. There was little doubt in my mind that I'd probably achieve more today by staying under my nice warm blankets than I would by going to meet Iulian. He wouldn't mind if I stood him up, he was probably sick to death of assisting a man in the fruitless pursuit of footballers and had a far more intellectually rewarding way of spending his time.

One idea saved me, at least temporarily, from this bed-ridden gloom, and it was simple enough. Working on the assumption that the presidents of these football clubs shared the same character traits as Grigorii Corzun, I contrived a new approach which would appeal to the largest part of these men. Their egos. It might be a long shot, but it had one significant thing going for it – it gave me a reason for getting out of bed.

At the Journalism Centre I ran my new idea past Iulian.

'I'm not sure that this will work,' he immediately retorted.

Such a frustrating response, and I'm afraid I was lacking the patience of the first week.

'Well of course you're not sure,' I whined, barely concealing my irritation. 'I'm not sure either. But if we only did things in life that we were sure of, the world would be a pretty dull place.'

Moldova, in fact.

'Come on Iulian,' I continued. 'Let's give it a go. Let's call The Green One.'

Valeriu Rotaru was the president of FC Constructorul, the club from which I required the services of one player – Oleg Sischin. Everyone knew Rotaru by his nickname – The Green One, which was coined from the fact that his football team wore bright green shirts. According to the sports journalist Leonid, this man had quite a reputation. His business dealings aside, in the world of football it had been alleged that he had beaten up referees whose decisions had displeased him. Whether or not this was true Leonid did not know, but certainly the Green One commanded a great deal of respect. At least you knew where you stood with him. As far away as possible. This was not a man who was keen on delegation, being president, owner, manager and coach of Constructorul, and on the occasions when he was ill, he would hand his coaching role over to his daughter. Who else could he trust but someone of his own blood? The Green One clearly had an enormous ego, and consequently was exactly what I was after. I had lost my mind of course, but being on the very brink of surrender, I was willing to try anything. This man was about to be the guinea pig for my new plan. A new plan which involved some deception.

'That's amazing,' said Iulian, hanging up the phone. 'He has agreed to see you, but it has to be right away because he is going to training later this afternoon.'

'Blimey, and you told him the things I asked you to say?'

'Yes, I think that's why he wants to see you now. Let's go.'

Iulian grabbed his coat and tossed mine over to me. Things had never happened this quickly here before. The new plan was working rather well.

We struggled out of the busy maxi taxi outside the offices of FC Constructorul, offices where we'd received an unhelpful brush-off on our first visit on my second morning. Things were very different now – we were the guests of the head honcho. Nevertheless I hesitated as we reached the doorway.

'What's the matter?' said Iulian.

'I'm just going over in my head what I'm going to ask him. I'm a little nervous.'

'Me too. Try not to make him angry.'

'OK.'

We were taken up a flight of stairs by an uncharismatic security man whose unfaltering glumness made him a natural for the job (he'd always have struggled in showbusiness.) We were shown into a bright, airy office and told to wait. I sat down on one of the black leather seats and began rehearsing my questions, while Iulian rigged the camera up on its tripod.

After an uneasy few minutes there was a noisy babble of Russian outside the door and then in came a large beer-gutted man in his fifties with a well-worn, almost gnarled face. The Green One. A slightly perspiring Iulian made feeble introductions.

'Mr Rotaru – Tony Hawks.'

We shook hands, and in so doing we momentarily united two utterly divergent lifestyles. Mine – gentle and creative; his – peremptory and aggressive. Feeling rather weedy, I tried too hard to produce a firm handshake and this resulted in a contortion of my facial muscles giving me the appearance of someone about to go into a seizure. It may have been the firmest grip I could offer but my hand was still crushed by the strength of The Green One, who no doubt had more experience in the art of adversarial greetings. For me, this was a new experience. I had never met this type of man before. You tend not to run across them that much during recordings of Radio Four panel shows or book signings in Chipping Norton.

Our host moved over to his desk, sporting a figure which belonged more in a restaurant than a track suit. I suddenly found myself wondering why it is that overweight people wear track suits. Do they feel this gives them the appearance of being fit and sporty? If so, then theirs is an admirable self-delusion. The gut may be huge, but the track suit somehow proves they're still in touch with their bodies (even if they haven't seen their genitalia for a month) and they know that the gym is only a cab ride away. Mr Rotaru went one better by wearing a track suit and, rather splendidly, smoking a cigar. Now what did *that* mean? Probably that he owned the gym.

'Is the camera running?' I asked Iulian, who nodded back. 'Right in that case, let's start the interview.'

Iulian took up his translating position and I cleared my throat and posed my first question for the President of FC Constructorul who was eyeing proceedings with some suspicion.

'Mr Rotaru, you are trainer and president of this club. Is it difficult to perform both roles?

Iulian duly translated.

'*Da,*' said Mr Rotaru.

'I see. And is it true that two years ago you won the championship?'

Once again, Iulian's translation, followed by a blunt '*Da*'.

'I see. And was that a proud moment for you?'

Another '*Da*'. This wasn't going well.

Mr Rotaru shuffled in his seat and fidgeted with the papers on his desk. He drew a long puff on his cigar. Were we beginning to try his legendary brittle patience? I took a moment to glance at the camera gently whirring behind me. It looked small and unimpressive. Was this really the kind of camera the BBC would provide for making a documentary about football in Moldova? I was relying on The Green One's displaying a naivety in television technology consistent with his name, as well as my own performance being of such aplomb that it would be hard to imagine that I was anything other than a top TV sports pundit. Just at this moment neither of these were apparent. The yarn we had spun was in danger of unravelling. For the second day running I found myself enduring an uncomfortable and potentially explosive liaison with a powerful Moldovan entrepreneur. This was so far from my original perception of what winning this bet might involve. I had envisaged meeting the jovial semi-professional players as they left their respective workplaces, and arranging to play them at tennis, before going on to dine and drink with their family and friends. Not this. It was all going horribly wrong.

'Mr Rotaru,' I continued with an external pluckiness which belied an underlying fear. 'Was winning the title an enormous personal achievement for you?'

To my relief, I heard new sounds, not merely the begrudging '*Da*' which my interviewee had produced up until now. For some inexplicable reason this question prompted an altogether more enthusiastic approach and he began to speak with some passion and with such speed that Iulian's translation could hardly keep pace. The floodgates had opened and suddenly we were awash with the torrents of his ego – yes, winning the championship had been a personal achievement, after all he had only formed the club five years previously, and entirely out of his own money. His was the only privately owned club in Moldova, and to see them playing in Europe after the championship win had made his heart swell with pride. They may have lost to Galatasaray but this was nothing to be ashamed of since the Turkish club had gone on to beat Manchester United in one of the later rounds.

'Do you think that you can win the championship this year?' I asked, with an enthusiasm drawn not from any real interest but from signs that the bait had finally been taken.

The Green One spouted facts and statistics about the coming season, clearly now having decided that this interview was for real and that the British public were about to see what a wonderful person he was. He began to enjoy being in the spotlight, even though we didn't actually have one. Fraudulent film crews rarely do.

At one point I interrupted his boastful peroration by asking him how much he paid his footballers and he proudly replied that they received in the region of $3,000 a month. A generous figure given that the average monthly wage in Moldova was $30-40. Much of this sum, it turned out, was made up of generous bonuses earned when the team had good wins, but The Green One had his own spin on the bonus system. If his players lost a match that he felt that they should have won, he would fine them by exactly the same amount as the bonus would have been. For a man who had grown up under the Communist system he had a keen and almost brutal understanding of incentive. He did not motivate his players by seeking to engender any kind of team spirit, but rather he let hard cash do the talking. The winner takes it all. Evidently he and Mrs Thatcher had more in common with each other than not looking their best in a track suit.

'How do you pay your footballers,' I asked, 'given that there are no gate receipts, sponsorship deals or sales of TV rights?'

The Green One's answer was unashamedly frank. He paid for it out of his own pocket with laundered money. In this country, he maintained, you could not make money officially because then you would lose all of it in taxes. A shocking remark, not because it revealed anything that I hadn't already suspected, but because he was prepared to make it on camera for broadcast across the United Kingdom. No caution, no guilt, no fear, no conscience. He was too powerful for any of that stuff. This guy could pretty much do what he wanted. He was one of an emerging Ruling Class in Eastern Europe whose success appeared to be based on stretching the rules to their own advantage.

The phone rang and the Green One excused himself to deal with the call, which he did with a brisk efficiency. I tried not to allow myself to think about what unscrupulous action he had just authorized and instead endeavoured to compose myself for the next question. The big one. The reason why I was here in his office.

'As well as making this television programme,' I offered rather meekly, 'I am also in this country to try and win a bet. Have you heard anything about this?'

'*Nyet*,' came the eventual reply.

'Right, I will let Iulian explain.'

I looked across and cued Iulian with a nod. Poor Iulian. I was providing fresh material for an answer to the question 'What was the worst job you ever had?'

The Green One listened attentively, at one point bursting into laughter, surely at the mention of the nude singing of the Moldovan national anthem. Then his face recovered and returned to its factory setting of stern invincibility. He relit his cigar, which had not survived his previous ramblings on the greatness of his football club, and he just sat there quietly. I became worried by this lack of reaction. Was he suddenly suspicious of my motives? I felt a need to fill the silence.

'Of course, the bet is just an excuse for me to find out more about Moldova and it's football.'

I waited patiently during the Russian reply which still gave me no inkling as to his present disposition towards me.

'Mr Rotaru says,' began Iulian's translation, 'that Moldova makes you welcome and he says that in this country we have always known how to greet our guests and how to say goodbye to them.'

This sounded okay, but I was a little concerned by the ambiguity of the latter part of the statement. How did Mr Rotaru say goodbye to his guests? Especially the ones he didn't like. Was I about to find out?

He spouted some more Russian which left me anxiously awaiting elucidation from my humble employee.

'Mr Rotaru says,' said Iulian finally, 'that you have his permission to play tennis with his midfielder Sischin, and that you can do this whenever you like once they have played their game against Roma Belţi.'

If this was an immense relief, then even better news was to follow. Mr Rotaru thought it would be good exercise for Sischin to be playing tennis on one of his days off and that before we left he would give us his home phone number so that we could ring and arrange the game.

Furthermore we could come and watch the match against Roma

Beltsi which was taking place the following day, and I could meet Sischin afterwards if I so desired. I sat back in my chair unable to prevent a smug grin from forming. To think that this morning I had been close to giving up.

Unexpectedly and unreasonably, I left the office of The Green One quite liking him. And it wasn't just because this man had given me what I wanted. He had charm. Once he had begun to relax he had been a genial host and it had become difficult to imagine him as having a cruel or violent side to his nature. Then it occurred to me that charm is an essential tool for the attainment of real power. The ruthless dictator needs to be able to manipulate, to lull his potential foes into a false sense of security, and he can do this easier behind the smokescreen of courteous affability.

All ruthless dictators have the knack. Take Saddam Hussein. Whenever I watch him on TV he always strikes me as having the appearance of a rather benign fellow – cuddly even. He's the best. He can be the genial host one minute and then pick up the phone and order someone's assassination the next. From good to bad in 6.4 seconds. That's what's got him where he is today. Those with the good grace to be consistently evil never really get on. But then it's a cruel world, isn't it.

Dinner with the family provided further evidence to support that premise. Following a discussion in which I remarked on the extraordinary discrepancy between the wages paid to The Green One's footballers and the average Moldovan monthly wage, I discovered that for those who worked for the government it wasn't only the size of the wage packets, but whether you actually received one *at all* which was the real problem. Dina had not been paid since May. This I found difficult to believe since it was October now. Grigore also had received no wages for two months.

'But how do you manage?' I asked.

'The patients look after my farver and my muvver,' explained Adrian.

I learned that a primitive and unofficial social structure had developed in which patients brought gifts of food or money each time they made a visit to the doctor. They had to – all that was on offer from the government were empty promises and they are difficult to live off. Sometimes the government would pay workers in goods and commodities rather than money. Dina's mother, a pensioner in the countryside, was regularly paid in sugar, rice or flour. Once she even took a carpet instead of half a year's pension. It was quite common for factory workers to receive their salaries in the goods they produced, like boots, stepladders or light bulbs. I was even told of one poor fellow named Vitalie who worked in a factory which made bicycle pumps and all he received at the end of each month were hundreds more of these infernal things which he had to try and sell at the market. Perversely, his survival depended on inflation.

I went to bed feeling rather guilty about my life. Here were my good and kindly hosts working hard in run-down under-funded hospitals and not even getting paid for their troubles, and here I was swanning round the place spending my time stubbornly trying to prove a point by winning an infantile wager. As I lay in bed, drifting from consciousness, my somnolent mind filled with unanswerable questions. What was going on? Who had dealt us such contrasting hands? Had He shuffled properly? How was it all going to end? Should I buy some bicycle pumps to take back to England? So many questions and only the letter Z could provide the answer.

'Zzzzzzzzzz.'

Not for the first time, sleep had come to the rescue.

Today was to be my last with Iulian for four days. Right at the outset he had told me about this previous booking that he had – translating at a conference – but I had forgotten all about it.

'It will be interesting to see how I manage without you,' I said as we strolled to the Republican Stadium. 'You have become my voice and my ears in the last two weeks.'

'Yes, it will be interesting.'

The Republican Stadium was sensibly located for the home ground of a Chisinau football club. It was in Chisinau. This was where FC Zimbru had slipped up. They probably lacked the persuasive qualities of The Green One, who had managed to secure the national side's ground for his team's home matches. Iulian and I had somehow failed to find the proper entrance on to the spectators' terraces and found ourselves approaching the pitch by walking down the players' tunnel.

For a moment I shared the same tingle of nerves that the players must get as they walk side by side towards the magic green carpet which awaits them. My imagination took hold and as we left the tunnel I was about to wave to the expectant crowd who were anticipating yet another tantalising performance from the wunderkind Hawks, when rousing music began to blare from loudspeakers and the real players ran into the centre circle and began waving to the crowd. Had there actually *been* a crowd the whole thing would have been far less tragic. All around us empty seats. Just a small pocket of around a dozen Constructorul fans who looked suspiciously like the fans I had seen shouting encouragement to FC Zimbru just days before. I began to wonder whether Moldova only actually possessed twelve football fans and that they had to move around the place in various disguises switching allegiance whenever required. Maybe they were mercenaries and they cheered for the highest bidder, and today The Green One had secured their services. Maybe he would fine them if they didn't chant loud enough.

Constructorul, in their distinctive green shirts, began the game well, launching promising attacks which unfortunately came to nothing.

'Mr Rotaru is expecting a big win today,' said Iulian. 'Anything else and he won't be happy.'

I looked over to the Constructorul bench and there was the big man, his face filled with anxiety. He was dividing his time equally between shouting furiously at his team and taking long drags from his cigarette, and generally behaving in a manner unlikely to reduce blood pressure. He looked like someone who could suddenly clutch his heart and keel over at any minute. This would have bothered me more if I hadn't already been in possession of Sischin's phone number.

The football match turned out to be just as bad as the one I had watched just days earlier. As the uneventful game drew to a close I realised that I had now watched over two and a half hours of Moldovan football and still not seen one goal. In the eightieth minute it fell to Sischin, whom three little boys had helped us to identify, to put this right. Constructorul had won a rather dubious penalty and it was Sischin – lithe, dark haired and handsome – who had been selected to take it. This was no surprise since he had been a class above the rest of the footballers on show. His deft touches and visionary passes belonged in an another arena. He deserved to have a crowd watching him play.

Sischin stepped up to take the kick. The goalkeeper jigged and bounced up and down on his line like a puppet on a string and Sischin composed himself. Then he did something I suspect he hadn't done for years. The bastard missed the penalty. He hooked it wide of the left-hand post. Like me, he hung his head. I turned to Iulian.

'Fucking unbelievable.'

'This is not good, certainly.'

Football, as they say, is a funny old game, although funny wouldn't have been the adjective I'd have chosen on this day. Infuriating would have been nearer the mark. Following the missed penalty Sischin went on to get himself booked, and although Constructorul did scrape a 1-0 win with a scrappy last-minute goal, once again the post-match atmosphere was not likely to be conducive to effective socialising. In spite of this I still insisted that Iulian and I waited outside Constructorul's dressing room in the hope of meeting Sischin and letting him know about our intended phone call, but after forty unforthcoming and very cold minutes I conceded defeat on that one. The Green One's post-match team talk had outlasted my body's heating system. Maybe it was taking him so long because he'd become confused as to whether to give his players a bonus for getting a win, or fine them for playing like donkeys. Either way they'd be unlikely to come out of it with more than a bicycle pump each.

'Have a good conference,' I said to Iulian as he left me at the stop for the maxi taxi. 'I'll see you on Monday. You will promise to keep trying Sischin's number, won't you?'

'If I have time, I shall be very busy in the next few days.'

Trust me to have hired somebody who had a life.

'Do your best.'

'OK.'

And with those two letters, he meandered off into the uncompromising darkness of the Moldovan night. It was Wednesday evening and I had no realistic prospect of playing any footballer until at least Monday, especially now I'd lost my translator. I was faced with a new and in some ways more challenging problem.

I had four days' holiday.

11
Living Like a Moldovan

On the Thursday morning, the prospect of four totally free days seemed daunting. Predictably enough, there hadn't been a flood of suggestions at the Journalism Centre for how to pass this time.

'Have you been to Orheiul Vecchi?' American Tom had said. 'That's great.'

But that had been it. Period.

Unfortunately it was a period I had to fill.

Unlike Romania, Moldova has no tourist industry. Only one consideration has hampered its development and that is its total lack of anything whatsoever to offer the tourist. No mountains, no coastline, no water sports, no transport, no quaint little villages, no night-life, no streetlights, no cuisine, no smiles and no bloody idea. This place really was as unlike Venice or Ibiza as you could possibly imagine.

I'd had one thought, that I could spend this time in St Petersburg trying to track down the player Alexandru Curtianu, but this had been dismissed when I discovered that the Russian Embassy took four days to issue a visa. I also considered visiting Romania, since the mountains of Transylvania and the resorts on the Black Sea were within reach, but both these trips would involve miserable twelve-hour train journeys as well as administrative problems given that I didn't have a re-entry visa.

So, Moldova it was. Unless I went home, of course. Gave up and went back to England. Hard though I fought it, I just couldn't help but consider this as a very real option. I mean, what was I doing? Soon I would have been here for over two weeks and still not played one footballer. I certainly wasn't having fun, and that was something this adventure was always meant to be. Was there really any point in pursuing this absurd task any further? I felt like a dog hanging on to a stick, close to exhaustion, with its gums growing bloodier by the minute. I didn't need this any more – I was ready to go lie in my basket, have someone throw me a biscuit, wrap me in a blanket or pat me on the head. Did I really want the damned stick that much anyway? It wasn't worth anything, was it?

At breakfast with the family, which somewhat disconcertingly involved the consumption of pasta, I put a brave face on things.

'What will you do today?' asked Adrian.

'Oh, I have lots to do up at the Journalism Centre.'

'And when will you play your first footballer?'

'Soon.'

Soon. A good word 'soon'. It sounds so much nicer than 'fuck knows'.

'Will you come to my English class at school?' asked Elena, pleasingly changing the subject.

'What for?'

'You can teach us and talk to us in English. I have told all the other children about you and they want to meet you.'

'Really?'

'Yes, please come. I have asked my teacher and she says that it is OK. Why don't you come tomorrow morning?'

'Er . . . all right then, I suppose I could make time.'

After the family had left the house and distributed themselves evenly among the city's hospitals and schools, I went for a run in a nearby park to try and figure out just what to do. Sometimes I find that the physical exertion and gentle rhythm of the feet on the ground can help focus the mind. On this occasion I both ran and thought hard.

The reason ought to have been not wanting to lose my bet with Arthur, or that I didn't want to concede that my philosophy of optimism was hopelessly flawed, but in the end it was neither. Something else entirely made me decide to hold on to the stick. For the first time since I'd got here, somebody had *wanted* me for something. Elena wanted me to come to her school. Oh I know it was only a tiny thing but it meant so much. On no other occasion since I'd set foot in Moldova had anyone asked me or invited me to do anything. It had always fallen to me to make things happen. I had always been the instigator and this had become both exhausting and disillusioning. Now however, an 11-year-old girl had changed all that. By issuing the invitation to her school she had showed that someone cared. Elena cared about me. It didn't matter if no-one else did, this was reason enough to stay put. For the moment at any rate.

As the day progressed things continued in the same positive vein. When I called the Journalism Centre and was given a message that Marcel had invited me to Orheiul Vecchi on Saturday, I was stunned. Nothing for two weeks and then two invitations in a day. I began to wonder whether this sudden upturn in my social life had anything to do with the fact that I was without Iulian now and that being alone meant that people made more effort. Maybe I should have done this earlier.

I walked to the National Tennis Centre in the hope of picking up a game, and on my arrival I was lucky enough to bump into my old French-speaking chum Jan, who arranged for me to play with a promising young 15-year-old, Alexandru. After an hour's practice he beat me rather soundly in a tie break. Suddenly I was only too aware that I was out of shape and that I would need to perform much better than this if I was to win my bet. Maybe I could use these four days to get my game up to scratch.

After the game, the outgoing and rather cheeky-looking Alexandru taught me how to score tennis in Romanian. In a few minutes I knew all I hoped I'd need for my upcoming encounters.

Cincisprezece zero
Trezece zero
Patruzece zero
Avantaj Hawks
Ghem Hawks

Alexandru, oddly assuming that I was some sort of authority on the game, asked me if I knew why tennis has such an unconventional scoring system. Yes, good question, this had been something which had always bothered me. Why fifteen? Why

All I knew about Moldova were the names of eleven men printed in the inside back page of my newspaper.

Travel in Moldova was never straightforward.

My trusty interpreter Iulian – we were quite a team.

'We are not like the early Beatles – we are like The Flying Postman *now*.'

'You will stay with two doctors and their two children. Typical Moldovan. You will like them.'

Naroc!

Grigore's friend Anatole, proving that Colonels have extremely long left arms.

Marin produced a smile so cheesy you could almost smell it.

Marin Spynu.

Alexandru Curtianu.

Sergei Rogaciov.

Denis Romanenko and Iurie Miterev.

Ion Testimitanu.

Sergei Stroenco.

Oleg Fistican.

Vitalie Culibaba.

Oleg Sischin.

Radu Rebeja.

'Tony has spent six months chasing Moldovan footballers around the globe and he is now here to make a rather dull presentation of his evidence.'

Nudity was what the crowd wanted and nudity was what they uniquivocally got.

deuce? Why love? Advantage this, advantage that? Back in London, an afternoon in the library had done little more than reveal to me that no-one is entirely sure, tennis being a very old game which originated in France before people bothered to write things down much. The method of scoring by 15s is believed to be medieval in origin, and 40 is used as an abbreviation of the original 45. 'Deuce' is a corruption of the French *à deux,* indicating that one player had to win two consecutive points for the game. No-one is certain about the origin of 'love' being used for zero, but it either came from *l'oeuf* – meaning egg and being the shape of a nought – or the fact that the word 'love' had become equated with 'nothing' in such phrases as 'a labour of love' and 'neither for love nor money'. (It says something of the savagery of the times that 'love' could have come to mean 'nothing'.) It was called a 'service' because the task of beginning the rally was carried out by a servant for his master. The canny player might have used this to his advantage: 'Ah, my good Lord Salisbury, I am so looking forward to the game. Have you met my servant, Sampras?'

Alexandru didn't look entirely satisfied as I attempted to translate the gist of all this into simple English.

'Did you follow that Alexandru?' I asked.

'The most of it, yes,' he replied.

'You know what I always say,' I continued. 'I think it would be better if we took what thc umpire says at the beginning of every match as a piece of advice. "Love all". If we did, then the world would be a much better place. It's only as shitty as it is because we're all trying to get the advantage.'

A baffled Alexandru eyed me blankly.

'I do not understand.'

You're not alone there, Alexandru.

Elena was thrilled. Maybe she'd thought that I wouldn't turn up, but her little face beamed with excitement as I met her outside the school gates.

'This is my friend Mariana,' she said, gesturing to a pretty girl who did a kind of half curtsy. 'You must come inside now, Miss Tudoreanu is expecting you.'

She was too. She ushered me into the class and proceeded with her lesson much as if I was a school inspector. Had that actually have been my métier then I would have been well impressed, as the attentive children took it in turns reading from a text book. Soon I found myself engrossed in the gripping story of Uncle Oscar and Aunt Agatha.

'"My Uncle Oscar was a very nice man",' began Elena, who in volunteering herself as the first reader had raised her arm with such enthusiasm that she must have nearly pulled it out of its socket. '"Every morning on Monday, Tuesday, Wednesday, Thursday and Friday he usually took the seven forty-five bus and started for work . . ."'

Only the occasional corrections from Miss Tudoreanu prevented me from losing myself totally in the dramatic events of Uncle Oscar's life.

'"Uncle Oscar went to the bank early in the morning and returned home rather late. He didn't go in for sports. He liked music but didn't play the piano, the violin, the flute or any other instrument. He practically never went to the theatre or to the cinema and he didn't visit exhibitions or museums either . . ."'

He was quite a guy this Uncle Oscar. Had anyone secured the film rights to his story, I wondered?

For all my reservations about the communist system, education appeared to be one domain where they had got things largely right. The schools had been well funded, the teachers had been highly respected members of society, and the kids were well disciplined. I hate to sound like a conservative old fogy on this one, but children *need* discipline. They bloody love it. They just can't get enough of it, and, from my experience, they don't. I am now at that hellish age where you go to parties and people bring their children along. Consequently too many times at too many barbecues and for too many years have I had my afternoon ruined by some spoilt little brat trying to poke my eye out or pour ketchup in my hair. There's a lot to be said for a regime which rewards that kind of behaviour with a lengthy stint in a Siberian gulag. At least at barbecues under a communist regime you'd never hear the sentence; 'Sweetness, don't insert the meat skewer there, I don't think Tony likes it.'

As the lesson drew to a close, Miss Tudoreanu turned and addressed me.

'Tony, will you finish the lesson by doing a short talk for the children?' she asked, taking me quite by surprise.

'About what?'

'About London. Maybe you could talk about the British Museum.'

Before I had a chance to explain that I knew absolutely nothing about the British Museum, I had been ushered to the front of the class and been announced in such a way as to suggest that I was the world's leading expert on the subject.

What followed was a curious mixture of bullshit and fabrication. My hope was that none of the children was really listening, and instead they were allowing the curious foreign sounds coming from my mouth to become the background noise to a world of daydreams. However there remains the worry that one day there'll be a Moldovan teenager inside the British Museum demanding to see the Crown Jewels and asking where the Beefeaters are. I finished my talk and the kids cheered and applauded rapturously. They'd been an easy audience to please. Frankly, all I'd had to do was not be Miss Tudoreanu, and I though I say so myself, I'd carried it off with some aplomb.

In the coming days I made absolutely no progress in the attainment of the goal which had brought me here, but significantly I began to feel more at home than I had before. Instead of breeding contempt, familiarity was beginning to instil a nagging respect and fondness for the place. I started to see behind the grim faces of the people on the streets and to realise that there was a smile within which couldn't be coaxed out by a mere pleasantry. This was a land where the people had suffered, were still suffering, and expected to suffer tomorrow. This culture had no room for benign social platitudes. This was not a society where you urged people to 'Have a nice day' because they would simply turn round and say 'No thanks, I've already made other plans.' I was discovering that you had to be patient and wait for people to open up instead of trying to force it. Trust, like so many other commodities here, was not something which was acquired easily, but once it had been earned then the doors would begin to open.

The family began to warm to me in a way that I had not expected. Maybe there was an empathy between us which hadn't existed when I had first arrived in their country, rather cocky as I was, and full of the joys of spring. Perhaps since things had gone wrong and become a struggle, I had started to display a humility which made me more accessible to them. At the dinner table we laughed more. Sure the language was still a barrier, but I found the route to their funny bones through big visual slapstick gags. Dina, on watching me mimic a vodka-sodden man I had seen stumbling from a bar one afternoon, said that I reminded her of Mr Bean. (It was at this point that I decided to tone my performances down somewhat.)

I was now included in family outings. Adrian began to shun the confines of his room in favour of conversation. For Elena, who had always been on my side, I could do no wrong, especially since her popularity rating had greatly increased at school after the guest appearance at her English class. Grigore, who still seemed to be genuinely surprised each day when I returned to the house not having become fluent in Romanian, became more tactile, patting me on the back or putting his arm round me each time our fruitless attempts at communication ground to a halt. The barriers were down. I was starting to feel like one of the family.

On one occasion I was invited down from my room to share in a toast to Grigore's old schoolfriend Anatol, who had called round after just having been promoted to colonel in the army. As he stood proudly in his full military regalia, he made an unnerving sight for a Westerner like me who had only ever seen figures like this represented as the enemy. A brandy later, however, we felt comfortable enough to pose for photos together and put each other right on a couple of common misconceptions which we both held about the other's politicians. I now knew that Gorbachev was a prat, and Anatol that Margaret Thatcher was completely bonkers.

Marcel was the opera singer brother of Andrei from The Flying Postmen, the overly loud fellow I had met briefly on my first morning. He had promised to organise a car and a driver to take us out to Orheiul Vecchi where he was going to let me film him singing the Moldovan national anthem from a cliff top. I couldn't think of a better way of presenting to Arthur the musical piece which he would have to perform. The only difference between the two renditions would be that Marcel's would be performed with his clothes on, and that Arthur's would be crap. I allowed myself an inward chuckle at the thought of this, valiantly failing to acknowledge that the way things stood it was far more likely that I'd be the one who'd be doing all the naked singing.

It was a beautiful crisp autumn morning. Marcel had promised to pick me up from the house at nine o'clock. At ten o'clock I became a little concerned. At eleven o'clock I gave up on him. Unreliability, I had discovered, was another Moldovan trait. Twice Corina had arranged for a journalist from a newspaper to come and interview me about my business in Moldova but on both occasions no-one had shown up. They never rang to apologise, give an explanation or attempt to arrange another appointment. Seemingly there was nothing newsworthy in an English comedian coming to Moldova attempting to beat the national football team one by one at tennis. The mind boggled as to what you had to do before a Moldovan newspaper would deign to write a few words about you on an inside page. I had questioned Corina on this and she had replied that the press had been controlled for so long that it had not yet found its own true voice.

'You have to remember,' she'd said rather poetically, 'that for more than half a century we have been like caged birds. Now the cage is open we don't know how to fly.'

This one sentence helped me to understand so much of what I had been experiencing here.

'Can you get to Orheiul Vecchi by bus?' I asked Adrian, who was only too pleased to take a break from his Saturday morning chore of hoovering the house.

'I think it is possible, but I thought that Marcel had arranged a car.'

'He may have done, but he hasn't bothered to come here in it.'

'This does not surprise me. I think that he is a strange guy,' commented Adrian, who had formed this opinion of Marcel as a result of speaking to him on the phone in the course of setting up this morning's non-event.

'Right, I may have been let down,' I announced proudly, 'but it is far too nice a day not to make something of it, so I am going to go to Orheiul Vecchi by bus.'

'I think that this will be difficult,' said the cautious Adrian.

'It may be so,' I said, adopting the statuesque posture and weighty tone of a great adventurer about to embark on his boldest journey yet. 'But you will see that I will succeed, for I do not know the meaning of the word "failure".'

Instead of eliciting the smile I had hoped for, this remark prompted a swift return to hoovering. Although Adrian had dispensed with his initial frostiness, he was still the only one in his family whom I hadn't really been able to make laugh. He was proving to be a tough nut to crack.

The first part of the journey was easy enough. I had become something of an old hand in the art of maxi-taxi travel, and so when I arrived at the bus station I felt confident enough. Why shouldn't I be? I'd been here twice before on my trips to Soroca and Transnistria, and not had any difficulties. Admittedly I had been with Iulian, but really how hard could it be to buy a ticket and take a bus somewhere? The ticket hall and waiting room were packed with people, the hurly-burly of Saturday morning travel being something I hadn't witnessed before. I joined the queue for tickets at kiosk number fourteen and after ten minutes I found myself at the front. However on each occasion when I was about to begin my transaction with the woman in the booth, a fellow traveller barged unceremoniously in front of me. This continued until there was no-one left to slide in front of me and I was finally able to address the woman who was seated behind the scratched piece of glass which separated us.

'*Orheiul Vecchi, va rog,*' I said in my best Romanian.

The woman shook her head. I repeated myself. She shook her head again. What was she saying? That Orheiul Vecchi didn't exist? That I had made it up? I had one more go.

'*Orheiul Vecchi, va rog.*'

This time she just pointed into the distance. This was no use. I didn't want directions, I wanted a ticket. I stood before her looking bemused until she said something in Romanian which I failed to understand. Seeing that I was a foreigner, she repeated it louder and faster. I nodded, turned round and wandered off having decided that this lady didn't like me much and that I might have more luck at kiosk fifteen.

I don't know whether the rules of queueing were entirely different in this country, but I certainly wasn't getting the best of them. I was being particularly badly served by the rule which stated that every time an Englishman reached the front, then provided you approached briskly from the right and pushed him rather impolitely with your left hand, you got served next.

During the ten minutes in which I was tantalisingly close to getting served, I observed the woman inside the kiosk and drew some comfort from the fact that however fed up I was becoming, I would never manage to look as pissed off as she did. Her ID photo, which was stuck to the window, made her look rather ugly, and to be fair, this was flattering. Her name was Lolita Levchenko. *Lolita* – that name which conjured up images of sensuous nubile beauty. Well, used to. This middle-aged and obese Lolita, bless her, waited until the very moment I was about to announce my intended destination before she decided to go off and make a phone call. A long one, and not to her agent regarding the modelling shoot in St Tropez, I'd wager.

'*Orheiul Vecchi, va rog,*' I said when she eventually returned and had finished dealing with the bloke who'd just shoved his way in front of me.

'*Casa patruzece,*' she said, gesturing off into the middle distance.

Ah. This I understood. It meant I had to go to kiosk number forty. Quite why, I was unable to establish, but from the vigorous pointing she was doing with one of her stubby little fingers, it seemed that kiosk forty appeared to be in another building entirely.

I followed the direction of her finger but all this did was lead me outside and into the busy marketplace where people were busy wandering around with chickens and other livestock tucked underneath their arms, or stuffed in bags. Guessing that this wasn't kiosk forty I went back inside. However, after four circuits of the building I'd still had no luck, so I went outside again where a man tried to sell me a live turkey. I declined the invitation to purchase, partly because what I really wanted was a bus ticket to Orheiul Vecchi, and partly because only a fool buys the first turkey he sees. (The really wise buyer will browse through *What Turkey* magazine before he sets foot anywhere near the market.)

This market place was brimming over with people, and for a moment I was carried along by the forward momentum of those around me. Everything appeared to be on sale here. Clothes, electronic goods, tools, kitchen implements, live animals, fish, and even a stall selling drugs and medication. Iulian had told me a few days earlier that most of the drugs on these stalls had been donated to the government by foreign aid agencies but had found their way on to the streets as a result of this country's institutionalised corruption. The poor folk swarming around me now were having to pay for what had been a gift to their country, and as a result some were having to sell their turkeys to keep the family healthy.

The momentum of the eager shoppers dumped me in front of a single storey pre-fab building and I looked up to see the numbers 40-44 written above four glass windows. Aha! Kiosk number forty was here. In their wisdom, the relevant authorities had evidently decided that selling tickets at random locations would make life far more interesting for the traveller than if they housed them all somewhere as obvious as the bus station.

I joined a queue, now resigned to the inevitable lack of respect that the locals would show for it, and in a mere twenty minutes I found myself dealing with a woman who didn't immediately send me somewhere else at the mention of Orheiul Vecchi. She even spoke a little English and drew a little map for me, explaining that I needed to get two buses, one towards Orhei and another at the point where the road branched off to Ivancea. Provided I got off at the right place, this second bus would eventually deliver me to my desired destination. It sounded tricky, but surely not beyond the orienteering skills of someone who'd already successfully located kiosk forty.

I showed the kiosk lady's map to the driver and he made lots of positive sounds which seemed to be consistent with this being the correct bus. The girl who was getting on behind me also nodded in confirmation. Good. I was on my way, and it had only taken a little more than an hour and a half . All the seats were full so I made my way to the back of the bus where there was adequate standing room. I leant on a little ledge above the spare tyre which was below the rear window, and readied myself for the view of the city as we left it behind. The girl who'd got on behind me stood close by and she gave me a sweet little smile, revealing some badly neglected teeth. She was probably a little surprised to see the likes of me travelling alone on a bus. The few Westerners who did visit this country tended not to avail themselves of public transport, having been warned that the dilapidated buses were nearly always overcrowded, especially on a Saturday morning. This one wasn't too bad though – I may not have had a seat, but there was a little room to move about and I'd experienced worse.

Twenty minutes later we were still in the bus station but with twice as many people on the bus. The driver had crammed an insane number of people on to his vehicle, the weight of whom were now pressing me against the rear window. Had I wanted to turn around it would have been physically impossible for me to do so. I was trapped. I wanted to get off but I couldn't. My crotch was being rammed into the spare tyre with such vigour that it probably suggested to onlookers that I had developed an immense physical attraction for it, and was not being shy about making this known. The girl with the unkempt teeth was now being crushed alongside me, but this didn't prevent her from offering another attempt at a sweet smile. I'm afraid I just couldn't return it with one of my own. I didn't feel relaxed enough. It felt too much like I was having sexual intercourse with a tyre. And a bald one at that.

With the driver finally satisfied that the bus was full, now that he was the only one on board still afforded the luxury of movement, we set off. It was not a comfortable ride. (Tyres rarely are.) After half an hour, just when extreme discomfort was giving way to pain, and when the friction of body against tyre was threatening to melt rubber, we stopped at a small village called Drasliceni, where a good number of passengers alighted. I could breathe freely again and now there was enough space around me to see just how profusely I'd been sweating. It was the beginning of November. How did the locals suffer these journeys in the height of summer?

As we continued on our bumpy way, largely through drab and unremarkable countryside, I made a firm decision to abandon my original plan. There was no way I was going to leave this bus and then immediately get on to another. I would not willingly submit myself to any more of this torture. This bus was going to Orhei, not Orheiul Vecchi, but as far as I was concerned that was a good enough destination for a day's outing. On the map it looked like a good sized town and there must be something of interest there. I'd have a wander, a late lunch, a beer and then leave. The only other bus I was going to catch today would be the one that took me home.

A further hot and not altogether pleasant hour of travel passed, during which I was on the receiving end of more smiles from my female travelling companion. She seemed to have a soft spot for me, in spite of having seen how intimate I'd been with that tyre. Obviously not the jealous type. She had a nice face and was quite pretty, at least until she smiled, when the inadequacies of Moldovan dentistry became only too apparent. It was somewhat disappointing for me, a man who had always put a 'nice smile' right up there in what he looks for in a woman, to find myself in a country where observing one was such a rarity. True, the less shallow individual would have been able to recognise the real beauty within – to see *beyond* the teeth, but I'd been successfully brainwashed by the gleaming beaming glistening grins of the Western TV ad, and I was having trouble finding merit in what I saw as a mouth full of flaws. This was something I needed to get better at; like being tidy and getting Moldovan footballers to agree to play me at tennis.

The bus stuttered to a halt and the girl tapped me on the shoulder.

'You – you go here,' she said, a little sheepishly.

Go here? I looked around me. Surely too many people around to take a leak here, I joked feebly to myself.

'You go here,' she repeated, 'Now. Here.'

I realised what was happening. Not knowing about my change of plan the girl was drawing my attention to the fact that we'd arrived at the fork in the road where I should change buses.

'No thank you.' I said, 'I have decided to stay on the bus and go to Orhei for the day.'

She didn't understand, and repeated her instruction with a little more urgency. Never mind, the bus would move on in a second and this little moment of awkwardness would be over. Just as I was about to have another go at explaining my revised itinerary, I heard a commotion at the front of the bus and looked down the crowded aisle to see that the driver was on his feet, having switched off the engine and climbed out of his compartment. He was shouting at someone and waving his arms about. What had happened? Had some kind of family feud erupted?

The minor fracas nudged its way towards becoming something of an incident when the passengers around the driver began to join in with the shouting and gesticulating. The object of their attentions seemed to be someone near me but I couldn't make out who. The impatient driver started to force his way down the bus, still calling out at volume. The passengers who had initially remained outside the dispute were now becoming frustrated that their journey was being held up, and they began to vocalise their displeasure, the overall result being something best described as a din. Still it was not clear who was the object of all this clamour, but whoever it was, the noise levels and unanimity of feeling were such that this person would soon need to present a very persuasive argument in their defence.

Then something quite terrible happened. Stupefyingly shocking. I realised that it was *me*. *I* was the one who everyone was shouting at. *I* was the one who was holding up the bus. I shivered. For those of you who haven't experienced a bus full of Moldovans shouting at you, I assure you that this is how you respond, regardless of outside temperature. As I looked down the bus, all I could see were animated faces and a frenzy of waving arms, accompanied by a soundtrack of baffling foreign sounds. It was overwhelming. What was happening? What had I done? I had no answers. My mind was only able to produce one thought, and it seemed to stamp itself like a newspaper headline over this vision of turmoil before me.

BOY, DO I NEED IULIAN RIGHT NOW!

He could explain to me what on was going on, and he could tell the others that I was a nice chap and that I hadn't killed their president or done whatever it was they were upset with me about. I was innocent! I couldn't be treated in this way, did these people not know that I was a fully paid-up member of Amnesty International? My only hope was that my female admirer could save me.

'What is it? What do they want?' I called across to her.

'They want you go. You go. Go here. Go now,' came the reply.

'But why?'

'Because you go here for Orheiul Vecchi. We go Orhei. You go Orheiul Vecchi.'

Was this all it was? Was the driver and the entire bus up in arms because they wanted to ensure that I didn't miss my connection? It seemed unbelievable and totally out of character with my Moldovan experience to date – that anyone should care – but it seemed to be the case. I began waving my arms back at them.

'No, no!' I called out. 'I've changed my mind. I want to stay on the bus and come with you to Orhei!'

The response was extraordinary. As one, the bus fell quiet even though no-one had appeared to understand what I'd said. The passengers turned and looked to the driver for his reaction. They were going to be led by his response. He stared at me for a moment and then gestured to the door uttering an emphatic statement. A few passengers chimed in with some words of support. I was in a difficult position. These people were trying to help. They were trying their damnedest to get me to the place where I'd said I wanted to go. They were going out of their way to make sure that I didn't go out of my way. I had only seconds to make a decision. The bus had been stationary for too long now and the bus driver would surely have to continue taking his passengers to their destination soon. Did I leave the bus and therefore satisfy the driver and everyone else who was on it? Or did I hang on and leave them all frustrated and disappointed that they had been unable to prevent me from fouling up my journey? OK, not quite *Sophie's Choice*, but it's right up there.

I looked out of the window and saw more than a road junction in the middle of the Moldovan countryside. I saw a man, a foreigner, an Englishman, called Tony, stranded – unable to squeeze on to a bus, falling prey to bandits and shivering in a ditch as the night closed in. That did it, I was staying. I looked up at the driver and I shook my head to him. He shook his. I dropped my eyes to the floor. I was making it abundantly clear that I wasn't budging. I heard the driver mumble something under his breath, and observed from the corner of my eye as he threw his head back in frustration and turned to make his way back to the driver's compartment. A murmur of disapproval. Then the engine starting. The girl looked at me.

'You come to Orhei?' she asked.

'Yes, I come to Orhei.'

I was going to Orhei.

'Where you go now?' asked the girl, as I stood in the area of wasteland that appeared to be Orhei town centre.

'I don't know. I thought I'd get something to eat. Is there a restaurant in Orhei?'

'Restaurant? No, I do not think so.'

'No restaurant? There must be one, surely?'

'Maybe. Come with me.'

Maybe. How, I mused, had I ended up in a country where the answer to the question 'Is there a restaurant?' was 'maybe'?

As we climbed some steps to the part of town where this restaurant might be, I learned that my companion was Rodica, a 21-year-old who worked as a secretary in Chisinau and was returning to Orhei for a weekend visit to her parents. Her knowledge of English was so limited that establishing this information filled the entire ten-minute walk to the ugly concrete block outside which she was now leaving me.

'Thank you,' I said. 'You are very kind.'

'And you are very nice.'

'Thank you again.' I pointed to the run-down building to our left. 'Is the restaurant in here?'

'I think so.'

Looking at the building I could see why there was an element of doubt. It was falling to pieces and looked deserted. If, in having met the nice Englishman, Rodica had something of a story to tell, then she certainly wasn't going to dine out on it. Not in this town, anyway.

'Well, goodbye then,' said Rodica, rather plaintively.

'Yes, goodbye,' I said, shaking her hand.

Lovely Rodica. She'd been so kind, and but for an accident of dentists we could have been made for each other.

'Do you have a telephone number in Chisinau?' I asked, drawn to the idea that I should repay her hospitality by taking her out for a nice meal there next week.

'Yes I do,' she replied, beaming broadly, and as a result not really presenting herself at her best.

With some enthusiasm she wrote her number neatly on a piece of paper and handed it to me.

'Thank you,' I said, 'I shall call you.'

'I hope so. Enjoy you meal.'

'OK. Goodbye.'

Rodica smiled again and then turned from me, rather self-consciously. I watched her walk away, back to the world of her mother and father, back to the world of her youth. Did I detect a slight spring in her step? Had she construed the taking of her number to be a friendly gesture which had broken the monotony of a routine day, or as a sign that I might be some kind of Western knight in shining armour, ready to whisk her off to a land where the restaurants outnumbered the problems? At the street corner she looked back and saw that I was still watching her.

'I hope you can clean good your trousers,' she called out with an accompanying wave, before disappearing between the buildings which formed the jaws of the adjoining street.

I looked down and saw that the entire crotch area on my trousers had been blackened by the rubber from the bus spare tyre. It looked ugly and it looked unsavoury. It looked like I used my leisure time with an unwholesome creativity. Maybe that was why Rodica had not chosen this occasion to introduce me to her parents:

'This is Tony from England. He likes to fuck tyres.'

That's me. Always ready to be an ambassador for my country.

'So how did you like Orheiul Vecchi?' asked Adrian, as we sat down in the kitchen, the kettle toiling towards boiling point.

To my relief I'd been able to sneak upstairs and change my trousers before bumping into any family members.

'I didn't go to Orheiul Vecchi. I went to Orhei,' I replied.

'But Orhei is boring.'

'Yes, that's why I got the bus straight back.'

'It is a shame that you did not go to Orheiul Vecchi.'

'Yes.'

'Orheiul Vecchi is interesting.'

All right, don't rub it in.

Actually, Adrian was displaying a mischievous side here. He'd realised that I'd completely failed to reach my intended destination, in spite of only that very morning boasting that I didn't know the meaning of the word 'failure'. In his own gentle and unassuming way he was making a point. In the unofficial and undefined tussle which was taking place between the two of us over the credibility of my positive philosophy, Adrian had scored valuable points. His lead, which was already substantial, was to be extended later that night.

The occasion was a recital of Rachmaninov at the Filarmonica, Chisinau's Concert Hall. One of Dina's patients, a violinist in the city's prestigious orchestra, had given her a couple of tickets for tonight's recitation and I was invited to accompany Adrian to the concert, if I so desired. Looking through my diary and finding myself unexpectedly free of social engagements that night, I happily accepted.

The Filarmonica was yet another example of austere Soviet architecture. It was physically cold (the absence of any heating meant that the audience would remain in their coats throughout the evening's proceedings) and as Adrian and I filed in to take our wooden seats, it felt like we were attending school assembly rather than a musical recital. The only concessions to the aesthetic were a huge chandelier hanging from the ceiling and some second-rate portraits of famous composers on one of the walls. We sat down.

Hard seats. The dim lights began to dim still further. The concert was about to begin.

I'm no connoisseur of classical music but I've been known to be surprisingly moved by its live performance. Rachmaninov's Concerto for Piano and Orchestra No. 2 in C minor provided another such occasion. As well as the passion of the music, there was the visual spectacle to be enjoyed – the unison bowing of the string section, the extravagant flamboyance of the solo pianist, and the enthusiastic arms and flashing white baton of the conductor. It was by turns, spellbinding, soothing, inspiring and uplifting. Certainly there were flaws in the performance, notably the musicians not having learnt the piece and having to bring the sheet music on with them, and Rachmaninov's second movement having been unashamedly plagiarised from the Eric Carmen hit 'All by myself' (Rachmaninov was well known for this – he did the same with the theme to the South Bank Show), but I was prepared to overlook these details. The whole thing was rounded off perfectly when the cymbal player, who had stood with an admirable stillness throughout, finally got to do a bit of crashing in the climactic crescendo which preceded the interval. I'm sure he was thinking, as he walked off stage with three crashes in forty minutes under his belt, 'I was magic tonight.'

'How did you enjoy it?' I said, turning to Adrian.

'It was great.'

'I thought so too. What happens now?'

'Well, we wait for the second half.'

'Shall we go to the bar?'

'There is no bar.'

'Oh. How about ice cream? Do you want an ice cream?'

'There is no ice cream.'

'Oh. Well there must be tea or coffee?' Adrian shook his head. 'Or someone selling programmes?' Another shake of the head. 'So what do people do in the interval?'

'They wait for the second half,' said Adrian, with deadpan delivery.

To me this seemed absurd.

'Well I'm not just going to sit here, I'm going to take a little wander. Do you want to come?'

'Why?'

'Well, it'll make a change from sitting here. Something might happen.'

'I don't think that anything is going to happen.'

'You mustn't think like that, Adrian. If you think like that then nothing *will* happen. I believe that if you think in the right way, then you can *make* things happen. Just watch me. I'm going to get up and wander round a bit and I think that something is going to happen.'

'What kind of thing?'

'I'm not sure. I might bump into someone I know. I might fall in love. I might become involved in a political discussion. We'll see. Do you want to come?'

'No thank you. Nothing is going to happen.'

'We'll see about that.'

I got to my feet and struggled past the rest of the people in the aisle who seemed to share Adrian's view that leaving your seat was an act of madness. I made my way out to the foyer, hoping to see an animated throng milling around discussing the merit of the work they had just witnessed. Nothing. Just three blokes making their way to the toilet and the woman in the cloakroom slumped on a chair and watching her feet as if they were a TV channel. I climbed a flight of stairs only to meet a uniformed man whose stern shake of the head suggested to me that upstairs was closed, so I returned to the foyer and waited. Something was going to happen. Something had to happen. I had promised it to Adrian.

Nothing happened. Of course it didn't. Adrian was right, I was wrong – and I just had to face it. However, I couldn't just go straight back to my seat, I had to try and save face somehow, so I made my way back into the auditorium and started to march down the central aisle. Having clocked that Adrian was watching me, I proceeded to carry out a succession of elaborate mimes depicting a man who had just seen a number of his very good friends dotted around the theatre. It was not a subtle performance – one of which Mr Bean would have been proud. I pointed, waved, laughed, and kept tossing my head back in amazement that I should encounter quite so many of my friends here in this Chisinau Concert Hall. Before me, a sullen mass of bodies in big coats viewed me as if I'd lost my mind. I didn't care because to my delight I was scoring a bigger victory than I ever could have expected.

Adrian was laughing. Not smiling, not giggling, but laughing big time. I couldn't believe it. I looked in wonder as he wiped the tears from his cheek and beckoned me urgently back to my seat. I shrugged to him and smiled. I felt great. I wanted to proclaim 'My work here is done' and then just disappear.

But there was a bit more to do just yet.

'I must have come to the wrong place,' I said to myself as I looked out over a football pitch devoid of players.

And yet I seemed to have it right. It was Sunday afternoon, this was the national athletic stadium, and the football should have started by now. The big sign by the halfway line suggested that this was the correct venue.

MOLDOVA GAZ V NISTRU

But no sign of any players. I cautiously approached a group of men all clad in leather jackets and enquired as to the whereabouts of the footballers, but no-one spoke any English and no progress was made.

'*Parlez-vous français?*' I threw in hopefully.

'*Oui, un peu,*' replied a solitary voice.

A short man with a well-groomed moustache, who was the source of these sounds, explained to me in sketchy French that the match wasn't being played because the team Nistru hadn't bothered to turn up. This was more like it! This is exactly the kind of thing I had been expecting from domestic Moldovan football. Sloppy amateurism. It was just unfortunate for me that none of the players I required played their football for slack outfits like Nistru. Teams who don't turn up to matches probably aren't going to be that protective of their players.

'Vitalie Culibaba – *il joue pour Moldova Gaz, n'est ce pas?*' I asked, beginning to reveal my true reason for being at the ground.

'*Oui.*'

By turning up to this game, and thus having achieved something which had been beyond the capabilities of FC Nistru, I was to be handsomely rewarded. The man with whom I was sharing this scrabbly Gallic exchange now revealed himself to be the manager of Moldova Gaz. Delighted at the news, I immediately went into my old 'I'm a BBC TV sports journalist' line and produced my video camera by way of proof. I began filming him and asked a few vaguely journalistic questions as he basked in the glory of the camera's gaze. His colleagues looked on, impressed. Just as I had done with the Green One, I added the details of my other agenda here in Moldova as an afterthought and once again I was rewarded with the home phone number of the relevant player and the manager's blessing for the playing of the tennis match.

'*Merci beaucoup*,' I said shaking the manager's hand. '*J'espère que tous vos jeus seront assez facile que ce match contre Nistru.*'

He smiled, a *what did all that mean?* smile, and gave a friendly little wave to the camera as he and his entourage made their exit.

I kept the camera running and panned round to shoot the empty football pitch only to find the lens filled by a big happy smiling face, its red wine-stained mouth spluttering some greeting or other. I drew the camera away from my eye to see that I'd been focusing on a large middle-aged fellow with a bulbous nose and ruddy complexion, who was flanked by three enthusiastic looking youths.

'Hello London!' said one of them, directly down the camera lens.

The others looked on as if I held in my hand the answer to the secrets of the universe. The camera had acted as a magnet and drawn them to me, and now they wanted to wave playfully and send greetings from the Moldovan people to those in Britain. And who was I to stop them? To my surprise, the lads spoke pretty good English and fired continuous questions at me.

'Do you drive a BMW?'

'How much money do you earn?'

'Do you have a big house?'

'What is your name?'

I chose this last enquiry as the one most worthy of a response.

'My name is Tony,' I replied.

'Ah Tony! Tony Blair!' chimed in the most vocal of the lads, to much amusement. 'My name is Spartak. These are my friends, Iura and Leonid, and this is our friend Emile who we met this afternoon.'

On hearing his name, the older man Emile put his arm around me and began beckoning me somewhere.

'Emile says that he has never met an Englishman before,' explained Spartak. 'He wants you to go and have a drink with him.'

'Where?'

'His house. We are all invited.'

'OK.'

And so I traipsed off to Emile's house with my new-found friends. In between further questions about life in England and exactly how many people drive a Mercedes Benz, I was able to learn that the lads were students at the university, and that Emile was happy and drunk.

When we arrived at Emile's abode, which was a rather sweet little cottage set in a small courtyard behind the football stadium, he immediately took us down into a cellar filled with bottled gherkins. There is a line to be drawn with regard to the number of gherkins that it's healthy for a man to keep, and it was a line which Emile had unquestionably crossed. On all four walls, shelves from floor to ceiling were stacked full of bottles containing this unsavoury looking vegetable. For a moment I was struck by the unpredictability of life. By rights I should have been watching a football match now, but here I was in a dingy cellar with Moldova's very own super-hero, Gherkin Man.

'Emile wants you to take some wine,' said Spartak. 'He makes his own.'

Oh mercy, no. This I could not take. Gherkin wine? Please no.

'Give me your camera,' said Iura. 'I will film you.'

I handed the camera over, just for a moment wondering whether I would ever see it again.

'*Este vin*,' announced Emile, offering me what looked like a pint mug full of red liquid. '*E foarte bun!*'

Any relief at the colour of the liquid was tempered by the size of the receptacle from which I was required to drink it. As I took hold of the mug Emile grabbed my elbow and tried to force me to down the whole thing in one. My stomach still required gentle treatment and my instinct was not to indulge Emile by drinking a pint of his dodgy home-made wine. However despite resisting as best I could, I was still forced into a huge mouthful. Ugh! Foul, just as expected. Spartak and Leonid cheered, Iura filmed, and Emile grabbed me and planted a huge wet smacker of a kiss on my cheek. Alright, it may not have been the kind of kiss that had started to feature in my dreams of recent nights, but nonetheless it had its worth. It was another sign that Moldova was beginning to accept me at last.

Having extricated myself from the over zealous hospitality of Emile, and experienced an alternative tour of Chisinau courtesy of my student chums, I stopped at a call box to report in to Iulian.

'Great news Iulian,' I announced proudly. 'I have another home phone number – Vitalie Culibaba.'

'This is good Tony,' replied Iulian. 'I have had a lot of success today too. I called Sischin and he says that he will play you on Tuesday. He also gave me the number of the goalkeeper Denis Romanenko, who is a really nice guy. He says he will play you tomorrow and he will bring Radu Rebeja and Iurie Miterev with him too.'

'You mean I am playing three Moldovan footballers tomorrow?'

'Yes. You'd better get an early night.'

12

No Sets Please, I'm Moldovan

I looked out of my bedroom window and observed a fresh, clear autumn morning; one which looked like it was going to prove Iulian wrong.

'I think it is going to rain tomorrow,' he'd said to me the previous night as we finalised details for today's matches.

'Iulian, you do realise that you're a *I think it is going to rain tomorrow* person? Let's just imagine that things might go how we want for once.'

'OK,' he'd said, with absolutely no conviction.

I made my way down to the kitchen with more than a tingle of nerves in my stomach. D Day had arrived. I was only too aware that if I lost to any of these three footballers today then the bet was lost. By the front door, I met Adrian who was thrilled that I was finally about to play my first tennis matches.

'Don't you dare come home without winning!' he said as he started out for college.

I marvelled at the change in his attitude. I watched him as he headed for the bus stop, convinced that he looked more upright, more eager. Could it be that he was even excited by the prospect of a new day?

There was a more positive environment awaiting me at the Journalism Centre too. From outside the door, I heard a big booming American voice coughing decibels into the normally tranquil office. Big Jim had arrived.

Jim was a healthily round figured man with a keen, interested face, on which he sported a grey moustache similar in design to those plastic clip-on ones from Christmas crackers. He was chairman of some kind of broadcasting governing body back in Minnesota, and was in Chisinau to assist the Moldovans in setting up commercial radio stations. I learned later that he'd started out life presenting the breakfast show on Radio KSTT in Iowa before working his way to the top of his profession on the administrative side. He never told me what KSTT stood for though. It occurred to me that American radio stations are always called things like Radio WBQX or WKIM but we tend never to find out why. From what I've heard of American radio, they all ought to be called Radio WTCB[3]. I liked Jim. His upbeat approach boosted my confidence just when it was needed. His response on learning the nature my business in Moldova was unequivocal.

'You'll win that bet, Terry, no question.'

This sentence summed up the two things I liked most about him. His positive attitude, and the fact that he persistently got my name wrong. All around him people would refer to me as Tony, but Big Jim was deaf to these sounds. For some reason he'd locked on to Terry, and was not prepared to countenance addressing me any other way. Terry may not have been my given name, but it was certainly the one I'd been given by him.

'Well, good luck, Terry,' he said, as Iulian and I headed off for the courts. 'Go out and do your stuff!'

On the way we stopped off to buy some beers, on the assumption that it's not just British footballers who are partial to the stuff. I would have bought a Page Three model, and a tabloid photographer for brawling purposes, but they'd sold out. That's state-run shops for you.

Since the courts at the National Tennis Centre were being used all week in a training camp for promising young juniors, Iulian and I had been forced to find another location for the matches. After a little to-ing and fro-ing we had secured the use of one of the courts within the grounds of the Republican football stadium, a fitting venue given the profession of my opponents. The courts, which were sandwiched between the stadium's stands and the road, were looked after by a

[3]We Talk Complete Bollocks.

man called Sergei, whose chiselled features and rough-hewn hands suggested that factory life had preceded his recent foray into commercial sport. He seemed a nice enough guy and what's more, he wasn't charging me an excessive amount for the hire of his court. OK, I might have been paying slightly over the odds compared to a Moldovan, but then I was a wealthy guest in this country, so why not? Sergei's slight adjustment of the going rates contrasted sharply with The Arsehole of the Universe in Transnistria, who appeared to assume that everyone in the West was a millionaire and consequently fair game for wholesale exploitation.

Sergei's face lit up when Iulian explained to him what was about to take place on his patch.

'He is a big football fan,' Iulian informed me. 'He says he knows all the players.'

In this regard Sergei was untypical. Most Moldovans show little interest in their national side, preferring to follow the fortunes of either Romania or the Ukraine, depending on their ethnic background. Sergei, however, knew all the players' names and was quite delighted that they were going to appear on his tennis court. He smiled broadly, as well he might. His court was being hired out at a good rate and he was going to get to meet all his heroes. Not a bad gig.

Sergei watched me with interest as I paced nervously, awaiting the arrival of my first celebrity guest. It was ten past two and the first player had been due to arrive at two o'clock. I did my best to resist thoughts that I was about to be stood up, but I couldn't help myself. By quarter past two I'd convinced myself that I'd been naive to expect professional footballers to give up their free time for a game of tennis, especially when there was absolutely nothing in it for them.

'Ah – Iurie Miterev!' exclaimed Sergei with excitement, referring to one of the three young men emerging from a car which had just pulled into the car park adjoining the courts.

I looked over, awestruck. Could it be true? Was I finally about to do battle with a Moldovan footballer on a tennis court?

The three men made their way towards us, and it became obvious which one was the footballer. The tall, fit-looking one. My immense relief at the arrival of a player was instantly superseded by fear, especially now I could see that Iurie Miterev was a fine physical specimen, and one which looked likely to make formidable opposition. Even though only a few days earlier I'd done enough of it for a lifetime, I was close to crapping myself again.

Iulian made the introductions and I shook hands with the object of my fear, who then made his way into the wooden hut which Sergei called a changing room. While he prepared himself for battle I met his two friends who happily accepted the offer of a beer. I tried to get Iulian to establish from them whether Iurie Miterev had played much tennis in his life, but the two men just shrugged and then giggled a bit. Terrible thoughts crossed my mind. Why were they laughing? Was it because I was about to get stuffed by Iurie, who was an ace with the racket? Was Iurie going to be the best of all of the players? It would be Sod's Law that the first one I played would be the best. I tried to think back to what Natasha, the gypsy card reader from Soroca, had said about Miterev. The more I thought about it, the more I became sure that he had been one of the players that she had told me not to play. Hang on, wasn't he one of the footballers who she had said would try and poison me? Maybe that's why he had the two guys with him – they'd help him dispose of my corpse when he'd finished with me. I would have to be very careful. Very careful indeed.

Iurie emerged from the dressing room wearing a red top and green shorts, but with no steaming test tube spewing toxic fumes into the atmosphere. Good, no evil potion. And no established tennis kit either. This I took to be a good sign. For a moment I was reminded of the junior tennis tournaments I used to enter in the summer holidays when if a player turned up with better tennis kit than you, then the assumption was that they would be the better player. Sometimes you'd be half way through the first set before you'd suddenly realise that their game wasn't as impressive as their brand new rackets and expensive Fred Perry tennis wear, and that you could actually beat them. On occasions it worked the other way. A player would turn up with one racket, odd socks and a tatty T-shirt and turn out to be extremely talented. A bluffer. You had to watch them.

Conversations were significant too, especially in the nervy pre-match walk to the tennis courts. Big talking, boasts of tournaments won or difficult opponents thrashed, all played their part. Similarly, players might say things which can suggest a poor level of play is to be expected. Many years after my junior days, in a celebrity-am tournament at the Queen's Club, I was due to play in a match with a radio presenter who some might say was no longer at the peak of his career – to protect his identity let us call him David *'Doddy'* Hamilton. As we walked to the courts David looked at me and said:

'What have you got *two* tennis rackets for?'

I knew from this that he did not play very much, or hit the ball hard using much topspin. (A player who does will accept the possibility of breaking a string at any moment, and will therefore keep a spare in readiness.) As we got to the courts and took out the balls, David turned to me and smiled confidently. Suddenly it dawned on me that he was probably a bluffer who had plenty of spare rackets stashed in his car. As it happened I needn't have worried. David's career was in a much healthier state than his tennis.

I was pleased to see that Iurie had gone one better than David *'Doddy'* Hamilton. He had no tennis racket at all. This augured well but I was still uneasy. Maybe he was a bluffer. Maybe he played so much he'd broken all his rackets and they were off being re-strung. Maybe he'd traded his rackets in to pay for the poison.

While Iulian set the video camera on its tripod, I handed Iurie my spare racket and we made our way to our respective ends of the court. Battle was about to commence. After travelling over a thousand miles and grovelling for more than a fortnight, could it be that I'd then fall at the very first hurdle? Miterev, a colourful figure in his green and red, looked unsettlingly eager as he waited at the opposing baseline.

I hit him the first ball. A high, gentle, looping one aimed at his forehand. I watched keenly as he shaped up to it, taking a big and hugely worrying back-swing. This guy was about to strike the ball very hard indeed. His face, a picture of concentration, was almost grimacing as his racket head made contact with the ball, and . . . bang! . . . he hit it clean over the back fence. His two beer-drinking chums fell about laughing and I let out a huge sigh of relief, while Iulian scurried off to retrieve the recently expelled yellow projectile.

Iurie's next attempt at striking the ball, although in marked contrast to the first, was still no better. This second shot bounced several times before it reached the net. He needed to find some kind of middle ground between the two shots, but I knew this was something he'd be unlikely to achieve in the course of an afternoon. Thank God.

After Iulian had returned for the fourth time from retrieving one of Iurie's 'big' shots, he oversaw a short meeting at the net between Iurie and myself at which it was decided what form the match should take. My initial suggestion was that we should play one long set – the first to nine games, with a tie break at eight all. Iurie, however, was not keen since he had to go to training later that afternoon and was pushed for time. He suggested that we played one long tie break – the first to eleven points. At first I was reluctant to agree to this. In the sudden death situation of a tie-break I felt that I might fall victim to a freak passage of inspired play by my opponent, and not be afforded the opportunity to stage a spirited comeback. However, after giving it a moment's thought, I agreed, largely for two reasons. First, so that I could conserve energy given that I had three matches to play in one afternoon, and secondly, because Iurie was crap. So crap that it really made no odds whether we played up to three, or a thousand and three.

As we changed ends after the first six points, with the game tantalisingly poised at 6-0 to me, I passed a perspiring Iurie at the net and took good care not to allow him the opportunity to administer any poison. It would have been daft to have thrown victory away as a result of downright carelessness. I knew what he was capable of.

Playing at a different end made little difference to Iurie's fortunes and in fact if it hadn't been for my serving a double fault and deliberately missing a forehand, it would have been a whitewash.

'11-2. Match to Tony,' declared Iulian from the net, readying himself to film the handshake which would provide my evidence to Arthur.

'One down, ten to go,' I mumbled to myself as I made my way to the net.

Iurie was magnanimous in defeat, and showed no signs of disappointment as I thanked him and offered a beer which he gladly accepted. I would have joined him and wallowed in the unexpected joy of having a victory behind me, had it not been for the arrival of a plush BMW pulling into the car park. A rather elegant lithe figure emerged from the car in a green track suit.

'Radu Rebeja!' announced an enthusiastic Sergei.

At the same moment another man, clad in a black leather jacket and carrying a sports hold-all, walked off the street and into the car park.

'Denis Romanenko!' said Sergei, who was starting to remind me of John Motson.

As the two men walked towards us, I wondered if this could really be. So much of my experience in Moldova had been about blows and setbacks that it seemed hard to believe that these guys were really coming through for me. As I shook their hands, I couldn't stop myself from doing a kind of Japanese bow, such was my gratitude to them for having shown up.

Both men greeted their team-mate Iurie, and while he let them know that the experience of losing to me was painless enough, I took a moment to study my opposition. Radu Rebeja, the team's left back, was slim and handsome, and Denis Romanenko, the goalkeeper, resembled a boxer losing a fight against baldness. He seemed the nicer of the two, smiling warmly and appearing to be up for having a bit of fun, while Rebeja looked a little fed up and keen to get his match out of the way. The most noteworthy observation however, was that neither player had their own tennis racket. Promising, I thought.

Radu Rebeja wanted to play first, since he was already in his track suit and Romanenko needed to get changed. I handed him my spare racket and he ambled up to the far end of the court, occasionally swinging the racket in a manner which suggested that it was an unfamiliar item to him. After a ludicrously short warm-up Rebeja announced that he was ready.

'Let play begin,' announced Iulian, in all the relevant languages.

Miterev and his two chums, now getting well stuck into the beers, shouted encouragement to their fellow countryman. Had Rebeja not demonstrated an ineptitude for tennis to rival Miterev's, then the tie-break wouldn't have been over by the time their colleague

Romanenko had emerged from the dressing rooms. Splendidly, however, this wasn't the case. Radu Rebeja was *worse* at tennis than Iurie Miterev. No mean feat, I tell you. For all his good looks and stylish appearance, put a tennis racket in his hand and, no doubt about it, he looked a bit of a prat. He scrabbled, grovelled, scooped, swished, slashed and swiped, but still did no better than Turkey in the Eurovision Song Contest. 'Nul points' was the best that he could manage.

'11-0. Match to Tony,' proclaimed Iulian, to sniggers from the three strong crowd.

Radu took it all a little ungraciously. Managing a smile was too much trouble, and he showed no interest in having a beer or sticking around for the big game with Romanenko. Instead he said his goodbyes and took off in his big black BMW. Let's be fair though, he probably had better things to do. I didn't care. Even if he wasn't Mr Sociable, he was still my hero. He'd turned up, and that was all it took to acquire that status.

Denis Romanenko was altogether a different personality. Enthusiastic, effervescent, energetic, jovial and most pleasingly of all, crap at tennis. I had wrongly assumed that Radu Rebeja had provided a rock-bottom performance. Denis was able to plumb the depths of inadequacy still further. His problem was quite basic. He simply couldn't get the ball over the net. Iurie and his pals were consumed with laughter as whatever method Denis adopted produced the identical result of ball bouncing five times before reaching the net. Sergei was so distressed at his hero's performance that he felt the need to intervene, and stepped on to the court to give a short coaching lesson. Denis was a quick learner and was soon hitting the ball over the back fence.

I beat Denis Romanenko 11-4. I gave him four points because I liked him so much. As we shook hands he declared that he wanted to play another tie-break, thus displaying a surprising appetite for a game which he had so convincingly failed to master. Immediately, Iurie Miterev jumped to his feet and demanded that he too be given the opportunity of a re-match, and so it was that the afternoon was whiled away amidst beer, footballers and an extraordinary mélange of appalling stroke play.

Denis and Iurie were great guys and I wanted so much to spend time talking with them, but the language barrier was such a hindrance. It was such a shame, because here were a couple of people who I would have loved to have got to know better. By the time we said goodbye, I had learned that the match they'd played at Wembley had been a great thrill for them, and that the English player who had most impressed them had been Paul Gascoigne, but regretfully I still knew little about their lifestyles, their aspirations or whether they were planning on joining a tennis club forthwith.

Iurie and his chums said their goodbyes while I did some more needless bowing, but Denis hung on for another beer and said he would try and help me to contact the other players I needed. Iulian was to call him later when he might be able to provide some useful numbers.

When he finally said goodbye I felt an enormous swell of affection for him. Unlike Rebeja, he left on foot, having no shiny black BMW to speed his exit. He was cool enough not to have to hurry because he was the sort of guy you wouldn't mind hanging round for. Nine times out of ten the geezer in the flashy sports car needs that speed so that he can get to where he's going before everyone pisses off without him. Not Denis Romanenko. Moving at his own pace meant that he had more time for other people. I reckon he knew that if you speed about the place then you miss out on the views.

I took my time walking back to the Journalism Centre. No point in rushing – too much to savour. In one afternoon I had seen off more than a quarter of the opposition. Given the standard of the footballers thus far, there was no reason to suspect that I was going to lose this bet as a result of encountering a superior tennis player. It was just going to be a matter of getting the guys on to the court.

'I have just beaten no fewer than three of the Moldovan national football team at tennis!' I proclaimed proudly from the centre of the main office of the Journalism Centre.

I'd been looking forward to this moment. A chance to show the sceptics that I was on my way. I'm not sure what response I was hoping to illicit – maybe a cheer or perhaps a spontaneous round of applause, but all I got were six raised eyebrows and one slightly begrudging 'Oh, this is good.' A moment of despair. Just what did I have to do to get this lot excited?

'Hey! Way to go, Terry!' came the rescuing voice of Big Jim. 'I understand you've been giving these Moldovan soccer guys a hiding!'

Boy, was it good to have this guy around. He knew how to enthuse. That's what he should be teaching over here, I thought, forget all that radio nonsense and teach these people how to enthuse.

'Three soccer players in one day?' he continued. 'Why you gotta be one helluva tennis player, Terry!'

Not strictly true, but nevertheless it felt wonderful to be on the receiving end of some praise, even if it had to be accepted under a pseudonym.

'I have some more news, Tony,' offered Iulian, hanging up the phone, his universally deadpan delivery making it almost impossible to predict whether what was coming was going to be good or bad. 'Testimitanu and Fistican have agreed to play you tomorrow and Sischin and Culibaba have said they are available on Wednesday.'

'Wow.'

'Hey, Terry,' added Jim, 'looks like you'll have this all wrapped up by the weekend.'

Back at the house, Grigore couldn't believe it. He'd worked late the previous night and been off to work early in the morning and so he'd had no inkling that I'd been about to engage in some tennis matches at last. Elena jumping around and hugging me had been his cue to make enquiries. A good fifteen minutes elapsed before he fully understood what I had achieved, and then he shook his head in disbelief. When he passed on the news to his wife, Dina announced that she would cook a celebration meal in my honour, one at which I was to acquire yet another name.

'My farver says,' said Adrian, on completing a tasty fruit salad, 'that after your three victories we have a new hero in Moldova as well as Stefan cel Mare. It is you – Tony cel Mare.'

'Tony cel Mare,' I repeated. 'Tony the Great. Yes I can live with that. I promise to try and live up to my name.'

'I think that you will,' said Adrian.

What had happened here? I'd made him laugh once in the concert hall and now he'd undergone a complete change in personality. After dinner, I sought to take advantage of it.

'Adrian, would you make a phone call for me?' I asked, handing him a phone number on a piece of paper. 'It's someone who hardly speaks any English.'

'Of course,' he replied.

'When you get through, ask for Rodica.'

Surprisingly she'd been on my mind in those moments of relaxation between playing Moldovan footballers. In my head I'd redesigned her teeth and I'd begun to see her real beauty. Her kindness deserved to be rewarded – with dinner for two – and surely I deserved a date with a beautiful woman as a reward for beating my first players?

'OK,' agreed Adrian. 'But what do I say when I have Rodica?'

I hesitated.

'Ask her if she wants to come to dinner with me tomorrow night.'

Adrian went quiet.

At that moment we had switched lives. I'd become the nervy teenager and Adrian the experienced and responsible adult.

'Who is Rodica?' he asked, almost disapprovingly.

'She's a girl I met in Orhei.'

'Ah, so that day was not all a failure,' he teased, almost like a parent savouring a child's embarrassment.

'This is what I keep telling you – if you go for it, things happen,' I asserted, trying to re-establish my status as a grown-up.

'What do you want me to say to h—'

Adrian's query was halted as the phone was answered at Rodica's end and he was suddenly required to switch to another language. A conversation began and I, a man well into his thirties, began to watch the endeavours of a 17-year-old boy who'd been instructed to ask a girl out for him. Not the proudest moment of my life. I made a mental note to try not to ask 'Well, what did she say?' when the phone call was over, and sat back in my chair, letting the foreign sounds wash over me like the piped music of a hotel lobby. Then, rather abruptly, Adrian hung up the phone. He looked at me with his old pre-laugh face, impassive and unpenetrable, and said nothing. I broke the silence.

'Well, what did she say?'

Damn, I wasn't supposed to do that.

'I did not speak with her. This was a drunken Russian man who was speaking rubbish. Are you sure that this is the right number?'

'Well, it's the one she gave me.'

'Oh. Well, maybe we will try again tomorrow night.'

Yeah, and maybe not, I thought to myself as I undressed for bed. I wasn't going through that again. If Rodica was going to be asked out, then from now on it would be me doing the asking, language barrier or not. I'd been reminded what it felt like to be a teenager again and it hadn't been at all pleasant. No longer would I lament the loss of youth.

'Being my age is alright,' I said to myself as I arranged myself under the blankets, in search of the position that would ease me into unconsciousness.

I felt warm, mellow and respectably tired, but most of all, and for the first time since I'd arrived in Moldova, I felt content.

It's amazing what beating a few footballers can do for your state of mind.

The next morning I was woken by the front doorbell. I looked at my watch and saw that it was 5.45 am. Too early to be a social call, surely. I heard voices and wrested myself from the warmth of my bed to watch what was going on from the window. Grigore was in a dressing gown addressing two rather shady-looking figures in black leather jackets. I immediately felt concerned. Were these mafia figures? Was Grigore being threatened? An apparently clandestine dialogue continued for some time until one of the men walked slowly to the car and returned with a huge fish which he then handed over to a grateful-looking Grigore. I went back to bed a little confused by the whole thing. Why the secrecy? It was only a fish.

'It was probably poached,' said Iulian, in answer to my question on the subject, as preparations at the Journalism Centre began for a second day's play. 'I have no doubt that these guys were saying thank you for some treatment which Grigore had done for their children.

They know that the government does not pay him properly so this is what they do.'

'I see, so you have a kind of secondary economy which bi-passes money.'

'Yes. This is because money is more scarce than fish.'

While I was trying to work out whether this remark was profound or merely a truism, my thought processes were disturbed by a familiar sound.

'Ah Terry! How are you today? Ready to beat more of those soccer guys, I hope? How was your evening last night? Did you celebrate?'

'Yes.'

I was struck by how easy it was to converse with Big Jim. He just asked consecutive questions to which one could answer yes or no, although it was nice to reward his enthusiasm with some of one's own.

'The family I'm staying with,' I added, 'paid tribute to my achievements by naming me after the great Moldovan hero Stefan cel Mare.'

'Great idea. So they call you Terry cel Mare, eh? I like it, it's got a good ring to it.'

As we arrived at the courts, I could see from Sergei's expression that he was eager to discover who I had lined up for today.

'Ion Testimitanu and Oleg Fistican,' I declared.

'Varry goot,' he said in a thick accent, thrusting both thumbs in the air. 'Testimitanu – varry goot. Fistican . . .' he paused, commencing an agonising and entirely unsuccessful search for more English words, 'Fistican . . . varry goot.'

We could have talked for hours had Iulian not interrupted our flow from the back of the court where he was setting up the camera equipment.

'I think the tripod is broken,' he called out.

A short examination indeed confirmed that one of the legs had been damaged and that the tripod was no longer stable when at its fully extended height.

'We'll just have to film from a lower angle,' I suggested.

'OK,' said Iulian. 'When you get back to England you could

probably get it fixed.'

I studied the shoddily manufactured broken tripod which had never been the sturdiest piece of equipment.

'It would probably be cheaper to buy a new one,' I thought aloud.

'What do you mean?' asked an astonished Iulian.

I tried to explain that the combined cost of parts and the labour would almost certainly mean that repair wasn't a viable option. In the course of this explanation I began to question the wisdom of an economic system which allowed a situation like this to prevail. It was plainly absurd. We didn't repair things, we threw them away and bought new ones, never mind that we were exhausting the world's resources in the process. It was just plain daft, and yet we in the West were urging these fledgling former communist states to follow our example, and they were happily doing so, assuming that we must know what we're doing because we drive more BMWs than they do.

Camera in place, Iulian went off to make the necessary phone calls to ensure the presence the following day of Sischin and Culibaba, while I was left to await the arrival of today's footballers and make small talk with Sergei. It was not enlightening. All I managed to establish was that there were ten or so things which Sergei thought were 'varry goot' before an athletic-looking fellow in a grey track suit entered the courts by the far gate. Sergei informed me that this was Oleg Fistican, reiterating just how 'varry goot' he thought he was.

Fistican was a number of things – good-looking, gregarious and fun being three of them – but in the realm of tennis he sank to new depths of ineptitude in the boggy field of Moldovan footballers' tennis. This man, let loose on court waving a racket around, made Miterev, Rebeja and Romanenko look like tennis professionals. His initial response on being handed a racket was to swing it with such violence that it looked like he was attempting to ward off attack by a swarm of bees. His lack of co-ordination during this unconventional warm-up was such that he dropped the racket twice, a sight which hardly filled his English opponent with trepidation for the forthcoming contest.

Several players in the past have adopted a two-handed stroke on both forehand and backhand sides, Monica Seles probably being the most well-known. Fistican turned out to be another, although he didn't appear to have based his game on Monica's, the only similarity being the grunt which he emitted after having swung and missed the ball completely. This he did with impressive regularity. Oleg was king of the air swing. It is said that Pete Sampras once broke fourteen sets of strings during forty minutes of practice, something it would have taken Fistican a lifetime to achieve given the infrequency of contact between ball and strings.

Just as the tie-break was about to begin, something telling happened. A football dropped into Fistican's end of the court, having been kicked over the wall from a practice match on one of the adjoining training grounds. It bounced once before Fistican controlled it on his chest, flicked it up in the air with his knee and then volleyed it back over the wall with exceptional skill. Up until this moment, anyone watching Fistican's tennis performance would have assumed him to be a man devoid of any ball sense or hand-eye co-ordination, but the simple truth was that he had technique in one sport but not in another. Technique mattered, and it was beginning to look like this had been something Arthur had underestimated when he'd made our wager.

Iulian returned from his secretarial duties in time to see the last point of the tie-break in which I served and Fistican, with racket held out with both hands in front of him like a begging bowl, scooped the ball up into the air. He was oblivious as to its whereabouts until it landed rather unceremoniously on his head, seconds later. A fitting end to a truly comic performance. Oleg the clown shook his head, laughed and then skipped to the net to shake my hand. What a splendid fellow. My fourth hero.

I was able to recognise my fifth hero with no help from Sergei, since he'd been the one footballer I had met before, albeit very briefly outside the coach after Zimbru's disappointing draw with Olimpia Belţi. The distinctive shaven head of Ion Testimitanu glistened in the autumn sun as he made his way across to our court.

'Hello Tony,' he said.

Wow, he remembered me. Still, I suppose you would.

Ion was proudly sporting a Bristol City FC track suit. With Iulian's help, he explained that he'd had recent trials with the club and he was hoping they'd sign him soon.

'Bristol is nice,' I said, 'although it rains a lot.'

Ion had to do without this vital information because Iulian didn't bother to translate it. He had standards, and 'Bristol is nice although it rains a lot' had clearly dipped below that which was worthy of his skills.

Ion, like all his colleagues so far, had no tennis racket but said that he had played a little tennis while on holiday one year. This experience was reflected on court where he gave the best performance to date, but still offered pretty feeble resistance, losing 11-4.

'Thank you so much for helping me to try and win my bet,' I offered as we shook hands at the net. 'Maybe I will see you in Bristol.'

'Maybe,' he said, trying to give the impression that he'd understood.

Maybe I really *would* see him in Bristol – when he'd learnt English, and I could take him out for a meal as a way of saying thank you. A thank you which would probably have to do for all the team.

Rodica, however, would have to remain unthanked. Iulian's attempts to get her on the phone had only resulted in repeated and fruitless conversations with the drunken Russian.

'Maybe this is not so bad,' said Iulian. 'If you had met her then I think she may have become hopeful. Many girls are looking to Western men as an escape route from this country.'

'Ah, so she may just have seen me as her Bristol City.'

'Exactly.'

Maybe it was best for her this way. There's nothing worse than having a couple of trials and not getting picked. It's happened to me enough times.

The third day of tennis was to follow the exact pattern of the previous two – charming and co-operative footballers turning up with no racket, succumbing with magnificent ease on the tennis court, wishing me luck and then wandering out of my life forever.

'Today I claimed the scalps of Oleg Sischin and Vitalie Culibaba,' I announced back at the Journalism Centre after the victories had been secured.

'Great, so that's seven and O,' said a genuinely thrilled Big Jim. 'You got these guys on the run, Terry.'

'Well, it sounds good Jim,' I replied, 'but I've just done the relatively easy part. The seven players I've played so far, all live in Chisinau. Forgetting about the one in Russia and the one in Israel, I've still got two to get in Transnistria.'

'Well, I'm sure Iulian can organise that. He's a very able guy.'

'I hope so. He's trying right now.'

We both looked across to an earnest Iulian who was in the closing stages of a telephone conversation, the result of which he was about to relay to me.

'That was our old friend Grigorii Corzun,' he said, hanging up the phone.

'The Arsehole of the Universe?'

'The same. The trouble is he's living up to his name. He says that he was deeply insulted that you did not stay at his hotel. He says you drank his brandy and then you just left. He says that you want something for nothing, and that he thinks you are not sincere about wanting to go into business with him. Why should he let you play his footballer? He says that you can forget it. There is no way.'

This was shattering news.

'Those were his exact words?' I enquired. '*You can forget it – there is no way.*'

Iulian nodded, and my heart sank.

'There's gotta be a way,' said Jim. 'There's always a way.'

He was right, there is always a way. The trouble was I just couldn't think of one. Jim hadn't met Corzun and he didn't know what a determined, powerful and bitter individual he was.

The prospects were bleak. I'd got used to being on the receiving end of bad news but this seemed so final. Had this setback come earlier in my trip then I might have felt better able to deal with it, but now, after weeks of drawing on all my reserves of energy, enthusiasm and resolve, this new problem felt like one hurdle too many. I slumped in my chair, winded. The heroic figure who had just beaten seven footballers in three days, now a picture of defeat.

'This is not good,' I said, in homage to Iulian's gift for understatement.

'You gotta get the press to help you on this one,' suggested Big Jim, who had assumed the mantle of lone positive voice. 'You gotta use the media to expose this guy as a wrecker of dreams, as a killjoy.'

Ah yes, the Moldovan press and media, who make appointments and never turn up. They'll really make things happen, I thought, dejectedly.

'Maybe Jim. We'll see,' I said, putting on the bravest face available. 'There's got to be a way round this one. There always is.'

But in my heart I knew the bet was lost.

13

'My Muvver has had an Idea'

Dear Mr Grigorii Corzun,

I am sorry that you think everyone in the West is a millionaire, and that you have built a hotel in the middle of nowhere. I regret too that I will not be able to persuade anyone from England to spend something in the region of $200 a night to sleep in your plush but ultimately tasteless bedrooms, but I'm afraid that other than yourself, I don't know anyone stupid enough. Furthermore I am disappointed that your small-minded revenge for my unwillingness to become a partner in a business bringing tourists to one of the shittiest places on earth is to refuse to let Sergei Stroenco play me at tennis.

You should know that I have christened you 'Arsehole of the Universe', a sobriquet which you consistently live up to. (By the way, if you don't know what 'Arsehole' means, look it up in the dictionary where it says; ARSEHOLE: Person who spends £25 on a beer and a sandwich in Manchester.) As a result of your asinine ways I have to concede that I have lost my bet, and I now have to face a seventeen-year-old boy whose faith in a better future had somehow become inextricably linked with the success of my project. You have not let me down, but rather one of your young people. Not a first for you, I shouldn't wonder.

I wish you no ill, but I do hope that one day you stub your toe quite hard on the corner of your bed and suffer acute pain, albeit momentarily. Please think of me when this happens.

Yours with a Mancunian beer and sandwich in hand, (cost £3.90).

Tony Hawks.

I didn't send the letter, partly because I couldn't be bothered to go and get the stamps and partly because Iulian told me it only had a 50/50 chance of reaching its destination, such were the vagaries of the Transnistrian postal service. Nevertheless writing it had been a cathartic process and one in which I'd needed to indulge. I felt better for it, if only marginally so. I still had to tell Grigore, Dina, Adrian and Elena that I had failed, and that was not a prospect I was relishing.

The blame for failure didn't lie wholly at Grigorii Corzun's door. Shortly after his rebuff, the other Transnistrian club, FC Sheriff, had called to say that they would not allow their player to indulge in extra-curricular tennis activities either, thus rendering Sergei Rogaciov totally unplayable too. Transnistria had not been kind to me.

Drawing on the last vestiges of fighting spirit within me, I put one more suggestion to an exhausted Iulian.

'Maybe our friend the goalkeeper Denis Romanenko could help? He may know the home phone numbers of the two players and we could side-step their pig-headed clubs.'

Two hours later we had discovered that Denis had no number for Stroenco and the one he had for Rogaciov was his parents' number, and they told us he was staying in club accommodation and could only be contacted through official channels.

Game over.

'Iulian, it's time to go shopping' I said. 'We're going to buy my flight ticket home.'

'It's all over folks,' I said rather sheepishly at the dinner table. 'The bet is lost. I've tried everything but I just can't get the two players in Transnistria.'

When Adrian translated, Grigore and Dina looked shocked. As shocked as they'd looked on my arrival when I'd first told them what I was intending to do. I'd been so relentlessly positive throughout my stay that seeing me so resigned to defeat was difficult for them to comprehend. Eyebrows were raised and little shrugs of the shoulders were accompanied by short bursts of Romanian which remained untranslated. The mood was sombre.

'I'm sorry, Adrian,' I said as I got to my feet at the end of the meal.

'It's OK,' he replied. 'I think that it is not your fault.'

It probably wasn't, but that didn't make it easier for any of us to bear, and subdued goodnights rounded off an uncomfortable evening.

In my room I did my best to fend off the gloom, telling myself that I'd done well to beat seven footballers when I'd been on the brink of giving up without a single player defeated. I had made interesting discoveries about a new and challenging part of the world, and somehow I'd become part of a warm and wonderful family. It was just too bad I hadn't managed to be their Tony cel Mare.

It was now Thursday morning and the earliest flight I'd been able to get back to London was on Saturday, so whoopee, I had two more days of holiday. On the first of these I decided to have another crack at Orheiul Vecchi, but this time doing it the easy way by getting Iulian to book a taxi to take us out there.

'What exactly is Orheiul Vecchi?' I asked Iulian as the car moved from the greys and blacks of the city into the soft shades of autumn countryside. 'I never bothered to find out before. I wanted it to be a surprise when I got there.'

'It is a monastery built into some cliffs.'

'What's it like?'

'I don't know, I have never been.'

Many had spoken highly of this place, which was only 45 minutes by car from Chisinau, and yet Iulian had never bothered to pay it a visit. Iulian's dream, I suspect, was not to look for beauty within his country, but to secure a way out of it. For me this was flawed thinking. Wouldn't it be better to look for what we want *where we are*, and not in some other place? Nevertheless, it must have been painful for Iulian, only the day before, to have watched the ease with which I'd purchased my ticket out of Moldova. Maybe I should have been more sensitive and done it alone.

As the taxi drove us further from human life along dirt tracks instead of roads, I began to realise how crazy I'd been to try and reach this place alone, and by public transport. Orheiul Vecchi was not a town or village as I had originally imagined, but little more than a small church perched on a clifftop, towering above a fertile river valley. Disappointing it was not, however, such was the drama of its location – a remote pin-prick of civilisation precariously balanced atop a wild, rocky and expansive terrain.

We stopped at a solitary house at the foot of the cliff where Iulian secured the services of Lilia, who became our personal guide for as little as ten lei, the equivalent of £1. Her lengthy tour was interesting, informative, and in Romanian. Had I made it here alone, days before, I would not have benefitted from Iulian's translation and would have missed out on a truly fascinating history. Humans had lived on this site since the days of the cavemen, and later the Dacians had built a large town in the valley below, now completely buried under the debris and waste of subsequent centuries. Lilia took us to an ancient arrangement of stones which the Dacians used as a sacred site to worship their myriad gods. She explained that every five years the elders of the community would have brought the most accomplished and well-respected member of society here and sacrificed him to the gods by pushing him from the cliff edge on to spears which were facing upwards in the valley below. To die in this way was considered the highest honour. For me, it has shortcomings as an incentive scheme. If the reward for success is being impaled on sticks, then I'm sorry, but aren't most people just going to call in sick for another week?

The highlight of the tour was the cave monastery which had actually been carved *inside* the limestone cliff in the thirteenth century by Orthodox monks who had sought a hermit-like existence in an attempt to get closer to God and avoid persecution. A dozen or so monks had been holed up in here, in the crampest of conditions, each of them having little more than a tiny cell to sleep in. To have willingly chosen living arrangements like this, either required exceptional faith or downright stupidity – or both. Day after day, night after night, they prayed earnestly in an attempt to commune with God and hear His voice, a voice which was almost certainly saying, 'Look, you really don't need to go to all this trouble you know. Have a pizza and chill out.'

That evening the family were in buoyant mood. It was difficult to fathom what could have brought about such good cheer.

'My muvver has had an idea,' announced Adrian at the dinner table. 'Earlier today she was in a car with the muvver-in-law of one of the national team players, and this lady was talking of the qualifying game which is coming up for the European Championships. They have a match in Belfast against Northern Ireland in just a few weeks.'

'Yes. So?'

'Well, just now my parents and I have been talking-'

'And me too!' piped in an affronted Elena.

'Yes, and Elena too,' continued Adrian. 'And we thought that it would a very good idea if you went to Belfast and played the footballers there that you cannot play here.'

I was stunned. A quite brilliant thought, and one which had simply not occurred to me.

'What a fantastic idea!' I cried out, almost overwhelmed. 'Dina, thank you so much. Thanks to all of you. Thank you. Thank you.'

'My farver says that we should drink Moldovan champagne, because tonight your bet is alive once again.'

And we did too. Quite a little celebration we had. A beaten-up guitar was produced from somewhere and Grigore sang and played with an unexpected proficiency. As he launched into an old Russian ballad, I noticed a glint in Dina's eye which suggested to me that this song was special to them both, and one which had probably played a part in their courtship many years ago. They exchanged knowing looks and for just the briefest of moments, they were two medical students again, young and in love – their progeny and the odd English guest merely onlookers, privileged witnesses to that special force which had brought them together and sustained them through the years. As the drink hit its mark I sat back in my chair and observed the scene before me. The troubadour Grigore and his beautiful wife surrounded by two wonderful children.

Together they shared something special, and for a moment I found myself wanting what they had. A little surprising. I hadn't thought I'd say that about anyone in Moldova.

It wasn't until much later, when I finally stumbled into bed, that I was struck by the full significance of what had happened that night. Not only had the family's plan set my task back on track, but it had been the first time in my entire stay that anyone from Moldova had been anything other than reactive. Up until now I had always been the one making the suggestions, inventing hairbrain schemes or pushing for this or that. Finally someone else had come up with something, and bloody good it was too. It seemed odd that this moment hadn't arrived until I'd actually given up on things. Maybe it was because this was the first time that I'd appeared vulnerable and really in need, and this was something with which Moldovans could empathise. Or maybe the help arrived because they didn't want me to fail, and they didn't want me to fail because they cared.

With the bet resurrected, it was back to work, and my last day replicated my first, with a visit to the Moldovan Football Federation. Andrei, the team's translator, looked pleased to see me.

'How are you?' he asked. 'And how have you got on?'

'OK thanks,' I replied perkily. 'I've had some success. In three weeks, guess how many players I've managed to play?'

Andrei became pensive and did not rush his response.

'Well, I suppose,' he finally ventured, 'that you have played seven.'

'Extraordinary – that's exactly right Andrei, how did you know that?'

'I did not know. This is just what I supposed that you may have achieved in this time.'

How disappointing – he'd got it dead on. Somehow this lessened my sense of achievement.

I explained to Andrei about the Northern Irish leg of the plan and he took me to meet Vasile Vatamanu, the team's PR officer, who was rotund in physique and robust in speech. It was pure speculation, but I got the impression that over the years he might not have been averse to the odd glass of vodka.

'Mr Vatamanu says,' translated Andrei, 'that the national coach is sympathetic to this kind of thing, and he thinks that we will be able to help you in Belfast.'

It struck me as unusual that my desire to take on the players at tennis could be described as 'this kind of thing'. Did Mr Vatamanu deal with similar requests on a regular basis? If he did, then this might add weight to my initial prognosis that he showed a keen interest in vodka.

The best news of all was that my elusive Transnistrians, Stroenco and Rogaciov, were both in the squad for the match, as was Alexandru Curtianu, the guy who played in Russia for Zenit St Petersburg. If things went to plan in Belfast, then I would have the scalps of all but one of the players, Marin Spynu, who'd been dropped from the national team since the Wembley match, and was now playing his football in Israel. It just might be that a trip to the Holy Land would be needed to see the bet to a successful conclusion.

As a result of taking a short cut suggested by Iulian, by the time I got back to the Journalism Centre everyone had gone home except Big Jim who was working away at his laptop computer.

'Terry, I hear you're off tomorrow,' he said, spinning round from his computer screen. 'I understand you're now going to Ireland and then Israel.'

'That's the plan.'

Well, I gotta take this opportunity to wish you the best of luck. Maybe you should call up Tony Blair and get him to help.'

'He might have one or two other things on his mind.'

'Well, you know what they say – "If you don't ask, you don't get."'

While Jim expounded on what was achievable if you 'went for it', I pulled a flip chart into the centre of the room and wrote on it in large letters:

GOODBYE EVERYONE, AND THANKS
Tony cel Mare

As farewells go, it may have been a little impersonal but I wasn't sorry it was happening this way. With the exception of Corina, who was away on business in Romania, I hadn't made much of an impression on the guys in this office, and I was happy to slip away quietly.

'Maybe you oughta write it again,' suggested Jim. 'That "Terry" looks like "Tony" to me.'

'Oh I think it'll do,' I said, still loath to reveal the truth.

'It's your call. Well, goodbye Terry.'

'Goodbye Jim.'

A huge handshake.

'Look me up if ever you're in Minnesota.'

I probably will too.

For someone who doesn't like goodbyes much, this wasn't a great day for me. The maxi taxi stop on Boulevard Stefan Cel Mare formed the backdrop for the next valediction. Lucky old Iulian was to be rid of me at last. As he stood before me, I felt strangely numb – unable to fathom which emotion I ought to be feeling. We'd worked closely together and shared many laughs as well as disappointments, but nevertheless not much warmth had developed between us. We respected each other, and that was about as far as it went. I liked to think that Iulian would remember this time with the mad English guy with fondness, and that some of my positive thinking might have rubbed off on him, but somehow I doubted it. Iulian enjoyed being pissed off. He didn't need anyone to come along and mess that up.

'Good luck,' he said, as we shook hands.

'Good luck,' I offered, by return.

We'd both need it, but one of us had already been blessed with a healthy dose of it simply by virtue of where he'd been born. I wouldn't take that for granted any more.

It was all rather touching. The family had thrown a dinner party specially in my honour, the culinary main attraction being the huge fish which I assumed some patients had poached especially, and the surprise guests being Corina and her husband Aurel, who'd just returned from Romania that day.

'So my prediction was out by one,' said Corina, having been brought up to speed with recent events. 'I said that you would play six players and I hear that you have now played seven. And won!'

'But of course I won,' I responded modestly. 'How could you ever have doubted me?'

'I am sorry,' she laughed. 'But seven is not enough – don't you still lose the bet?'

I explained about the planned trips to Belfast and Israel.

'You really want to win this thing don't you,' she remarked, almost in disbelief.

'I think I do, yes.'

I was in little doubt about this, and who could blame me? After having gone to as much trouble as I had, I didn't really want the further inconvenience of having to get my tackle out on Balham High Road.

It was a fine meal, and if the wine flowed more fluently than the conversation then it was for no reason other than the language barrier. Presents were exchanged; I gave flowers to Dina, and Wimbledon T-shirts and key rings to everyone else. I was on the receiving end of an abundance of Moldovan chocolates and wine. Grigore thanked me for the influence I'd had on his children and I thanked him for his family's kindness and support.

'I think that we have been good for each other,' I said via Adrian.

Dina and Grigore nodded. Just as I did, they knew that relationships don't get any better than that.

At midnight, merry in every sense of the word, I climbed the stairs to my room only to hear Adrian's voice calling up behind me.

'Tony, I fink that our house will be empty without you,' he said quietly and sincerely.

I found myself quite choked, and struggling for words.

'Thanks Adrian,' I managed.

It wasn't enough but it would have to do.

Despite my taxi arriving at five o'clock in the morning, all the family were up to see me off. I hugged them in turn, discovering a genuine affection in each embrace. Win or lose the bet, these doorstep squeezes would be enough to have made it all worthwhile.

As the taxi reversed away from the house, its headlights illuminated a family waving goodbye. They were lit beautifully. This could have been the final shot of an Oscar winning movie.

Except that it wasn't time to roll the credits just yet.

14
Sausages

Leaving Moldova wasn't as easy as it might have been. My bag was weighed at check-in and I was given the astonishing news that it was 23 kg overweight and that I would have to pay $225 in excess baggage charges.

'Two hundred and twenty-five dollars?' I whined to the guy from Air Moldova who had been summoned especially. 'My bags and their entire contents aren't worth that much.'

This was probably the truth, given that I was carrying my video camera as hand luggage.

'These are the rules,' explained the deadpan official, a young guy in his late twenties. 'This is what you have to pay.'

'I'm not paying two hundred and twenty-five dollars. It's absurd,' I complained. 'Besides, I've only got 50 dollars left.'

Three weeks in the country had emboldened me and I wasn't going to be taken for this amount of money. Not without creating quite a fuss anyway.

'You must pay,' he insisted.

'Not if I make my luggage lighter,' I announced, much to the puzzlement of the official.

I proceeded to empty my bags of all the bottles of wine and brandy which I had bought in the last few days, or been given on my last night. I looked up at the official and smiled.

'There. Now you can have a party,' I proclaimed.

'What do you mean?'

'Well, I'm not going to pay 225 dollars for the privilege of taking these bottles home with me when they're probably only worth around 50 dollars. You keep them. You and your friends here can have a party.'

I looked up at some of the official's co-workers and signalled to them that this alcohol was soon to be all theirs. It was news which did not seem to displease them. However the official remained solemn.

'We have enough wine in this country already,' he said.

'Well, now you have a bit more because I'm not paying two hundred and twenty five dollars to take it with me.'

My attitude was somewhat disarming to my adversary. He recognised that I was an awkward customer but he had clearly never come across one before whose awkwardness manifested itself in a desire to give alcohol to him and his colleagues. There was nothing in the book on how to deal with guys like me. Confused, he went off to seek advice, taking my now much lighter bag with him.

Ten minutes later he returned looking a mite relieved.

'Your bag is now only five kilograms over,' he said. 'I will do you a deal. You can take your wine and your brandy and I will only charge you for the five-kilo excess.'

It sounded like a good deal. Especially since agreeing to it meant that I could go home. And I wanted to go home.

'OK, we're in business. Charge away,' I said a little cheekily.

The official then filled a page of his notepad with calculations before turning to me and announcing;

'You have fifty dollars to pay.'

Fifty dollars? What a coincidence. His extensive calculations had produced the exact figure which I'd earlier revealed as being what I had left in my wallet. Why didn't they just forget about all this excess baggage palaver and just introduce a rule where they confiscate any money you have left over?

'OK,' I conceded, 'here's your money.'

So far as I was concerned it was a scam, but at least my rather brazen actions had got the price down to an acceptable level. Now when I got home, I could make use of one of the bottles in my luggage to drink two toasts to Moldova – one to some of the beautiful people I had met, and one to the relief of finally being out of the place.

'So have you done it then Hawks?' asked Arthur, as we met for a drink in the same pub which had seen the birth of the whole preposterous wager.

'Not exactly. I have to go to Northern Ireland next,' I replied.

'What for?'

'To get some more of the footballers.'

'Christ. I suppose you'll have to go to Timbuktu after that.'

'No, Israel.'

He looked at me, totally unable to fathom whether I was joking or not.

'So how many have you beaten so far?' he enquired.

'Just be patient, Arthur. I'll tell you the whole story when I've completed it. Until then, you just work on that tan. And make sure it's an all over one.'

Two weeks later, following my first game of tennis back on English soil against my friend Tim (who always provides considerably more opposition than your average Moldovan footballer), a pot of tea was being shared back at my place when a fax arrived from Iulian in Moldova.

Bad news Tony. I just spoke again with Andrei from the Moldovan Football Federation and he says that the national trainer does not think that their schedule in Belfast will allow them time to play you at tennis.

I am sorry. I guess this means you have lost after all.

Regards Iulian

I hung my head. I was staring defeat in the face again. When I had left Moldova, things couldn't have looked rosier, but now my hopes had been dashed by a simple fax. Tim, who knew that I was already a bit pissed off after having just lost to him in a close tie-break, could now see that I was doubly gutted.

'Will you still go to Belfast?' he asked.

'I don't know,' I sighed. 'I mean there doesn't seem much point.'

'The point is to win the bet.'

'But the trainer has said no.'

'What was the exact bet with Arthur?' asked Tim, adopting a new upbeat tone of voice.

'What do you mean?'

'How was it worded?'

'Well, I have to beat the entire Moldovan national football team at tennis.'

'At tennis?'

'Yes at tennis. Tim, what's your point here?'

'Well, why don't you go out and buy yourself a Play Station and beat them at tennis on that? Their manager surely couldn't object to them sitting in front of a TV and twiddling a knob.'

'Are you serious?'

'Of course I am. The game's called *tennis* and if you beat them at *tennis*, then you're fulfilling the terms of the bet.'

'That's the most ridiculous idea I've heard in ages.'

'Yes, but that's no reason not to act on it.'

I hesitated. It was undoubtedly a straw, but it felt good to clutch at something. I was a desperate man. Having come this far and survived Moldova with seven scalps under my belt, it just seemed madness to concede defeat just yet. Besides, I'd bought my ticket to Belfast – I'd might as well turn up there. OK, without question Arthur would not count the defeat of a Moldovan footballer at a computer game as a legitimate victory, but it might just be that I could persuade him to allow some kind of independent jury to make a judgement on the matter, and who knows – they might just rule in my favour, especially given the time, effort and money I'd put into the project.

'All right then,' I replied finally. 'Let's go shopping.'

The man in Dixons, Oxford Street, had said that the Sony Play Station was so easy to operate even a two-year-old could do it. This did not make me feel any better when, after 45 minutes, I was still on my hands and knees in front of the TV, shouting at the instruction manual. I was badly in need of a two-year-old to explain a few basics, but all the toddlers I knew were busy at nursery lecturing their teachers on the relative merits of the 475MHz and K6-2 3D processor. I just had to figure it out myself.

I finally acquired toddler status when I read the instructions at a sensible pace instead of trying to rush through them so that I could begin playing the video game immediately. As with so many things, the trick was to be patient. My first match was against Pete Sampras.

It might have been better to have started with a weaker opponent, but I'd checked thoroughly the list of available opposition and I hadn't seen the names Luciano Pavarotti or Roseanne Barr anywhere. No, you had to take on pros, and frankly they don't get any tougher than Sampras. Even when he's only a drawing.

I lost 6-0, 6-0, in one of the more one-sided confrontations since US forces took on Grenada. What made the defeat all the more unpalatable were some of the hurtful remarks made by TV commentator Barry Davies. He had evidently been hired by the makers of the game to come into a studio one afternoon and record thousands of different comments which could then be slotted in at relevant moments in the match. I felt he was unfairly critical of my service, and I resented the impersonal way he referred to me as Player One. 'Oh dear,' he'd say. 'And what was Player One thinking of there?' or 'Player One really has to look closely at his service action. It's simply not good enough.'

After my 6-0, 6-0 loss to Cedric Pioline, Barry went too far.

'Oh dear, oh dear,' he pronounced, 'Player One simply doesn't have what it takes to compete at this level.'

'Look Commentator A,' I shouted at the TV screen, 'just give me a sodding break – I've only been playing for twenty minutes! Pioline's been playing the pro circuit for ten years!'

But Barry was right, of course. I was playing at the wrong level. Unwittingly, I had the machine switched to *VERY DIFFICULT*. Once I flicked the button over to *EASY*, I pissed all over Agassi 6-2, 6-2. (If only real life was this simple.)

After playing for two hours solidly, I felt I'd earned a cup of tea, especially since I'd just drawn level at one set all with Greg Rusedski at *MEDIUM* level. Barry was not impressed that I'd stopped. From the kitchen I could hear his continuing commentary.

'*Well is this nerves we're seeing here?*'

'I'm making a cup of tea, Barry, I'll be back in a minute,' I called from the kitchen.

'*Well, I don't like to call this gamesmanship from Player One, but there really can be no other reason for this delay.*'

'Give me a break man, I'm trying to—'

'*Oh I must say that this is bad sportsmanship.*'

'Look Barry, just fuck off!'

I could never live with Barry Davies. The man is too impatient, too judgmental. Two days holed up in a bedroom with him while I attempted to acquire a level of competence at a computer game, was enough to confirm this. As soon as this whole business was over he would have to move out. No two ways about it.

Painful process though it may have been, this brief foray into the tragic world of the maladjusted spotty teenager had provided me with a valuable new life skill, and as I left the house for Belfast on Monday morning I was fully in possession of the technique required to defeat any footballer in the world at Play Station tennis.

Not to mention two quite sore thumbs.

'Have you been to Belfast before?' said the taxi driver in a pleasingly strong Ulster brogue, as he delivered me from airport to city centre.

'Yes, I've been a few times,' I replied. 'The first was about five years ago when I did a show at the Arts Theatre during the Belfast Comedy Festival.'

It was on that visit that I'd discovered how the people in Northern Ireland have developed a unique sense of humour, presumably to deflect the pain of the horrors which all too regularly afflict them. I learned this the hardest way of all – in front of an audience of four hundred. Being in Belfast, I had wanted to perform at least some material which made reference to where I was, but I was only too aware that to do so was to walk into a comedy minefield, given the sectarian complexities of the place and the explosive political situation. Nevertheless, I'd come up with an idea which I ran past several locals who all assured me that it would go down 'just fine'.

On the night, twenty minutes into my performance I decided that I was being received well enough to risk it, and I took a deep breath and leapt from the metaphoric high board, not entirely sure whether the pool below me contained any water.

'I've had a lot of bad luck with my left shoe recently,' I began. 'The sole came loose and I kept tripping up over the bit that was flapping about at the front. Well, I was recommended a glue by a friend who assured me that it would hold the leather firm at the front of the shoe, but it had little effect. Then I tried a rubber under-sole but that too came loose . . .'

I won't bore you with the full extent of my ramblings on this extraordinarily trivial subject, but suffice it to say that I continued for as long as I felt I could still hold the audience's attention, before I delivered the line for which the whole preamble had been constructed.

'. . . and finally after trying my fifth different glue, I gave up and threw the shoes away . . . and you think you've had troubles up here.'

Silence from the audience. Oh God no! I'd been given the wrong advice and I'd gone too far. There'd be no way back from this. But then a chortle, followed by a guffaw, and sure enough, just like the cliché scene in a movie, the theatre was soon filled with laughter.

My most daring moment on stage had been a success, but it had been touch and go. That moment sums up the resilience of the people of Northern Ireland – that they could laugh at someone making light of the suffering which they had endured for a generation – and take it from an Englishman at that. I guess they could do it because their humour is black. It has to be. For many, laughter has been the only defence.

'How do you like Belfast?' asked the driver as we approached the disordered sprawl of grey buildings which are the city centre.

'I always find the people here so friendly.'

'That's our problem,' he said. 'We're friendly to outsiders but we hate each other.'

He dropped me at Ulster TV on the Ormeau Road, but not before we'd both endured heavy city centre traffic.

'I don't know why they call it the rush hour when everyone's at a standstill,' he remarked wryly.

I was back in a country where the sense of humour prevailed. Well, almost.

'Ah come in Tony, it's great to see you again,' said Shonagh, holding open the door to the offices of *The Kelly Show*, on which I'd appeared once before. 'Look everyone – it's the eejit with the fridge!'

'Ah Jaysus!' said Mary, 'And what's he up to this time?'

'He's playing Moldovan footballers at tennis,' piped up Helena from the rear of the room.

'Somebody needs to help that man. He's mad,' observed Patricia.

'What was Moldova like?' asked Alice.

'Well, let me put it this way,' I responded. 'It's a country where you'd be unlikely to see any adverts for soft toilet paper.'

My audience laughed. I liked it here. Five young women, all with a well-developed sense of fun, and all up for giving me a helping hand with my quest. Just like the Journalism Centre had been in Chisinau, this office would be the headquarters for my operations, the difference here being that I'd be surrounded by people taking an active interest and making positive suggestions.

'Why don't you call the Irish FA?' suggested Mary. 'They'll tell you where Rogaciov is staying.'

'Good idea, do you have the number?'

'Ah sure, we'll have it for you in a second.'

This was just amazing. I was surrounded by professional researchers. As far as they were concerned, problems were there to be solved. Something of a contrast to my recent Moldovan experiences.

Rogaciov was the problem which needed solving. Since the Wembley game he'd been dropped from the senior national side but he was still playing for the Under 21s. Their match was taking place at another time and in another part of Northern Ireland. Just as yet, I was unfamiliar with his itinerary. Over the phone, Trevor Irskine at the Irish FA was to provide me with all the answers.

'The seniors play on Wednesday night as you know,' explained the helpful Trevor, who at this stage believed himself to be chatting with a reporter from Ulster Television. 'But Rogaciov will be running out with the Under 21s tomorrow night in Coleraine.'

'Right. Well, I'll definitely come to that.'

'No problem – I'll arrange tickets. Why exactly is it you want to interview him anyway?'

'It's a very long story Trevor – if it's all right I'll explain when I see you.'

'No problem.'

I liked this guy. Everything appeared to be *no problem*. Perhaps that was because he didn't know exactly what I wanted from him yet.

'His name is Andrei Ixari,' I said to the pretty receptionist at the Holiday Inn. 'He's expecting me. He's the translator for the Moldovan national team.'

'Ah yes, Andrei,' she replied with a smile. 'I'll call him for you now. He's lovely.'

This I knew already. He'd probably been the most co-operative of all the people I'd met connected with Moldovan football. Now it seemed his good manners and boyish good looks were winning friends among pretty Northern Irish receptionists.

Andrei must have been wondering why I'd still bothered to come all the way to Belfast given the rather unsympathetic nature of the last message from the national team coach. When we'd spoken on the phone a few hours earlier, he'd been in the middle of a meeting and I hadn't been able to explain my proposed solution to this. If Andrei didn't have me down as a genuine British eccentric just yet, then surely that would change the moment I explained that I'd travelled all the way to Belfast to play three Moldovan footballers at Play Station tennis.

It was good to see his face again as he marched proudly from the lifts to the lounge area where I was waiting for him. He was flanked by the large amiable figure of Vasile Vatamanu. They both looked surprisingly pleased to see me.

'Welcome to the United Kingdom,' I offered, rather formally.

Mr Vatamanu said something in Romanian.

'It is really great to see you here at your home,' translated Andrei, dutifully.

Belfast wasn't my home, but I knew what was meant, and we all shook hands warmly. The two men seemed so relaxed, it was quite extraordinary. Naturally, having only flown in that day they would have been excited about being in a new land, but I wondered if they were experiencing a sense of ease at being free from the burden that was Moldova. I reckoned so. It was in their expressions. It was almost as if their facial muscles were warmed up and ready to break into a smile.

Our meeting was infused with uncharacteristic laughter, Mr Vatamanu being in jocular mood. He was the bearer of good news. Stunningly good, in fact. It was explained that the national trainer had changed his mind yet again and now he had no objection to my taking on his players at tennis, provided it was done the following morning. Naturally enough I agreed. I was hardly going to say 'No, I've set tomorrow morning aside for window shopping.'

I wasn't going to have very long. The two games against Stroenco and Curtianu would have to be played after their breakfast and before their sightseeing tour. This would mean fitting it in between 10.15 and 11.00.

'Will there be enough time?' I asked Mr Vatamanu, whose response was immediate.

'Mr Vatamanu says,' interpreted Andrei, 'that in this time you will be able to beat the players three times over!'

Mr Vatamanu let out a huge roar of laughter.

'Beating them once will be enough,' I returned with a smile.

Some things you want to do twice. Beating Moldovan footballers at tennis wasn't one of them.

'Are you fit and ready?' enquired Shonagh, as we met in the reception of UTV the next morning.

'I'm as ready as I'm ever going to be, and as fit as I need to be.'

Shonagh had kindly agreed to perform the role which Iulian had done in Moldova, and film the matches as evidence.

Leaving the taxi waiting outside, ready to whisk us off to the Belfast indoor tennis centre, we entered the Holiday Inn at exactly 10.15 am. The atmosphere was unusual, to say the least. Middle-aged Moldovan men were milling around the foyer wearing dark overcoats and a variety of inappropriate hats. It felt like I was back in Chisinau, except that the light wasn't dingy and the staff in the hotel didn't look like they'd just been sentenced to death. The milling men, I assumed, were team officials. There were far too many of them and, as I was soon to discover, they all wanted their say in the decision-making process.

'God, it's like a scene from a Cold War thriller,' said a stunned Shonagh.

'I had three weeks of this.'

'Rather you than me.'

Andrei finally appeared looking a little harassed. He explained that the players were still finishing breakfast and they'd be with me soon. It was now 10.20 and they were supposed to be back at the hotel having completed the games by 11.00. Time was tight, but I was powerless to hurry things along. Even though I was back on territory where I spoke the language and understood how to make things happen, I was still reliant on the good will of my Moldovan friends, and subject to their capricious and vacillating dispositions.

The foyer became even busier now that track-suited footballers were added to the ranks of those busily doing nothing in the hotel's reception area.

'This must mean that they've finished breakfast,' I remarked, as coolly as I could.

'It's twenty-five past ten,' observed Shonagh. 'I don't think you're going to have time to fit this in.'

'The important thing is not to panic in this situation. It'll all come together.'

My confident words belied my inner fears. This was all slipping away. If the games didn't get played this morning then that was it. No other available times.

'What's happening Andrei?' I asked as he moved past looking a little flustered.

'I will be with you in a moment,' he said. 'There is a problem that needs to be resolved.'

And with those words he joined a confabulation of officials, who were doing a great job of looking like Eastern European spies. Voices were raised, opinions declared, and arms waved about. They appeared to be discussing something of a calamitous nature. Shonagh looked across to me.

'Something bad has happened,' she said, gravely.

'I know. It's bit of a worry.'

For the next few minutes, as the crisis meeting before us continued, Shonagh and I speculated on the possible reasons for all this anxiety. Had their star player been injured? Had there been a break-in to one of the rooms? Had the Moldovan government been on the phone with some complicated diplomatic diversions?

Whatever the predicament, Andrei was dispatched to deal with it. I watched anxiously as this fraught figure made his way across the foyer for the umpteenth time in search of a solution. I took a moment to pray that whatever had been the cause for this exigency, it could be cleared up in the next thirty seconds.

Grimly, Andrei flagged down a passing waitress. We craned our necks to hear as much as we could.

'What is happening about the sausages?' he asked.

'I thought your man said that you didn't want sausages,' she replied.

'That was Mr Cepoi. Mr Danileant wishes for there to be sausages now.'

'OK. I'll go and get the sausages again.'

Andrei looked across to the huddle of spies and gave them the thumbs up. Their looks of concern appeared to be assuaged somewhat.

Shonagh and I shared a look of disbelief. It seemed scarcely plausible that disruption on this scale had been caused by little more than a lack of sausages. It would have been hilarious, had the consequences of the delay not been so crucial to the outcome of my wager.

Moments later the waitress emerged from the kitchens, and held a large tray of sausages in front of Andrci.

'Sausages,' she said, routinely.

'Yes, sausages,' confirmed Andrei, before ushering her in the direction of the officials.

We all watched anxiously to see if this body of men would accept them as sausages or whether one or two of them would demand scientific corroboration.

We were in luck. The waitress was greeted with a succession of approving nods and she was dispatched to the dining room followed by a line of hungry, track-suited footballers, relieved that the contents of their breakfast had finally been approved. The sausage crisis, it seemed, was over.

It was an agonising further five minutes before Andrei and Mr

Vatamanu finally emerged from the dining room with two footballers alongside them.

'We are ready now,' said Andrei. 'This is Alexandru Curtianu and this is Sergei Clescenco.'

The players shook hands with me, obediently.

'Mr Vatamanu says that you must go now to play tennis,' stated Andrei firmly. 'He wants the players to be back here by eleven.'

However, now it was my turn to have a problem, and it was a bigger one than sausages.

'Andrei,' I said, as the two footballers made their way out of the hotel, 'I think Mr Vatamanu has brought me the wrong Sergei.'

'What do you mean?'

'Well, to win my bet I have to beat the eleven footballers who played in the Wembley match. Sergei Clescenco didn't, but Sergei Stroenco did.'

'Ah, you want *Stroenco*?'

'Yes.'

Andrei suddenly looked flustered and went into an immediate conference with Mr Vatamanu before conveying the news to a bemused Clescenco, whose look of disappointment suggested that he'd been rather looking forward to this brief sporting diversion. Given the difficult nature of getting Moldovan footballers on to a tennis court, it felt rather odd to turn one down when he was on offer, but it needed to be the right one or it meant nothing at all.

Clescenco sulked his way off, managing what appeared to be a dirty look before disappearing behind the closing lift doors. It felt cruel, but business was business. Admittedly, on the presentation of my evidence to Arthur, it would have been unlikely that that he would have said, 'Hey, wait a minute! That wasn't Stroenco – that was Clescenco!' Nevertheless, having come this far it seemed important to do things properly.

Amazingly my Moldovan friends seemed to agree, and minutes later another track-suited footballer was paraded before me.

'Sergei Stroenco,' announced a proud Vasile Vatamanu, pointing to the bewildered, slightly balding young man in a track suit, who presumably had just been plucked from breakfast and told that he had to go and play some bloke at tennis.

We shook hands and I thanked him for his time, before ushering everyone out to the awaiting taxi. It was 10.40 am. Supposedly I had twenty minutes to complete the whole procedure. Of course, it was impossible, but as long as no-one else had realised that, there seemed little to be gained from pointing it out.

Mr Vatamanu looked positively excited by the proceedings as he eased himself into the taxi's spacious and comfortable front seat. There was no such luxury for the four of us who were struggling into the limited space just behind him. Curtianu, Stroenco and I snuggled in along the back seat while Shonagh, the valiant camera woman, spread herself across our laps. This did not seem to displease the footballers who were now beaming broadly.

Huddled in the back of the car as it hurried us to our sporting destination, I felt a sudden swell of pride. Here I was, wedged between the Moldovan team captain and the big stalwart of the defence, surely on the brink of adding their tennis scalps to an already impressive list. I was *doing* this. Little more than ten minutes ago it had seemed a distant prospect, but the sausage crisis was behind us and victory was once again within sight.

Despite being unable to serve at my normal pace because of a painfully sore right thumb, I encountered little difficulty in overcoming my Moldovan opposition, who offered predictably meagre resistance. Stroenco covered the court quite well for a big defender, but had clearly suffered from the lack of time he'd had to mentally prepare for the big game. This, coupled with a tendency to miss the ball completely with his racket, proved to be his downfall. Curtianu, reckoned to be the best footballer in the team, fell some way short of being the best tennis player, and this proved to be his.

Thus two more downfalls were safely in the bag, as Shonagh and I delivered the players back to their hotel, only twenty minutes behind their schedule.

'Thank you for the game,' said the extraordinarily polite and charming Curtianu, as he bade me farewell outside the Holiday Inn. 'And good luck.'

'You too,' I replied. 'I hope you win the big match tomorrow night – I'll be supporting you.'

Curtianu smiled and gave me the thumbs up.

A most impressive thumb, I noted. I was a little relieved that I hadn't been required to take it on at Play Station tennis.

15

My Name Is Stony

'Can I travel up to the Under 21 match in Coleraine with all of you, on your coach?' I asked Andrei, back in reception at the Holiday Inn, adopting the *if you don't ask, you don't get* approach, as advocated by Big Jim back in Moldova.

'I will ask Mr Vatamanu,' he replied.

I was fairly confident of success. Mr Vatamanu definitely liked me now. Just twenty minutes earlier he'd given me a small lapel badge bearing the emblem of the Moldovan national side. I cannot imagine there is a more sure-fire way of knowing that you've been embraced in a Moldovan's affections.

'This is no problem,' Andrei said on his return. 'The coach is leaving from here at 4.30.'

And so it was that at 4.20 pm I was wandering aimlessly around the reception area of the Holiday Inn, just as I had done for an extremely fraught half hour, earlier that very same day. I was more relaxed now – until, that was, I got the shock of a lifetime. Over by the lifts, I saw a familiar figure in a dark coat and wearing a flat cap more indicative of Yorkshire than Moldova. I focused on the face. *That* face. Although it was not frightening in itself, it still sent a shiver down my spine and into my pants, where it put my bowels on general alert. I was looking at my nemesis. Grigorii Corzun. Arsehole of the Universe. My sworn enemy.

Without thinking, and before I could be recognised, I rushed to the toilets where I intended to gather my thoughts and decide what to do. I closed the cubicle door, dropped my trousers, sat down, and commenced deliberation. I took solace in the fact that if a solution to my predicament was to be found then surely I was in the best place to find it. On the loo. Isn't this where all the truly great thinking is done? Wasn't it here that Galileo worked out the constancy of the time of a pendulum's swing? Wasn't it here that

Boyle finally declared the volume of a fixed quantity of gas at constant temperature is inversely proportional to its pressure? Of course it was. If you ask me, this had been where Sir Isaac Newton actually discovered gravity. The apple story has just been the version of events which have been sanitised for public consumption. After all, it does make far more palatable reading in a children's text book if Newton's moment of enlightenment arrived when an apple hit him on the head rather than as a result of the splashes produced by number twos in the toilet bowl. One version suggests that Newton was a great inspirational thinker and the other that he got lucky when his bowels were playing up.

Being on the loo definitely seemed like the right place to be. Apart from anything else, it was an appropriate facility on which to be seated given my fearful state of mind. I sat there, like Fagin in *Oliver Twist*, reviewing the situation. Not far from where I was *relaxing*, Grigorii Corzun was waiting in the foyer of the hotel, no doubt about to board the same coach to Coleraine as I was intending to take. This, I knew, was not good, not least because Grigorii Corzun bore no similarities to Vasile Vatamanu. He wasn't plump, he wasn't very nice, and he didn't like me. *At all.* His last words to me, delivered via Iulian, had not been of a complimentary nature. On the contrary, he'd been angry that I'd drunk his brandy, refused to stay at his hotel, and shown little enthusiasm for becoming his business partner.

But, I reminded myself, what did I have to fear? What could he do? He was hardly likely to have me killed. (Although should he have chosen that course, we were in a part of the world where practitioners in this skill weren't that hard to find.) I suppose what was really bothering me was that he could scupper the whole ship. Should he so desire he could badmouth me to the relevant managers, trainers or officials, and I would be *persona non grata* from here on in, and be refused access to Sergei Rogaciov, the one remaining player I still required who fell within Moldovan jurisdiction.

I reached a decision, and I left the lavatories knowing that I had to follow the courageous course. I hadn't done anything wrong or behaved dishonourably, so why had I been skulking around in the karsy? If he decided to make things difficult for me then so be it. I wasn't going to run away from this one.

In the foyer I saw that Grigorii Corzun was in conversation with two silly-hatted men. Taking a deep breath, I approached him as boldly as I could, head held high and proud, in a position designed to say 'I am strong and I am not frightened', even though I wasn't and I was, respectively. My plan was to embarrass him by being overly nice. I would offer my hand in friendship and he would be made to feel distinctly uncomfortable. A slightly eccentric method of getting even, but more than good enough for me. In my view, killing someone with kindness is always a better option than killing them with a shotgun. It's less messy, entirely legal, and you feel much better afterwards. I don't know why it isn't favoured more often.

'Hello Mr Corzun, it's nice to see you again,' I said politely, arm extended with hand proffered for shaking purposes.

The Transnistrian turned to see who was addressing him and was staggered by the sight before him. Surely not? The persistent Englishman had followed the players to Belfast?

'Hello,' he replied, managing to change *aghast* into *awkward smile*.

It seemed like he was completely unable to gauge which emotions he ought to be feeling, but I reckoned he was experiencing something between sheepish and uncomfortable. Good. No more than he deserved, given the way he'd treated me back on his patch.

Then the most wonderful thing happened. Mr Vatamanu, on his way from the lifts to the hotel's revolving doors, broke short his journey so that he could give me a big friendly pat on the back. He made a comment in Russian to Corzun, which although incomprehensible, I knew was about me, and felt sure was wholly complimentary. Mr Vatamanu moved off, giving me a comradely wave. Corzun looked both hurt and bewildered. Whatever his feelings towards me might have been, they now had to be tempered by the fact that I had the approbation of the PR officer of the Moldovan National Team. Corzun looked a little nervous. He was just a club man after all, and his presence on foreign jaunts like this one probably depended on an invitation from the Moldovan Football Federation. Could he be worried that I might tell them the story of his behaviour towards me in Transnistria? Could it be that the balance of power had shifted and that I was now the one to be feared?

Oh, I did hope so. It may not be gentlemanly to hit a man when he is down, but I couldn't resist it.

'I beat your player Stroenco yesterday,' I said, wallowing in this brief moment of glory.

Corzun smiled, and shuffled from side to side awkwardly.

'Goodbye then,' I said, suddenly remembering that we shared no common language and that any further digs would be lost on him anyway.

'Goodbye,' he managed with a feeble smile.

As I walked away, in my head I read out the final score:

GRIGORII CORZUN 1	TONY HAWKS 2
(Hawks, o.g.)	(Hawks 2, one pen.)

I sat at the back of the coach. Not because I had any desire to do any singing or smoking (things which, in my youth, had been compulsory when sitting at the back) but because I felt like an intruder among all these middle-aged officials, and I thought it better to keep a low profile than risk being ejected. I didn't want to give Grigorii Corzun, who was seated at the front, any opportunity to avenge his foyer humiliation.

As the Belfast rain pounded against the coach windows, I settled into my seat, relieved that the journey to the Under 21 match was going to be this easy, but a little concerned about what was going to happen once I got there. Earlier that day, as a result of information gleaned over the phone from Trevor Irskine at the Irish FA, I'd booked myself into the same hotel that the Moldovan team were staying in that night. My hope was that I would be able to play Sergei Rogaciov some time the following day, but acquiring the necessary permission wasn't going to be easy because the Under 21 team were run by an entirely different set of officials, none of whom knew anything about my intentions.

The coach delivered us through the main gates of the Showgrounds, the venue for tonight's game, and the Moldovan posse alighted to witness the damp coolness of the county Londonderry evening. They all headed straight for the hot dog stand. My initial impulse was to sneak around the back of the stall and advise the vendor to revise his prices for Grigorii Corzun, explaining that this was a man who'd once paid twenty-five pounds for a beer and a sandwich in Manchester.

I bought a programme, and found myself a seat in the stands, in readiness for the big game. As the players warmed up, I picked out the number eleven shirt of Sergei Rogaciov, and I was impressed by his balance and movement. I wanted him to have a good game tonight, but most of all I wanted him to avoid being carried off on a stretcher.

The players lined up for the two national anthems. This was the first time I'd heard the Moldovan one, and I decided that it had quite a nice little tune, but nonetheless I was keeping my fingers crossed that I would never have to sing it. Then the band struck up with the anthem for the Northern Ireland team. I was surprised by its familiarity. I knew it well. Of course I did – it was 'God Save the Queen'.

I had never seen a crowd stand and sing this mediocre song with such gusto and heart, but then I suppose this was because I had never been anywhere before where its rendition meant so much. In this part of the world, your attitude to this piece of music depended on from which half of the sectarian divide you heralded.

I don't normally stand for the national anthem, given that I'm not sure that I approve of what *it* stands for, but on this occasion I felt that not to do so might have incurred the wrath of those around me. Cravenly I rose to my feet and sang the mindless words.

> God save our gracious Queen
> Long live our noble Queen
> God save the Queen

Why *should* God save the Queen? Certainly ahead of anyone else.

Were we suggesting that there ought to be some kind of pecking order for God's protective hand? If so, what number was I going to come in at?

1. The Queen
2. Sir Cliff Richard
3. Tony Hawks

Maybe not. I'd surely lose third place to Dana, on appeal.

I felt that given the amount of interest the Queen was going to show in the outcome of this particular encounter between the Moldovan and Northern Irish Under 21s, she could have been safely omitted from the proceedings. However, a glance over my shoulder told me that it was probably advisable not to share this view with those around me. Instead, knowing that football crowds are a generic group of whom it is generally wise to stay on the right side, I begrudgingly played the role of patriotic royalist.

The match was largely uneventful and it ended in a 1-1 draw. Rogaciov didn't score, but neither did he get injured. So far so good. I took a cab back to the country club hotel, checked into my rather luxurious room, and relaxed and waited. At 10.30 pm I put in an appearance at the bar.

'Do you know if any of the Moldovans are back from the game?' I asked a man perched on a bar stool, assuming that everyone knew that this was where the team were staying.

The man, who was making healthy inroads into a pint of Guinness, responded with characteristic Irish bonhomie.

'Ah sure, they're back all right. They're all taking a meal in the other bar,' he said. 'Why do you want to know?'

I hesitated.

'Er, well it's a little complicated.'

The man eyed me thoughtfully.

'You're not *Tony* are you?'

'Yes, I am,' I replied, rather taken aback. 'Tony Hawks to be precise.'

'Jeez, I was talking to you on the phone earlier. I'm Trevor Irskine.'

'Trevor. Hello.'

We shook hands.

'Pull yourself a stool up. I'll get you a pint.'

Trevor was good company, not least because he and I shared the same problem. We both had to deal with the world of Moldovan football on a daily basis.

'My job is to look after them while they're here,' he said. 'Get them what they want, arrange the training facilities, organise sightseeing tours and all that kind of stuff. The problem is that four people are in charge, and every time a decision needs to be taken one of them says yes and three of them say no. It makes my job bloody impossible.'

He looked both frustrated and jaded, and he'd only been with the squad for two days. I resisted the temptation to tell him the full duration of my Moldovan sojourn.

'Yes, they can be difficult,' I understated.

'Difficult? I'd say.'

He took a swig of beer instead of saying what was immediately running through his head.

'The worst thing,' he went on, when the beer had hit its mark and provided a suitably soothing effect. 'Is that they think I'm bloody spying on them.'

'How come?'

'Well they've still got this Cold War mentality which means that they don't trust me. They think that I'm going to relay information back to the Northern Ireland squad about their training and their tactics. They have these little secret meetings up in room 30 when they don't want me to know what's going on. It's annoying, cos all I want is for them to have a good time.'

'I don't think having a good time is on their agenda.'

'I think you're right. What's frustrating is, individually they're all really nice, but collectively they're a pain in the arse.'

Two pints later we were still chatting, the most pleasing aspect of our conversation being the extent to which Trevor was prepared to embrace the cause of Hawks v Rogaciov.

'Don't worry, Tony, leave it with me,' he said, just before I turned in for the night. 'I'll talk to the necessary people in a minute and I'll make sure you play that guy some time tomorrow.'

The plan was very simple. Play Rogaciov after breakfast before the team left for their sightseeing tour of the Antrim coast. However, morning brought customary inconsistency from the Moldovan camp.

'I don't believe it!' said a frustrated Trevor, when I bumped into him in reception after a worthy cooked breakfast. 'They want to put back the sightseeing tour because they've decided that the players need to do some training this morning.'

'Training? All they're doing today is sightseeing and watching the senior team play.'

'Well, Ivan wants them to be in tip-top condition for both.'

'Ivan? Who's Ivan?'

'He's the trainer.'

Logical enough. That's why he had them training.

'How about the bosses?' I asked. 'Did you ask them last night if they agree in principle to me playing the match?'

'Three out of four said yes. I've still got to ask Ivan.'

'He's not Ivan the Terrible, I hope.'

'No,' he joked, 'more Ivan the Bloody Awkward.'

The morning was as frustrating as they come. A veritable test of patience. I waited on a seat in the corner of reception for two hours while Moldovan players and officials came and went, all of them variously displaying expressions of vagueness, downright confusion, disorientation and bewilderment. I was powerless, other than to sit and wait.

'What's happening?' I asked Catalin, the nice Romanian lad who was studying English at Trinity College and had been roped in as team translator.

'Nobody knows,' he shrugged.

Twenty minutes later I found myself momentarily empowered. Having returned to my room to fetch a book, I saw a familiar track-suited figure approaching me from the other end of the hotel landing. I had spent one and a half hours watching this guy the previous evening so I knew him to be Sergei Rogaciov. Here was a chance to by-pass all the red tape and to confront the young man head on. The only problem was that I knew he spoke no English.

Never mind. There was one sentence which Elena had taught me back in Moldova and which I had spent hours mastering. I had only really learned it as a joke, but now I found myself in the situation for which it was absolutely tailor-made. I could not waste this opportunity. As Rogaciov drew level with me, I raised my hand to gain his attention and announced;

'*Mā numesc Tony. Sînt din Anglia. Am fàcut un pariu, cà-i voi bate la tenis pe toţi din echipa naţionala de fotbal. Vreţi sà jucaţi cu mine?*'

Rogaciov stared at me and then he shook his head. Was this a refusal? Did he just not want to play me? Was he going to be the first Moldovan footballer to turn me down flat?

Not knowing what else to do, I repeated the question.

'*Mā numesc Tony. Sînt din Anglia. Am fàcut un pariu, cà-i voi bate la tenis pe toţi din echipa naţionala de fotbal. Vreţi sà jucaţi cu mine?*'

This time Rogaciov screwed up his face and shrugged. I think I knew what was going on now.

Although I thought I'd said '*My name is Tony. I am from England. I have made a bet that I can beat the entire national football team at tennis. Will you play with me?*', the appalling accent in which the words had been delivered meant that what Rogaciov had heard, in the equivalent of his own language, had been:

'*My name is Stony. I am from Angland. I have made a bott that I can seat the entire national football team at tonic. Will you pale with me?*'

Understandably enough, the young footballer stood before me looking like he'd cry if I said anything more to him in this strange language.

'You don't understand, no?' I tried in English.

He screwed up his face again, mainly because – he didn't understand, no. The poor fellow didn't need this. He'd probably just popped up to his room for a dump and hadn't expected to be intercepted by a strange man confronting him with a diverse range of unintelligible sounds.

Luckily for both of us, Catalin appeared and was able to enlighten Rogaciov as to what I'd been trying to communicate to him. When he had finished, the footballer looked no less comfortable. I doubted whether he had ever experienced a more surreal ten minutes.

'I have explained what you want him to do,' said the co-operative Catalin, 'but he says that he does not feel very well.'

'Oh dear. Can you tell him that it will not take long, and that if he doesn't play me, then I will have to strip naked in London and sing the Moldovan National Anthem.'

Catalin did so, and Rogaciov responded with an ambiguous look which could have been a display of any one of four emotions. Frustration, resignation, defiance or downright despair. He grunted a reply.

'He says that he will see how he feels,' said Catalin.

'Thank you. Thank you,' I grovelled in his direction. 'I am sorry to have bothered you.'

The successful resolution of this bet looked like it was going to require competence in *basic grovelling* rather than on having a powerful serve and good ground strokes.

I returned to my corner seat in the hotel reception a worried man. There was no getting away from it, if Rogaciov was ill, then Rogaciov was ill. No room for debate on the matter. I chastised myself for having taken on a bet, the outcome of which could be dependent on whether a 20-year-old was feeling off colour or not. I felt like a man carrying a vase which was so fragile it could shatter in my hands at any moment.

When Catalin explained that Rogaciov's general mood had not improved and that Ivan the Bloody Awkward was still living up to his name, I declared that I thought that the game was probably up, but Trevor was having none of it.

'Leave it to me,' he proclaimed, before disappearing outside into the car park.

Five minutes later he returned.

'It's all sorted,' he said. 'Mick the driver is going to stop the coach at some local courts and we can all get off while you play your match. We're going to make it part of their sightseeing tour.'

'But what if Rogaciov is still not feeling well?' I asked.

'He can't be that ill. He was playing international football last night. When we announce the match in front of all his mates, I bet he'll be up for it.'

'And what about Ivan?' asked Catalin.

'We'll ride roughshod over Ivan. The other three officials have said it's OK, so stuff him.'

It was an exceedingly lucky break for me that Trevor Irskine had become so determined that my match with Rogaciov should take place. It was almost as if the successful conclusion of this game of tennis would represent a small personal triumph over the Moldovan bureaucracy which had dogged him during the past couple of days. I had no complaints. His feeling that way was very handy. Very handy indeed.

When Mick pulled the coach off the road and parked it alongside the tennis court, I rose to my feet and did exactly what Trevor had suggested.

'Now we are going to take a short break from the sightseeing tour,' I proclaimed, waving two tennis rackets in the air, 'while we settle a very important matter. I am going to play Sergei Rogaciov at tennis!'

This was greeted with cheers from his team-mates, who had presumably only understood two words – *tennis* and *Rogaciov*. I marched down the central aisle and handed a racket to Rogaciov, who was now enjoying being the centre of attention and was responding positively to the reactions of his colleagues. From the front of the coach I heard Trevor's booming voice.

'Come on everyone, let's go!' he called, eagerly waving his arms to usher everyone off the coach.

Amazingly everyone responded. Everyone, that is, except Ivan. He sat there stony faced as his fellow countrymen filed off the bus with remarkable obedience. Trevor and I smiled at each other as we saw the players and officials making their way to the tennis court. Marvellous. The yiddish word for it is *chutzpah*, I believe. I glanced at Catalin, who was shaking his head in disbelief.

'Amazing – you did it!' he said, as I alighted from the coach.

'Not yet, I still have to beat him,' I replied.

'You will, you will.'

'Ever used one of these?' I asked, handing him my video camera.

'A couple of times, yes.'

'In that case I've got a job for you.'

Catalin, in his role as chief cameraman, was able to record a remarkable scene, as an entire squad of footballers and their attendant entourage lined the side of a tennis court to witness a distinctly one-sided tie-break. Rogaciov had made a remarkable recovery, truly rising to the occasion by walking on to the court with his racket held proudly above his head and chanting 'I am the champion, I am the champion!'

Fortunately for me he wasn't the champion, or if he was, then he was the champion of a version of tennis in which the ball was not required to clear the net. To be fair to Rogaciov though, he was one of the better Moldovan footballers I had played to date, possibly second best to Oleg Sischin, whom I still reckoned to have been the most talented. This having been said, it was no great accolade. Any innocent passer-by, on viewing Rogaciov's performance, would still have been moved to remark:

'Goodness, what a dreadful tennis player.' (And not necessarily in such polite language, either.)

I coasted home 11-3. The crowd cheered, Rogaciov smiled, Trevor punched the air, and I jumped for joy. Upon landing, I experienced an enormous feeling of relief. I had now played and beaten the three players I'd come here for, but it had been a tense affair. Too tense for comfort. Now, with the ordeal over and my noble quest still alive, I could relax and enjoy the rest of my stay.

I had never been sightseeing with a squad of Under 21 footballers from Moldova before, and I was reasonably confident that I wouldn't do so again. It certainly wouldn't be something I'd be requesting. They were a nice enough bunch of lads, but at this stage of their lives, theirs was not really a quest for knowledge. Consequently at the first stop, the Bushmills Whiskey Distillery, they displayed an interest in the whiskey-distilling process as minuscule as Ivan the Bloody Awkward's general desire to lend me a helping hand. We were in and out of that place before you could say 'Jack Daniels'.

At Portstewart, Trevor's offer of a beautiful shore-side walk was rejected following an overwhelming vote *against*, and instead a team photo was organised which, for some strange reason, I was invited to join. As I stood in the back row, quite clearly not a footballer, not Moldovan, and just possibly not looking under 21, I wondered what the players' friends and family would make of it in years to come.

'Who's that guy?' they'd ask, pointing at me.

'Oh that was an Englishman who played tennis against Sergei Rogaciov.'

'I see.'

'Now they *must* want to see the feckin' Giant's Causeway,' said a frustrated Trevor, who took it personally each time one of the stops on his tour was rejected.

I knew that I certainly did, never having seen it before. On the previous occasions when I'd been in this part of the world, a visit had been prevented either by a lack of time or having the burden of a refrigerator as a travelling companion. But now, as the coach drew closer to this extraordinary geological wonder – thousands of basalt hexagonal columns extending from the cliffs down to the sea – we were informed that Ivan had announced that he did not want us to stop the coach here because we did not have time to pay it a visit. Trevor couldn't believe it.

'He's only saying that if we stop here,' he moaned, returning to his seat beside me, 'they won't have time to go shopping in Belfast.'

'Maybe that's why he is the way he is,' I ventured, 'because he's the sort of guy who favours shopping for a track suit over visiting one of the earth's wonders. I don't think he's a very sensitive man.'

'Me feckin' neither.'

*

As the Moldovan party set off to enjoy the world renowned pleasures of the Castlecourt Shopping Centre, Belfast, Trevor and I said goodbye.

'Listen Trevor, I really do appreciate all your help,' I said. 'I honestly don't think I could have done it without you.'

'Maybe. Maybe not. Who cares? The point is you've done it. Now you've got to make sure you get the guy in Israel.'

'I promise to do my best.'

'Are you going to the game tonight?'

'You bet I am.'

'I'll probably see you there.'

The European Championship qualifying game between Northern Ireland and Moldova kicked off that night at Windsor Park, Belfast, at 8.00 pm. It was the first time I'd watched an international football match in which I'd played tennis against so many of the players on the pitch. Oddly I knew nothing about them as footballers, but suffice it to say that this was a sport in which they gave a much better account of themselves.

I watched the first half in the stands, seated next to a little old man who was grateful enough for someone to talk with, but was possibly just a little disappointed by the nature of most of my offerings.

'That was Oleg Fistican,' I'd remark. 'Nice guy – two handed on both sides – ooh and that was Curtianu with that shot – he speaks good English, you know.'

'Is that so?' he'd reply politely, instead of saying what he was really thinking: '*Look, I'm supporting Northern Ireland and I don't give a toss who the others are.*'

I think Moldova surprised Northern Ireland rather, leading twice in an exciting match which finished in a 2-2 draw. I particularly enjoyed the visitors' second goal.

'That was Ion Testimitanu!' I shouted. 'What a shot! That's probably good enough to secure his transfer to Bristol City, you know.'

The little old man turned to me, his face contorted with restraint.

'Is that so?' he just about managed.

*

For the last five minutes of the game I took advantage of the photographer's pass which had been arranged for me by my good friends at UTV, and I watched the game's final action from the touch line. This afforded me the privilege of rushing on to the pitch at the final whistle. Unlike the local press, who immediately bombarded the Northern Irish players for reactions and comments, my goal was entirely different. I headed for the Moldovan players that I knew – the ones I'd met in such a novel manner. Our second meeting was no less peculiar. As the players left the field, exhausted but delighted at the result, they were greeted by a vaguely familiar figure wearing a bright orange bib, offering his own congratulations.

'Well played!' I blurted to each one in turn. 'Three cheers for Moldova!'

The reactions varied. Some looked confused, others delighted to see me again, even in these unusual circumstances. I was particularly pleasantly surprised by the response of Radu Rebeja, who in Chisinau had been a little cool towards me, but here in Belfast that had changed.

'Ah hi Tony!' he said as he recognised me, adding while miming a tennis swing, 'Tony the tennis!'

'Congratulations Radu,' I said.

The player nodded, knowing that I had said something of a positive nature, and moved off to join his retreating colleagues.

I turned around to watch them; my former tennis foes, soldiering towards the players' tunnel, the back view of their shirts reducing them to mere numbers. Regretfully, to me, they had been little more. The protective nature of their employers had meant that the time we had shared together had been limited to brief spells at opposite ends of a tennis court. How I would have loved to have joined them tonight to celebrate their courageous performance, to have allowed beer to bundle and bully us towards that pleasantly inebriated state where communication transcends words.

But it wasn't to happen. The powers that be, fearing that their heroic players might have had the opportunity to go out and have a good time, had chartered a plane which was leaving for Chisinau at midnight.

Never mind. Perhaps I could get pissed with Spynu in Israel.

16
Holy Land

The selfish actions of Saddam Hussein nearly messed things up for me. He had incurred the wrath of the Americans by refusing to let UN investigators see if Iraq had as many evil weapons of destruction stashed away as they did. The US decided that air strikes were necessary, and Britain immediately agreed with them, in accordance with the 'special relationship' which required them to do exactly that. For a few scary days it looked like things would escalate horribly and that Israel would be targeted by Saddam's scud missiles just as it had been in the Gulf War. Fortunately for the interests of world peace, Saddam backed down after having the crap bombed out of him, but not before having claimed it as a 'magnificent victory'. This is an excellent tactic to adopt should you ever have the misfortune of being flattened by someone in a pub brawl – simply pick yourself up, say 'Well, that showed you!', and then walk proudly off to nurse your black eye in private.

Despite the rather alarmist withdrawal of UK tourists from Israel which had taken place during the air strikes on the recommendation of the Foreign Office, I elected to go ahead with my trip. My business was altogether too important to let the trifling matter of international warfare stand in my way.

I made one call to the Israel tourist office in London to check whether I needed visas and innoculations, and I got talking to a very chatty girl there called Nurit. I asked her whether she knew much about Israeli football and, on learning the nature of my trip, she got me to call a journalist she knew from an Israeli national newspaper called *Ma'ariv*. He loved the sound of what I was undertaking and arranged for a reporter to meet me in Tel Aviv, lay on transportation and to take me to meet Marin Spynu, provided I granted *Ma'ariv* an exclusive in the story. Well, of course they could have an exclusive! Especially if it meant I could knock this game off very quickly and then head down to Eilat to sun myself for a week. I reckoned I deserved to have it easy after all the tough times I'd had in Moldova. Surely I *deserved* a nice smooth run.

It was New Year's Eve and I had expected the flight to be pretty empty since the region was still considered to be dangerous, but the airline had compensated for this situation by laying on a much smaller plane than usual. Consequently it was packed. I failed in my attempts to get a window or aisle seat and ended up wedged in the dreaded middle seat of three, a position from which you enjoy absolutely no 'Armrest Rights'. If you are seated by the window then the armrest below it is clearly yours, and likewise the aisle armrest is the property of the aisle seat. However, where I was, neither armrest is yours by rights and you have to niggle, nudge and cajole in order to gain even temporary possession. Quite why the airlines have not got their act together to rectify this situation is quite beyond me. It seems that as long as your seat-back is in the upright position for take-off and landing they do not care what injustices the 'middle-seaters' have to suffer.

On the screen at the front of the cabin, the morning's news was broadcast to us and I watched how Iraqi anti-aircraft guns had attacked American and British planes which were patrolling the 'No fly zones'. I kept my fingers crossed that there would be no escalation of violence and that I wouldn't have to play my final game wearing a gas mask (apparently they hamper low volleys). A report from Israel itself outlined how the Palestinian peace talks were floundering badly. It seemed that the voices of the extremists were having a disproportionate influence over the moderate majority who just wanted to live in peace with their neighbours. The fanatics on either side appeared to be winning the day. It hadn't been so long ago that Yitzhak Rabin had been assassinated by a fanatical Jew who had been opposed to peace with the Palestinians, and what had happened? At the next general election the government had lurched to the right with Binyamin Netanyahu sweeping to victory on a wave of anti-Palestinian rhetoric, and the peace process was faltering as a result. It was a tragedy, but the murderous fanatic had achieved his aim.

It has always seemed a great shame to me that the moderate

cannot arouse the same passions that the fanatic can, but the fact remains that organised marches accompanied by chants of 'We'll talk and we'll talk until we find a compromise!' or 'Let's try and see this from both points of view shall we?' tend not to set the heart pumping and blood coursing through the veins. The suicide bomber is always going to grab the headline ahead of the decent chap handing in a signed petition. The hunger striker is always going to provide better copy for the newspapers than the bloke who just lays off cheese for a month. The trouble is that the moderate's hands are tied by his very rationality. And so it is that the peace-loving majority are pushed around by fundamentalists, fanatics and extremists. What about the poor old man in the middle?

Like me. With no armrest. I couldn't even *see* the armrest on my left such had been its wholesale smothering by the obese gentleman in the window seat. On my right, the woman had unilaterally taken both armrests by force with no consideration for my rights. I wanted to call in an air hostess to act as a UN arbitrator but I could see that too many meal trays needed to be collected to allow time for any meaningful mediation. Armrestless, I consoled myself with the knowledge that there would be other flights in the future, and until then the tray in the seat-back in front of me was all mine and nobody could take that way from me.

Three and a half hours later we landed in Israel. The armrest of the Middle East, the struggle for which was unrelenting and fanatical.

I had been to Israel once before, nearly twenty years previously, when I had worked as a volunteer on a kibbutz. My motives had not been so much to discover a new and idealistic way of life as to try and get off with as many girls as possible in one month. Some may argue that this was shallow, but I was a young man and I needed some experience in swimming before I ventured into deeper waters. It was during this period that I perfected my breast stroke.

It was also on the kibbutz that I discovered that both farm labour and early rising were not for me. On one occasion I had been allotted the dreaded job of 'Chickens' which was one that only came up a few times a year and involved gathering up the chickens which had reached an age and size which made them suitable for slaughter. Conventional wisdom had it that this was best done at 4 am when the birds would still be fast asleep. The flaw in this thinking was that at this time of the morning those charged with catching the buggers were also half asleep. In my case I was still drunk, the night before having been my twentieth birthday which I had celebrated in something of an alcoholic frenzy.

Kibbutzniks led us down to a huge warehouse where the doors were opened to reveal a vast square footage of sleeping chickens. It was impossible to walk among them without treading on them, so we had to be taught to slide our feet along the floor like we were skating. The 'chicken shuffle'. All around me kibbutzniks and more able volunteers than myself were avidly collecting up chickens by the handful and delivering them to the awaiting trucks outside. It was okay for them, they clearly hadn't come across the obstinate 'Mother of all Chickens' which I was trying to pick up. I had sneaked up on it stealthily enough but as soon as I had gone to grab it by the leg it had turned on me, pecking away at my wrists, clucking and flapping and generally not having the decency to 'come quietly'. I threw it back down.

'Right, you want to make this difficult do you?' I muttered.

I had several more attempts at securing the capture of this one chicken while all around me other volunteers were on their fifth or sixth load. I made one final determined effort and dived on the chicken, completely smothering it until somehow I was in a position to haul it out to the truck. Proudly, I handed it to the surly kibbutznik in charge of loading the cages. He shook his head. I offered it to him once more. Again he shook his head.

'*Shesh!*' he shouted.

'And the same to you mate,' I slurred back mutinously.

A volunteer alongside me explained that *shesh* meant six. What? He wanted six chickens? In one go?

'I can't give you six,' I moaned. 'You've no idea how much trouble I've gone to just getting you this one.'

'*Shesh*,' he repeated doggedly, pointing to all the enthusiastic chicken collectors around me.

Seeing them rather invalidated my next line of argument which was to be that six was impossible. All of them were carrying six. Three in each hand.

Fifteen minutes later, fifteen minutes of feathers, fury and frustration later, I handed the same grumpy kibbutznik my best offer. Three chickens.

'*Shesh*,' he said unrelentingly.

'Oh come on man, give me a break,' I whined. 'This is really the best I can do. I can't do six, I've tried.'

Regretfully I had to admit that I was just no good at picking up birds.

'*Shesh*,' he said, once again displaying his expansive vocabulary.

'Okay, I'll try for six but at least accept the three that I've brought you, it wasn't easy I promise you.'

But he would not. He wanted *shesh* and that was it. It was *shesh* or nothing with this bloke. If it hadn't have been for a kindly kibbutznik who took pity on me and started handing me ready-collected chickens by the half dozen then I don't know what kind of international incident would have ensued. For me Shesh-face, as I took to calling him for the rest of my stay, came to symbolise the Israel I had left all those years before – macho and uncompromising. Would things have changed?

The pouring rain, which God had laid on to make me feel at home, meant that the queue for the airport taxis was, by my reckoning, about one and a half hours long. I took a bus and alighted at Tel Aviv's crowded bus station. I found myself surrounded by teenagers with guns. Big guns, draped over their shoulders like sports bags, with magazines glistening with brass bullets. And not just the boys but girls too. Kids in Israel must to have grow up quickly. I allowed my eyes to settle on a particularly pretty girl, her right hand resting the top of her machine gun. Maybe I should ask her to dinner, I thought, she ought to be able to get us a good table.

I had forgotten that Israeli national service meant that every boy had to do a minimum of three years in the army and every girl fifteen months. They seemed to go everywhere with guns either because it was deemed not a good idea to leave them lying around, or because it made the citizens of this constantly threatened State feel that they were being protected. Then I remembered – it was New Year's Eve. I shuddered at the thought of how busy the average hospital's Accident and Emergency Unit would be back in Britain if teenagers went out to celebrate New Year's Eve carrying guns. It would certainly be an effective way of keeping the population down.

I met Daniela, my Israeli publisher at my hotel and went for a quick drink. She had fallen in love with my previous book having discovered it on a trip to England and was busy having it translated into Hebrew. This amused me greatly since I'd always wanted to be translated into a language which you read backwards, and also it made me feel rather important. I explained to her my reasons for visiting Israel, about the bet and how I intended to track Spynu down.

'*Ma'ariv* are virtually sorting it all out for me,' I said. 'Provided I give them an exclusive.'

Daniela looked horrified.

'You cannot do this,' she stated firmly.

'What do you mean?'

'I have a huge amount of coverage lined up with a rival newspaper for your book. If you do this for *Ma'ariv*, they will cancel everything. You must ring them now and tell them you won't do it.'

'But Daniela, they've organised everything – they're driving me out to meet the guy tomorrow.'

'Tony, I absolutely forbid you to talk to them.'

There was no use in putting up a fight. She wanted *shesh* chickens and that was that. All my hopes for an easy ride had been dashed. I would have to start from scratch. Happy New Year mate.

I suppose it had been a slightly odd decision to fly out on New Year's Eve but I was wedging this trip in between other work commitments and this was the only real way to give myself time – time that I would now definitely need after having received Daniela's bombshell. I asked her advice on where I should go to experience a typical Tel Aviv New Year's night.

'Well, what do you want?' she asked.

It was a good question and I really didn't have an answer. I had long since ceased to enjoy New Year's Eves. The problem was that in my teens I had enjoyed these evenings rather too much. They were invariably spent at parties where everyone was drunk and where at midnight it was quite acceptable to kiss absolutely any girl who took your fancy. This seemed to me to be a smashing idea, and there wasn't any catch. You could just go up to a girl and say 'Happy New Year' and then kiss them. I don't know how or why, but life had got so much more complicated since then.

A further problem with New Year's Eve is the inevitable feeling that you've made the wrong decision. Invariably on this festive night, you're invited to at least three parties but you have to plump for only one of them. At 11.30pm, as you find yourself listening to a carpet salesman extolling the virtues of a hard-wearing deep pile and stressing its advantages over a basic linoleum, you just might begin to wonder whether one of the other parties might have been the better option. Presumably this has been the way for centuries. Your average caveman probably saw in the New Year by sipping mead and wondering whether he might have been having a better time if he'd gone to Og's do, four caves up. Daniela dropped me at a wine bar where she knew the owner, and she said it should be fun. It wasn't. Nobody even bothered to count down to midnight. I had forgotten that in Israel there is relatively little celebration for New Year's Eve since it is celebrated in September with Rosh Hashannah.

No-one came up and kissed me, and I didn't approach anyone requesting a kiss either. The gun thing had probably taken the edge off my boldness. I walked back to the hotel a little disappointed. However much I tried to suppress it, perennially I still clung to the possibility that New Year's Eve was the night when at midnight someone beautiful might grab you, kiss you and share the thrill of a new and exciting mutual attraction. One of these days the New Year was going to begin with a bang.

My first full day in Israel was spent exploring the city, making phone calls and sunbathing. I basked contentedly as the Mediterranean lapped on to Tel Aviv's pleasant sandy shores and I was warmed both by the sun and the thought of everyone shivering back home in blighty. Then I felt guilty and ashamed. What about my friends in Moldova struggling through a harsh winter with power shortages and an ever-weakening economy? I sent them a loving thought and reminded myself what a lucky bastard I was.

I called all the contact numbers that friends had given me before I left and spoke to a whole host of different answering machines. I did get through to a guy called Yehuda who lived in Jerusalem and who was a reporter and TV journalist whose number had been passed on to me by Arthur. He sounded very interesting and I promised to look him up if I went to Jerusalem. I also spoke to a guy named Johnny who was an English guy who had emigrated to Israel with his wife and family. I'd never met him, but somebody (alas I'd forgotten who) had told me to give him a call since he might be able to help.

'Oh, hi Tony,' said Johnny, brightly, 'Philippa told me you might call.'

Philippa? I wracked my brains to try to think of a Philippa.

'Yes, good old Philippa – she sends her regards,' I fibbed.

'She's told me all about what you're up to and I think I might be able to help actually.'

My jaw dropped. I couldn't believe what I heard next. One of Johnny's good friends was a sports physiotherapist who knew the manager of Maccabi Kfar Kana very well. If I wanted him to, Johnny could make some calls and try and set up the game in the next few days.

'Do you really think you could do that?' I marvelled.

'I don't see why not.'

Twenty minutes later it was all organised. We were playing the day after next at a tennis club in a place called Zichron Ya'acov which was not far from where Marin Spynu lived. I really was a very lucky bastard.

I studied the map and planned the rest of my trip. I would visit Jerusalem, then head north to Zichron Ya'acov to defeat my final Moldovan footballer before making the journey south to the Red Sea resort of Eilat. I drank a beer which tasted especially good and looked out across the Mediterranean Sea. My quest was almost at an end.

*

Jerusalem is quite well known. There were a few unremarkable events which took place there a couple of thousand years ago which got it some publicity, but I suppose what really put it on the map was hosting the 1979 Eurovision Song Contest. Who could forget the momentous victory by the host nation with the inspirational song 'Hallelujah'? Unfortunately as a result of the musical triumph, people suddenly wanted a piece of this place and they began fighting amongst themselves over to whom it rightfully belonged. I'm lead to believe that the squabbles are still going on – no doubt still exacerbated by Dana International's triumphant win 20 years later.

Years before, I had paid a fleeting visit to Jerusalem after leaving the kibbutz, and I had stayed at a weird hostelry for travellers called the Petra Hotel. As I walked into the old town through Jaffa Gate, I saw the very same place and felt it was only right that I should check in there again. It had gone upmarket but only infinitesimally so. It now had a leaflet which boasted that it was the oldest hotel in Jerusalem, founded in 1830. Unfortunately it still had the original plumbing. The leaflet also reported that famous guests included General Allenby (the British general who liberated Palestine from four hundred years of Ottoman rule in 1917), Mark Twain and Herman Melville – the latter, it was claimed, had conceived *Moby Dick* in one of the rooms.

I decided that if my tatty, crumbly, unsalubrious chamber was anything to go by then this was an hotel where guests would be far more likely to conceive stories about whales than conceive any children. There was nothing whatsoever to put you in the mood, unless a leaking pipe which dripped on you when you went to the toilet, a dampness in the air, and a bed that bowed in the middle like a hammock, were the kind of things which got you feeling fruity. Still, it was cheap and I suppose you get what you pay for in this world. Unless of course you're a Moldovan taxpayer.

The Petra was half-hotel, half-hostel with dormitories as well as private rooms and even facilities for pitching tents on its large flat roof. Consequently it was not short of its quota of eccentrics – permanent travellers who have shunned convention in favour of being a bit annoying to people who haven't. They're a harmless enough lot I suppose, but they do feel they have acquired great wisdom along the way and insist on sharing it with you regardless of whether it is appropriate to do so.

I met one such person in the reception area of the hotel. A man dressed as Che Guevara and calling himself Zoraya was playing the guitar and singing one of his compositions, which made frequent biblical references and was totally incomprehensible. When he finished I applauded politely.

'Thanks,' he said in an American accent. 'For more information seek the Lord and read his work.'

'Have you got his address?' I asked.

'Yes, you dial H-E-A-V-E-N, and you gotta mean it. You gotta dial the right numbers. Where are you from dude? The United States of Confusion?'

'No, I'm from London, England,' I replied graciously.

'Let's talk about London for a minute – which is how long I want to be there. Stay in Israel man, stay in Jerusalem.'

'Well, I don't want to commit to that just yet, I've only just got here.'

'Hey, what do I know? I'm just a Jewish guy – I'm one of the locals. I gave Moses such a headache he had to take two tablets. Do you want me to do another song?'

No.

'Zoraya, unfortunately I don't have time to listen to another song, I have to meet a man called Yehuda who is going to show me round Jerusalem.'

'Your loss, man.'

'As long as this is my only loss in Israel I'll be happy enough,' I said, getting up and leaving Zoraya looking confused, well, *more* confused.

'See you again, man.'

Yes, that could happen. I'd have to be careful.

Yehuda was a Jerusalemite by birth, immensely knowledgeable and a liberal who was fiercely opposed to the Netanyahu government. His tour was both enlightening and moving. He was proud of his city but was only too aware that it needed to be shared.

'Our problem in Israel,' he said, 'is that we have ceased to view the Arabs as our neighbours. We have begun to treat them like the enemy.'

It was difficult to believe that earlier this century Arab and Jew had lived alongside each other peacefully. Maybe it had been easier then because neither held the reins of power. It wasn't until the British pulled out in 1948 that they began to properly knuckle down to the business of really hating each other.

'There was a wise Israeli called Professor Liebovitz,' continued my compelling tour guide Yehuda, 'who summed up Israel's predicament by saying, "No-one ever said that Sweden belongs to the Swedes, but their sheer luck is that no-one else claims Sweden is theirs."'

I think he was right. My knowledge of history is fairly sketchy but I can't recall ever reading about anyone bothering to part any seas to lead any peoples into Sweden. They knew that it was too cold, too boring and the beer was too expensive.

At the Western Wall (or Wailing Wall), that most important existing Jewish shrine where Orthodox Jews go about their worship with an uninhibited zeal, I saw the most incredible sight. One rabbi, in the midst of his gentle rocking motion of prayer, had to postpone proceedings while he dealt with an incoming mobile phone call. To my stupefaction he simply walked around this sacred area talking freely and receiving no admonishment whatsoever from his fellow worshippers. Did he have a direct line to God? Was he receiving important instructions from the Lord or was it his mother asking him to pick her up at the station? I knew this much – if it wasn't a sign from above, it was certainly a sign of the times.

Yehuda continued the tour taking us to the area of West Jerusalem which he called British Jerusalem, incorporating many buildings built by the British during their Mandate which lasted from 1917 to 1948. He showed me where he had walked as a child, where the barricades had been erected by the British troops, where the no-go areas had been and where, in his opinion, Jewish settlers had encroached too far into Arab East Jerusalem.

I felt privileged to be seeing this historic city with a new perspective – seen through the eyes of a Jerusalemite. I was taken in the car to places which only locals knew about – to the surrounding hills which offered spectacular views of a city which was perched at 757 metres above sea level. Jerusalem would truly be a heavenly place if its physical relief could only be matched by some semblance of political relief. I fear that is some way off. Unfortunately, unlike Stockholm, there are too many people within its ancient walls who think that God told them to be there.

That night as I slept in my unluxurious bedroom I had a terrible nightmare. I was at the Wailing Wall in full tennis kit brandishing a racket and ball.

'Oi!' I called to all the worshippers. 'I've got an important match coming up, so does anyone mind if I practise against this wall?'

Since everyone appeared to be nodding, I took it as a 'yes'.

Ahead of me, my father was attempting to paint a line along the wall at net height, while soldiers moved in to arrest us. Orthodox Jews pounded us with stones.

'What's your problem?' I cried. 'Can't a man practise tennis in this country?'

As I was frogmarched away with guns digging into my sides, I saw Arthur laughing mockingly.

'You're not going to win the bet from inside an Israeli jail!' he scoffed.

To my amazement alongside him was the gypsy woman who had read my cards in Moldova many months before.

'Heed my words!' she said. 'Don't play Spynu!'

Then all the soldiers, all the worshippers, and what seemed to be all the people of Jerusalem, began chanting, 'Don't play Spynu!', 'Don't play Spynu!'

I woke up trembling. I gathered myself and slowly established who I was, where I was, and what I was doing here. Easy. I was Tony Hawks, I was in Israel, and I was here to play Spynu. I shivered.

Jerusalem was cold in the mornings.

17
Bet Daniel

Zichron Ya'acov must be as close to the dream of the idyllic Jewish settlement which the original European emigrants would have had, its quiet delightful cobbled main street an oasis of peace in a troubled land. However, the problem with this place was that it was too well looked after, too quaint. It had been preened to such a degree that it felt like a theme park, not a real town. I instantly knew it must be a spectacularly boring place to live. A little bit of untidiness is a sign that there is some fun to be had. Years ago I had flown from Barcelona to Geneva and had found one airport slightly grubby with unemptied bins and foggy with cigarette smoke, while the other was pristine with glistening freshly polished floors. In one, the passengers sat around drinking coffee, laughing and joking, and in the other they sat in silence, concerned as to whether that sweet wrapper they'd just dropped might lead to an arrest. One was modern, tidy and efficient and the other was Spanish. I know which one I'd rather be delayed in, *por favor*.

Zichron Ya'acov was far too much like Switzerland for me to feel comfortable. According to my guide book it had been founded in 1882 by Romanian Zionist pioneers, one of two I hoped might have been Moldovan in origin. I liked to think so, it leant such a poetic, almost meaningful dimension to my otherwise irrational journey.

Johnny had recommended that I stay in a guest house called Bet Daniel.

'It's more of a retreat than a guest house really,' he had said over the phone. 'A haven for musicians, writers and artists.'

'And now tennis players. It sounds great.'

I asked the bus driver where I should alight for Bet Daniel and he dropped me by a path leading into some woods, and gave me some directions which I didn't even begin to take in.

There's a part of my brain which disconnects as soon as someone begins directions. It can only cope with the first instruction: 'Go straight to the end and then take a left at the roundabout.'

I'd be OK if they left it at that, but the instructions will always continue: 'Then turn left at the Shell garage, keep going up that road about a quarter of a mile until there is a bend in the road where you'll see a pub called The Rising Sun; make a right-' By this point instead of concentrating on the required data I am focusing on all sorts of irrelevant information. 'His hair seems to be receding rapidly,' I'll be thinking. 'I reckon he'll be completely bald in three years.'

Consequently on this occasion, as a result of having formed an opinion as to whether the bus driver would need to start combing across soon, I got completely lost in the woods. For me it was a surreal moment. I was carrying luggage around some deserted woods in a quiet backwater of Israel looking for the guest house which would be the base for my tennis match against a Moldovan footballer. How had it come to this? Should I have paid more attention in physics at school?

Eventually, along the meandering path I had chosen, I met with an elderly gentleman and I asked him if he knew where Bet Daniel was. He shook his head and mumbled in German. Then I did the same with a woman who also spoke to me in German. What had happened? Had the driver made a wrong turning and dropped me in Stuttgart? I passed a beautiful house set back from the trees where a blonde girl was hanging out washing to dry on the terrace. I called to her.

'Excuse me, is this a guest house?'

She stared at me blankly. I tried again.

'*Entschuldigen sie bitte, wo ist Bet Daniel?*'

Ah, that did it. She immediately rattled off some directions in German, with accompanying gesticulation which gave some clue as to their meaning. I failed to follow any of it, mainly because I was assimilating the information that this girl was boss-eyed. Five minutes later I found myself outside another house talking to another young German girl who also had dodgy eyes. Just like a teacher in an inner-city comprehensive, she had pupils which did their own thing. Surely I couldn't have stumbled upon a strange German religious community where cousins have relationships which involve more than just an exchange of presents at Christmas?

Later I was to learn that these people were from a Christian community who called themselves 'Bet El' (House of God), founded in the Sixties by a woman called Emma Berger who reckoned that God had appeared to her in a dream with instructions to bring some chums over to Israel and wait for Armegeddon. While they were waiting they got on with everyday life as independently as they could. They had their own school, their own factory and their own funny direction for their eyes to point in. Their presence here in these woods made me feel like I was in some kind of weird dream. Even Zoraya, the hippie from the Hotel Petra would have found it unreal, man.

Arrival at the guest house did little to hasten any sense of a return to reality. It appeared to have no reception area, no guests and no staff. I enunciated a loud 'Hello, is there anyone there?' but received no reply. Odd, the lights were on but no-one was home. The way this bizarre day was unfolding, the same could have been said of me. I began investigating the large living room which was dominated by a large Steinway grand piano stationed in a central alcove. The walls were cluttered with portraits of musicians, but one particular frame contained lots of old press clippings which revealed the history of this mysterious residence.

It seemed that it had been built as a retreat in 1938 by a woman called Lillian Friedlander in memory of her son Daniel, a highly gifted pianist. He'd been a child prodigy who as a teenager had been sent to study at the Juilliard School in New York, where the pressures and stresses of studying at this prestigious establishment had proved too much for his fragile artistic temperament and tragically he had committed suicide at the tender age of eighteen. The Steinway had been his piano. I sat at the stool before it, glancing up at the portrait which hung on the wall above. It was of Daniel, playing this very same beautiful instrument all those years before. I began to play an improvisation around minor chords which seemed to flow out of me with a strange ease. Somehow I was being caressed by the soothing ambience that existed in this alcove and I felt a rush of peaceful energy. It was weird. Was Daniel here? Was the music I was making some kind of call to Daniel's spirit?

Then I felt a compulsion to sing a song which I had written

maybe fifteen years earlier, somehow knowing that this was the exact moment it had been composed for. Daniel needed to hear it. The words came back to me as if I had written them that very morning.

> You hang there upon the wall, the portrait that sits before of us all
> What is it like to be, ignored by so many and noticed by me?
> What are your thoughts as you sit there all day, watching us fritter our lives away?
> Do you have problems just like ours, or have they been solved in your lonely hours
> On the wall

> (Verses two, three and four were sung as well. You needn't suffer them.)

My musical reverie was punctured by some applause at the far end of the room, coming from a lady in wellington boots who addressed me in Hebrew. This really was turning out to be a very odd day. She was one of the few Israelis I had met whose competence in English was on a par with that of the average Moldovan footballer. After a long struggle I managed to convince her that I was not a performer who had been booked to give a concert but a guest who wanted to check in.

'Could I see the manager?' I asked.

'*Lo*,' she replied.

Lo I knew meant 'no', my Hebrew studies having extended as far as establishing that the words for 'yes' and 'no' were *ken* and *lo*.

I had met a Japanese girl once called Lo and I'd always hoped that she'd marry an Englishman called Ken and go and live in Israel. How splendid their introduction would be to the Hebrew speaker.

Well, they say that opposites attract.

In the absence of the manager, I was shown to my room by the wellington-booted lady whose eclectic clothing left her resembling a fascinating hybrid of gardener, cleaner and South American revolutionary. The room was bohemian, which is a nice way of saying it needed decorating, but I didn't mind. All I wanted to do was some stretching exercises and sit on the bed and get my head together for the big match.

As I stood at the gates to Bet Daniel waiting for Johnny to pick me up and ferry me to the tennis court, I paced around nervously. At the back of my mind I was still haunted by the chanting from the cast of the previous night's nightmare. Much as I tried to get myself in a positive frame of mind, I still felt apprehensive and unprepared.

Johnny never showed, but instead a friend of his called Danny was my chauffeur to the tennis club. Apparently Johnny's wife had been involved in a car accident earlier that day and he was with her in hospital where she was being treated for whiplash injuries. Again the voices in my head – 'Don't play Spynu!'.

Danny's use of words was minimalist, and his manner suggested that he was pissed off that he had been talked into giving me this lift since he didn't really owe Johnny a favour. At the tennis club he announced coldly:

'The Moldovan is waiting for you inside.'

I felt like a spy. In tennis kit.

'We have booked you the indoor court,' continued Mr Charisma. 'You have it for one and a half hours. Johnny says that this guy plays a bit, so be careful.'

'Thanks,' I said, hoping I might get a 'good luck' but Danny only grunted before driving off.

I opened the gate and entered the tennis club only too aware of how the conclusion to my epic struggle lacked any sense of occasion. Having been denied the press interest which could have made this some kind of media event and perhaps even attracted spectators, I was arriving at a sleepy suburban tennis club with an entourage of nil. The only way the world would ever know that this classic confrontation had taken place was through the footage recorded on my camera which I was struggling to carry under my arm, along with a tripod. I was presenting an image more usually associated with an enthusiastic father eager to film his promising child, than a highly talented athlete honed and ready for action. Nevertheless I felt an element of pride that I had even managed to reach this point. There had been times in Moldova when contemplating the possibility of a match against an eleventh footballer would have seemed fantasy-land. Now it was happening. The commentator in my head took over.

'And so Hawks walks on to the court, a heroic figure, his elegant stride and solemn countenance exhibiting a preparedness for an encounter which means so much not only to him, but to us all. Quite some time ago Hawks took up this challenge on the people's behalf. The gauntlet was thrown down and he stooped to pick it up. A duel, and Hawks chose his weapons. Tennis rackets at dawn. And now he proudly strides out before us aiming to record a victory which will show us that we can look forward to a brighter tomorrow, where the smile replaces the grimace, where work feels like play, and where love conquers . . . Oh dear, he's dropped his camera.'

I had too. The photographic clobber beneath my arm had been gradually slipping groundwards but I hadn't stopped to re-organise such was the enjoyment I was deriving from this fantastic glorification of the moment. Back in reality and humbled slightly, I stooped to pick up the camera which fortunately was undamaged, and I made my way into the indoor court.

Marin Spynu was waiting on a chair by the side of the court, easily recognisable as a Moldovan footballer, not just because of his physical characteristics but because, like every Moldovan footballer I had met to date, he looked lost. I suppose the very brief of having to go and meet a strange Englishman on a tennis court was in itself disorientating. I approached him and shook his hand and we exchanged a few words which quickly established that he spoke no English. My Romanian, which had never been anything other than extremely poor, was now rusty as well. Conversation didn't flow. Then I noticed that Marin Spynu had an impressive-looking tennis bag from which he produced two tennis rackets. This was two more than any Moldovan footballer I had played to date. Arthur's words reverberated in my head.

'One of them is bound to be very good.'

Surely he couldn't really be right?

Spynu and I began knocking up. He casually opened with a heavily topspun backhand drive across court which landed within a foot of the base line. I scrambled it back, making full use of the racket's frame. He replied with a deft forehand drop shot employing an impressive amount of underspin.

Oh no! Spynu was good.

He was very good.

Clearly his experiences outside Moldova had involved spending a great deal more time on tennis courts than his former team-mates.

I immediately began to regret that I had not made more preparation for this encounter. The excesses of Christmas had left me with a slight paunch and a lack of fitness which looked set to be exposed in the coming hour and a half. As Spynu stood, poised to make the first serve of the match proper, I knew the size of the task ahead of me. I prayed that he was a player who impressed in the warm-up but made mistakes in a match situation.

The first point did little to suggest that this would be the case. He served out wide with accuracy and power before coming to the net to dispatch a backhand volley with ease into the open court. On the second point his serve was unreturnable. Already, only two points in, I felt an air of despondency creeping over me. He had no right to be this accomplished. However, I fought back well and found some confident passing shots which earned me break points against the serve – but Spynu played excellent volleys under pressure and then found two big serves to hold this first game. It was ominous that he was clearly the kind of player who didn't give points away cheaply – you had to win them. As we changed ends I was worried man.

Twenty minutes later I was in deep shock. I had lost thc first set 6-0. I hadn't played that badly, and four of the six games had gone to deuce, but Spynu had won them all. I was being whipped as easily by this guy as I had been by Pete Sampras at Play Station tennis. I wanted to spin this Spynu fellow around and flick the switch on his back from *very difficult* to *bloody easy*. What was happening right now just wasn't fair. He was sharp, hungry and match tight – and I was a bloke who had consumed too much Christmas pud and had assumed his opponent would be rubbish.

In the second set I drew on all my reserves and managed to produce something close to my best tennis. In a highly competitive set I sneaked through by six games to four. I'd been a little lucky and I was aware that for a short period Spynu had let his concentration slip.Despite my recent ascendancy I still felt that Spynu was the more likely to take a final set. But would there be time? The clock on the wall revealed that we only had fifteen minutes left before the lights ran out. Negotiations were necessary. I called my opponent to the net, pointed to the clock and announced:

'We only have time for a tie-break.'

Whether he understood or not, Spynu nodded, and I had won the advantage of not having to play a full-length third set, in which my lack of fitness would have become horribly exposed. This was sudden death and I had a chance. It was a tie-break I simply had to win.

Spynu, on the other hand, didn't give a toss, and was relaxed enough to be able to begin the final battle with an ace. I followed it with a double fault. I was feeling the pressure. A backhand return of serve from Spynu went for a clean winner leaving me 3-0 down. I was beginning to dislike this guy. This was not in the script. Spynu was playing his best tennis by far.

I fought hard but I failed to make up the deficit and at 3-6 I faced three match points. I needed a big serve. In my head I heard the echo of a thousand TV commentaries. *'That's what defines the true champion – the ability to find a big serve when they really need one.'*

My problem was that I wasn't Pete Sampras or John McEnroe. I was Tony Hawks – and anyway I had to accept that I wasn't a true champion. My junior career had proved that I had anything but the temperament to win tournaments. Rather than reach a peak my tendency was to save my worst tennis for finals day.

As I walked up to the base line to serve I realised that from a tennis perspective I had arrived at the most important point in my life. I had staked a whole philosophy on winning this bet, a philosophy on which I had every intention of basing how I was going to live the rest of my life. I looked up at Spynu. He looked relaxed. Of course he did. This was easy for him, it meant nothing, probably no-one even knew he was playing a game of tennis. For him it was just a break from training. All the pressure was on me and I desperately needed to find some strength within. OK, maybe I didn't have a big serve, but I had served aces in the past. Sometimes a well-placed serve could elude the returner as well as the powerful one. All I needed to do was find one of them.

Then it came to me in a flash – I should ask for Daniel's help. Had that not been an inspirational moment at the piano earlier that afternoon? Had there not been the definite feeling of a presence there? It wasn't such a crazy idea. It had to be done. So, as I stood at the base line in readiness to serve, I bounced the ball in front of me and muttered:

'Daniel, if you're there mate, it's me – Tony, the bloke who sang to you this afternoon. Listen, I need an ace, do what you can to help will you?'

And with those words I tossed the ball in the air, bent my knees, arched my back and launched all my energy into what was surely going to be an ace down the middle. The racket head made crisp contact with the ball as I whipped my wrist through to generate extra pace. It truly was the hardest serve I had ever hit.

It landed slap bang in the bottom of the net. I instantly realised what I had done wrong. I had sought assistance from the spirit of a temperamentally brittle concert pianist. Obviously, a better choice of deceased accomplice would have been Arthur Ashe, but I hadn't thought of him, and besides I hadn't sung to him that afternoon so he wouldn't really have had any vested interest in my success.

All was not lost, I had a second service to come. This time I decided to try and managc alonc with no hclp from the dead. This point was going to be played by me alone. It would be a test of my character. I knew I could win it.

I elected to surprise Spynu by coming into the net behind my serve in the hope of picking off an easy volley. It would be a courageous move and not one that he would be expecting. I would serve at his body, not giving him any angles to make a passing shot and hopefully cramping him up and leaving him unsure whether to take it on the forehand or backhand side. I breathed in, mumbled 'Come on!' to myself, bounced the ball one final time. And then I served.

It was a good one, exactly what I had hoped for. Spynu struggled to get his body out of the way and only managed to flick back a limp backhand with no pace on it. It all seemed like it was happening in slow motion. My eyes fixed on the revolving yellow sphere spiralling towards me. I swiftly changed grip for a backhand volley. I closed in on the net, the ball still hanging agonisingly before my outstretched forearm. As the ball and racket made contact, my supreme effort resulted in a final animalistic grunt of desperation.

I had executed a perfect volley. It landed within an inch of the junction of Spynu's base line and side line, beyond the reach of his outstretched racket. I felt an adrenalin rush and a moment of pride that, after all, I *could* deliver when the moment required.

Unfortunately so could Spynu, who dispatched a glorious winning backhand down the line.

I had lost.

The Moldovan looked apologetic and ambled to the net to shake my hand. He had been the magnificent victor in a game which meant absolutely nothing to him. If the roles had been reversed then he wouldn't have played so well, I bet. Or perhaps I should lay off bets for a while. I'd just lost a big one. A very big one.

As Spynu put on his track suit and packed up his things, I sat by the side of the court replaying the last point. I simply could not believe what had happened. I had fought my way back into the match only to have my opponent play an inspired tie-break. Spynu held out his hand to shake mine before he left.

'Thanks be to you,' he said in a shaky English accent. 'I am sorry.'

'It's OK,' I replied humbly. 'Thank you for a good game. You deserved to win. You were the better player.'

He shrugged and moved off, clearly not having understood. Damn, I could have said what I really wanted to say;

'Thanks for screwing up my bet, you bastard.'

Johnny still hadn't shown up and I wasn't in the mood to wait. I didn't really want to talk to anyone and especially someone with whom one of the main topics would no doubt be Philippa, our mutual friend who I couldn't remember. I walked back to Bet Daniel via Zichron Ya'acov's desolate town centre where I became solitary drinker in solitary bar. There weren't any good places to be at this moment, but I could have done with being somewhere that didn't feel like it had been purpose-built for melancholy. A theme park for manic depressives called 'GlumWorld'. Dispiritedly I stared into my Maccabi beer – a local Israeli beer when really I wanted a beer to match how I felt. A pint of *bitter*. The barman looked at me, still in my tennis kit and with my rackets on the floor beside me.

'Don't look so fed up,' he said. 'God, if you can't handle losing, then why play?'

It was just as well there were no army teenagers in the place. I could have grabbed one of their guns and shot him.

18

Tony of Nazareth

The lady seated next to me on the bus asked me what I was doing here in Israel.

'Oh I'm just on holiday – touring around having a look at the place,' was my cowardly reply.

My reserves of strength weren't sufficient to tell her the truth; 'Oh I just came here to play a tennis match.' I knew what her next question was bound to be.

'And did you win?'

I wasn't expecting much of Eilat. All I knew was that the sun shone there pretty much all the time and that if I was going to strip naked in London in the middle of winter then I might as well take advantage of this so that I could do so with a nice bronzed body. Most of the four and half hour bus ride was through desert landscape which, though stunning scenery, did little to raise my spirits. Nothing was growing. There was no rejuvenation. In my present mood I needed lush greens, rolling hills and gamboling lambs, instead of the lifeless shores of the aptly named Dead Sea. At one thousand feet below sea level this place is the lowest point on earth. So that was it. I had reached the lowest point on earth. I tried to console myself with the trite thought that sometimes you need to hit the bottom before you can come back up again, although I was well aware that this isn't always the case. (See Titanic for details.)

The bus made a fifteen minute stop in the resort of Ein Bokek. Well, the Israelis call it a resort but in reality it's just a few hotels built on the edge of the Dead Sea. It made Zichron Ya'acov seem like Las Vegas. People come here for the healing properties of the sulphuric hot springs, the beautifying properties of the thick black mud, and to float like zombies in a sea with a salt content six times denser than the Mediterranean. I walked down to the water's edge where a couple of Yorkshire lasses were wading hesitantly into the sea for their first 'swim'. Their boyfriends stood on the shore ready to catch the moment on film. The heavier of the two girls, called Laura, lowered herself into the water and was immediately buoyed up, her ample frame bobbing in the water like an apple in a bucket.

'Blimey, it works!' she screamed excitedly.

To me, her surprise seemed unjustified. Did she think that everyone who had come here to date had actually sunk, but that they'd all got together to concoct a story simply to fool her?

'This feels weird,' she exclaimed while reclining awkwardly on the water. 'This is a whole new feeling!'

Was it a whole new feeling? I looked at her there, lying on her back with her legs wide apart, and I don't know why but I doubted her for a moment.

According to Genesis,[4] it was along these shores that the Lord rained fire and brimstone on the people of Sodom and Gomorrah. The Lord, who seemed to have been ever so snappy and irritable around this time, also turned Lot's wife into a pillar of salt. Either that or Lot's wife had run off with another man and left a pillar of salt with a note pinned to it.

GOD HAS DONE THIS TO ME TO PUNISH YOU. TEA IS IN THE OVEN.
YOU'LL HAVE TO GET THE SHOPPING IN THOUGH – I FORGOT
(WE DON'T NEED SALT).

The bus journey continued south through the Negev in the direction of the Sinai desert. It was here that Moses had received the Ten Commandments from God, carved on to a tablet of stone. It is my view that a piece of that stone had broken off by the time chroniclers and historians found it, so there are vital bits missing from the commandments which we are urged to follow. For instance; Thou shalt not steal, Thou shalt not kill and Thou shalt not commit adultery – should read; Thou shalt not kill *time*, Thou shalt not steal

[4]It was the angel Peter Gabriel, I think.

glances, and thou shalt not commit adultery *that much*. Adherence to these would be so much simpler.

We arrived in Eilat ten minutes before the sun went down which is exactly the amount of daylight you need to get to know the place. The town is little more than a cluster of modern hotels nestled at the northernmost tip of the Red Sea. The most remarkable thing about it is that the airport is just a matter of yards from the beach. When it's time to leave you can simply pick up your bags and *walk* to the airport. Taxi drivers must hate this place. I dumped my bags at my hotel and strolled down to the water's edge. The Red Sea struck me as being particularly blue, but then I suppose the Blue Sea wouldn't have been a very imaginative name. The truth is that it had originally been named 'The Reed Sea', but the omission of an 'e' by a seventeenth-century English printer had turned it Red. The typographical error could have been worse; a 'p' instead of the 'r' and it would have ended up being called the Peed Sea. That would have made the swimmers think twice.

I went out that night looking for some fun but there was none to be had. Saddam's 'magnificent victory' over the Americans and British had fed people's irrational fear of getting bombed, so there were no big groups of pissy tourists to get lost among. Just a smattering of earnest travellers and long-haired Aussie divers. I had a meal in one of Eilat's many empty restaurants and walked back to my hotel feeling lost and alone. That night as I lay in my bed, I chanted a one-word mantra which I believed would lull me into a liberating slumber.

'Shit, shit, shit, shit, shit, shit, shit, shit, shit, shit, shit, shit . . .'

I wasn't taking this losing thing very well at all.

Over the next two days I tried to be a good tourist. I nurtured my tan, snorkelled and visited the Coral Underwater Observatory. None of it made me particularly happy. The trouble was that there was nothing around to snap me out of my present state of self-pity. I needed something to *happen*, or I needed to meet some people – anything to stop me feeling that all I was doing was killing time for three days until my flight left. It was crazy – I was spending my days sunbathing on the beaches of the Red Sea, occasionally swimming among exotic fish adjacent to the coral reefs, and all I wanted to do was go home. I couldn't help it, that was how I felt.

The *Jerusalem Post* turned out to be my ticket to freedom. This Israeli paper, which is printed in English, had enabled me to keep in touch with world events.[5] On my third morning of purgatory, I took tea on the hotel roof garden and thumbed through the sports pages to see if they would give any kind of update on the English football results. My eyes were drawn to a picture of two footballers locked in a tackle. There was nothing unusual in the photograph but the words written beneath it were intriguing, to say the least.

> **Lod's Yossie Arat is flattened in a clumsy tackle by Marin Spynu of Maccabi Kfar Kana, in yesterday's 1-1 draw.**

I studied the photograph more closely. The paper must have made a mistake. Neither player bore any resemblance to Marin Spynu. Mistakes happen all the time. I only had to look out over the Reed Sea for confirmation of that.

I put the paper down and returned to my tea, but my mind would not rest. If the paper had *not* made an error, and let's face it – that was also conceivable, then I had *not* played Marin Spynu. Could Johnny have screwed up and got the wrong player? Had his physiotherapist friend sent the wrong guy? I trawled my memory and recalled the conversation I'd had with Leonid, the sports journalist in Chisinau, who had told me that *two* Moldovan players were playing for this same club in Israel – Marin Spynu and Sergiu Nani. Could it just be that I had played the wrong one and the bet was still alive? I tried to block out all thoughts that told me that I was indulging in a large amount of straw-clutching.

As I dialled Johnny's number my heart was pumping hard, desperate to deal with the new levels of hope which were coursing through my veins.

'Hello, Johnny?'

'Yes.'

'It's Tony Hawks here.'

[5]For 'world events' read 'Bill Clinton and Monica Lewinsky'.

'Oh thank goodness you've called, we've been desperate to get hold of you, but we haven't known how to. We've been phoning England to see if anyone knew where you were.'

'Why?'

'Because that wasn't Marin Spynu that you played in Zichron.'

Yes! I punched the air.

'I thought as much,' I said, 'there was a cock-up and that was the other Moldovan – Sergiu Nani, wasn't it?'

'I wish it was that innocent,' he said, nervously. 'The fact is we played a trick on you Tony. The guy you played wasn't Moldovan at all. He was a local tennis pro. Arthur put me up to this I'm afraid. It was all a practical joke – but I was supposed to tell you after the game. It all went wrong when I couldn't get there. I'm sorry. I'm really sorry.'

How embarrassing, I'd been duped. The fact that this scam had been so successful was either a tribute to Arthur's initiative or to my gormlessness. I thought for a moment and then decided it was the latter. There had been clues which I had overlooked. For starters, the ease in which the whole match had been arranged. I should have known that something was amiss when it all fell into place so easily. Experience had shown that you couldn't just lift a phone and then be on court with a Moldovan footballer. You had to suffer, you had to sweat, and you had to grovel.

Another clue had been something the phoney Spynu had said to me after the match;

'Thanks be to you.'

No Moldovan had said that to me in all my three week stay there, when they did manage some English they always got 'thank you' right. 'Thanks be to you' was clearly the language of someone *pretending* that they couldn't speak English.

'Have you told Arthur what happened?' I asked, returning my attention to the guilt-ridden Johnny.

'Yes, and he thinks it's hilarious that you believe that you've lost. He says that he's not going to tell you that the thing was a set-up until you've finished singing the Moldovan National anthem – naked.'

'The sly bastard. I'll get him back for this.'

'How?'

'I don't know yet, but I'll think of something.'

'If there's anything I can to do to help, just let me know.'

'My, you switch allegiance pretty quick.'

'Well, I've messed up your trip – I feel awful.'

'You can do one thing for me Johnny – if Arthur calls, don't tell him that you've spoken to me.'

'OK. And listen, I've got you the mobile phone number of a guy called Faisal who seems to run the club Maccabi Kfar Kana, let me give it to you – it might speed things up for you.'

'Thanks.'

I took down the number, accepted yet more apologies, and hung up. I forgave Johnny. He was just a nice guy who'd fallen under the influence of evil for a short while, that's all. It could happen to any of us.

I went straight to the hotel reception and checked out. With a spring in my step I hot-footed it to the bus station, confident that I no longer required the heat of Eilat's winter sun. Now I was warm on the inside, where it counted.

According to the map, the village of Kfar Kana was only a few miles up the road from Nazareth so this seemed like the most logical place to use for base. It made perfect sense to me that a story such as mine, which had taken on such biblical proportions, should end here in the place where one of greatest and most famous stories in the world had begun. It was here that the Angel Gabriel brought Mary the news of her forthcoming virgin birth; it was here that Mary was charged with selling this information to a confused and slightly insecure Joseph, and it was here that Jesus grew up and worked as a carpenter.

Actually, it has always struck me as being rather odd that Jesus should have spent so long studying and honing his carpentry skills and then not used any of them during his ministry. We read how he turned water into wine, fed the five thousand and took a bit of a stroll on some water, but there's never a mention of him stopping off anywhere and putting some shelves up for anybody. Never once is he reported as saying:

'Arise now, and ye shall walk – oh and while I'm here, you don't want me to knock you up a bookcase to go beside the settee, do you?'

Being the kind of chap he was, I think that's exactly the kind of warm-hearted thing Jesus would have done, but the fact is that the chroniclers of his story were trying to market him as the Son of God and probably felt it was an easier sell if people didn't see him as the kind of bloke who carried a Black & Decker Workmate around with him wherever he went. If they'd have been invented then he surely would have done. That's Messiahs for you – they're just your average human being who happens to have a shedload of wisdom. The New Messiah will most likely be an ordinary type too: a plumber, a school caretaker or a postman. I wouldn't have a problem with that; I'd happily follow him just as long as he didn't have a great big bunch of keys on his belt. You have to draw the line somewhere.

I don't know what I had been expecting, but Nazareth was something of a disappointment. Roadworks were everywhere. Apparently the town was gearing up for 'Millennium Fever' and the expected rush of religious pilgrims and unhinged fanatics who intended to come here and commemorate the momentous occasion by doing anything from praying quietly to committing suicide en masse. Religious cults which incorporate suicide as an end to the day's activities seem to be becoming more and more common. I just wonder whether they mention it in their publicity when recruiting new membership.

JOIN THE CULT OF THE SOLAR TEMPLE
FOR EXCITING NIGHTS OF PRAYER, TABLE TENNIS
AND EVENTUAL SUICIDE

(Delete as applicable)
I prefer to be buried/cremated/used for dodgy experiments.

The first two hotels I called at were full, but the man in the second one, which was a Roman Catholic hospice, said that I should find a vacancy with the Sisters of Nazareth. The Guest House wing of a convent didn't seem like the most exciting place in the world to stay, but since I was growing tired of lugging my bags around, it would have to do.

The convent stood behind a forbidding wall and was arranged

around a magnificent courtyard complete with fountain and palm trees. Nuns criss-crossed it, eager to go about their business. For a moment I stood there, bags at my feet, dazzled by this exquisite scene. No doubt about it, I had missed my vocation. I should have been a nun. Maybe they'd let me join? I could found the tennis department. All I would ask is that they let me off 6.00 am prayers – I'd just pray twice as hard after breakfast.

'Your room is over on ze left,' said Sister Anne Marie in a strong French accent, clearly disconcerted by the way I'd been eyeing the place. 'Zair is a nine o'clock curfew.'

In by nine o'clock, righto. I would have to give Nazareth's Studio 54 a miss tonight.

That night I again ate in a restaurant where I was the sole diner. Single-handedly I was keeping the Israeli tourist industry ticking over. After a kebab designed to give courage, I called Faisal, the boss man of Maccabi Kfar Kana. I was nervous. If Faisal was obstructive then life would be very difficult indeed. My mobile connected with his and a precarious signal afforded us the kind of conversation two people might share who were shouting through a six foot thick stone wall. Everything was repeated four times and nothing was properly understood. Thank God for mobile communication. From what I could make out though, Faisal had not been hostile and I was under the impression that he had invited me to training in the morning. This would have been better news if the signal hadn't disappeared before I could find out where it was taking place. Never mind, I would think of something.

I returned to the convent at 8.59 pm, having been careful not to have wasted the time available to me in the free world, and I went to make a hot drink in the area designated as communal lounge and kitchen. Here I made the acquaintance of two Japanese guys and a Frenchman called Jean. The Japanese didn't speak much English and Jean didn't speak much sense. The combination of these two factors made for a painful twenty minutes. They say that a watched kettle never boils (from my experience I've found that the same is true if you don't push that little button in at the back) and boy was I watching that kettle. It turned out that all three of my new chums were religious pilgrims who were keen to quote the Bible whenever possible, Jean with an unstoppable enthusiasm. He was a nice enough chap and, to be fair, he did give me quite a lot of his biscuits, but I did have to suffer 'how he found God' in return. It was a fair trade though. They were good biscuits. Good biscuits were turning out to be about all I could hope for in the fun department on this trip. Oh well, just do the job you came here for, I told myself, after all I was closing in on the real Spynu.

According to the Gospel of John it was in the Arab village of Kfar Kana that Jesus performed his first miracle – turning water into wine at a wedding feast, a trick that is always going to see you pretty high up on the list when the invitations are being drawn up.

'Who shall we invite?'

'Well, Jesus would be good. He's ever such a nice fellow. And cancel that order with Oddbins.'

My miracle, though small in comparison, is still worthy of a mention. Having alighted from the Nazareth bus, I was standing in the middle of Kfar Kana's deserted main street unsure of what to do next, when a car pulled up in front of me and a young man got out and moved towards the bread shop behind me.

'Excuse me,' I asked, 'but is there a football ground anywhere round here?'

'Why do you want to know?' he replied.

'Because I'm going there.'

'Me too, wait here, I will take you in my car.'

This guy turned out to be Wasim, one of Maccabi Kfar Kana's footballers who was on the way to training. OK not water into wine, but not bad for a beginner.

What was to follow was quite at odds with my Moldovan 'football experience'. At the ground Wasim introduced me to a handsome-looking man called Mywan.

'Ah Tony, pleased to meet you. Faisal told us you were coming. You are most welcome.'

Mywan was a former player who was now the club's general manager. He was also so charming and friendly that I decided he was my hero.

'Would you like some tea?' he enquired.

Tea. I'd been offered *tea*. No-one in the Moldovan world of football had even come close to offering me a cup of tea.

'Ooh, yes please Mywan, I'd love one.'

A young lad was sent scurrying off to fetch me one and when he returned, I held the cup proudly in my hands. Each sip confirmed for me that I was among friends. I was introduced to Baruch, a big man whose figure provided his track suit with lavish contours. He was from Moldova and was both Marin Spynu and Sergiu Nani's agent, his implausible job being to facilitate the movement of footballers from Moldova to Israel. I assumed his company was called 'Wilderness Transfers Ltd'. I explained to him why I was stood here at an Israeli second division football club's training ground and he laughed heartily, especially at the mention of the naked anthem singing.

'So you played Miterev?' he said.

'Yes, he was the first one actually.'

'And Testimitanu?'

'Yes.'

'I was trying to bring him out here. What about Sischin?'

And so the conversation went on, the surprising arrival of this eccentric Englishman affording Baruch the opportunity to remind himself of the country and friends he'd left behind.

'Do you think Marin would agree to play tennis with me?' I asked, cautiously.

'I don't see why not. You know that he doesn't speak any English?'

'Yes, I was wondering if you might translate for me?'

'No problem.'

Mywan arrived with another cup of tea. I did like it here.

Coincidentally the real Spynu didn't look unlike the phoney one had done. Similar height, similar hair colour and similar features. Just as long as his tennis bore no similarities, I would be happy. Baruch introduced me to him and I was greeted with the now familiar combination of confusion and shyness. It transpired that neither he nor Sergiu Nani had heard a thing about me. Evidently to Moldovan footballers, an Englishman who had devoted months of his time traversing the world in their hot pursuit did not constitute news.

They didn't indulge in long phone calls with colleagues catching up on news and gossip. The Moldovan footballer says what needs to be said and then gets on with the business in hand with an air of resigned stoicism.

Baruch explained to Marin what was expected of him and he listened and nodded obediently.

'He will play you tomorrow morning,' said Baruch assuredly.

'Fantastic. Where?'

'In Nazareth. He lives there. In fact if you go with Sergiu and Marin now, they will give you a lift back to your hotel.'

Convent actually, but I didn't bother to correct him.

'Great.'

And so I left the ground in a car with two Moldovan footballers, having achieved more in a few hours than I had done in two weeks in Moldova. Mywan had given me a Maccabi Kfar Kana scarf and rosette, and invited me as a guest of honour to their next home game. I'd thanked him profusely and told him that I would do everything I could to be there, not having the heart to tell him that by then I would be back in England. I felt real regret that I would not have time to get to know these people better. They'd shown a genuine kindliness and desire to help. I hope they win the Cup.

It couldn't have been the way he had expected to see his Wembley team-mates again but Marin chuckled all the way back to Nazareth as I showed him the footage of them playing me at tennis on the small video screen on my camera. Now he had seen with his own eyes that I was no fraud. He must have been relieved to know that I had genuinely travelled the world in pursuit of the Moldovan national football team and wasn't just some loony who had turned up at the training ground.

'You can drop me here,' I said, after the car had successfully negotiated Nazareth's roadworks and drawn up alongside the Church of the Annunciation.

'OK, we see you tomorrow at 10.30 at the tennis courts,' replied Sergiu in his hesitant English.

'Yes, 10.30,' I confirmed, getting out of the car and looking up at the towering edifice beside me. 'It's a fine church isn't it?' I declared in an attempt at parting small talk. 'Did you know that it's the largest church in the Middle East?'

'Yes, at 10.30,' replied Sergiu.

I hoped that Spynu played tennis as well as Sergiu spoke English.

I took breakfast at 8.30 am and set off for Nazareth's only tennis courts on the stroke of nine. It was way too early but I had taken the precaution of building a 'getting a bit lost' hour into my schedule – after all, directions to the courts had been provided by a Moldovan with only a sketchy command of English. As I left the convent there was a coachload of American Christians at the entrance waiting to check in. They looked at me askance as I left this holy sanctuary dressed in white shorts, holding two tennis rackets and a video camera, and wearing a green and white 'Maccabi Kfar Kana' scarf around my neck. I wasn't the average pilgrim, by any means.

'Morning – lovely day for it,' I said, knowing that by addressing them directly it would contribute still further to their discomfort.

'Good morning,' replied one bold one. 'And may God go with ya!'

'Thanks.'

I wasn't sure if God was going to come with me, but He'd shown an interest in this part of the world before, and this morning's action on a Nazarene tennis court might offer Him some light relief from organising floods, typhoons and earthquakes. I felt confident of winning. Even if Spynu was good, I had the competitive work-out of the tough match against the fake Spynu behind me, and I reckoned I was in good shape. My only concern was that for some reason he might not show up. My flight home left the next day. It was now or never. *Please* don't let me down Mr Spynu, *please*.

A jovial Arab taxi driver took me to Nazerat Illit, the modern Jewish neighbourhood on the outskirts of ancient Nazareth, where sure enough, exactly where Sergiu had said, a reassuring spread of tennis courts greeted me. The commentator in my head began again:

'And so Hawks has a reprieve. He has already tasted defeat and he knows he doesn't like it. Surely this morning, in this holiest of places, when the final act of his epic struggle is played out, victory will be his. There is no crowd, but that does not diminish the significance of this moment. Hawks is carrying the hopes of the world on his able shoulders. If he wins then the world will be–'

'My God, shut up Tony!' said another, more balanced, voice in my head. 'You're losing your mind. Just play Spynu and sod off home.'

Yeah okay, maybe you're right. A touch of humility wouldn't go amiss.

Marin Spynu had humility in abundance. At a delightfully punctual 10.30 he strode unassumingly on to the tennis court with his friend Sergiu, and shook my hand, revealing just a hint of a smile. I noticed the good news straight away. He had no tennis racket. I handed him my spare one and he made his way up to the far end of the court and we began hitting with each other. Well, to be more precise, I began hitting and he began missing. To my relief, Spynu did play tennis as well as his compatriot spoke English.

Fifteen minutes of tennis was played which was worthy of the crowd it had attracted. One. In fact, technically it wasn't even one because Sergiu had taken on the role of ball-boy throughout the whole one-sided affair. At match point, I put in a good first serve which Spynu was only able to return into the net, and I leapt the net in triumph. A slightly embarrassed Spynu shook my hand and I waved to an imaginary stand of adoring fans.

'I have done it!' I cried. 'I have beaten the entire Moldovan National football team at tennis.'

I had too. And the film was in my video camera which would prove it.

I was deeply grateful to Marin Spynu. He had been the eleventh Moldovan footballer to have walked on to a tennis court purely to facilitate the completion of a stranger's whimsical bet. There had been nothing in it for any of them, and none had expected anything in return. No big egos had barred my route, instead they had all been pleasant and co-operative and, most pleasingly of all, reassuringly bad at tennis. I could unequivocally reach the following conclusion:

MOLDOVAN FOOTBALLERS ARE A NICE BUNCH

It seemed bizarre that I had spent so much time in pursuit of these footballers and so little time actually getting to know them. Hey, maybe one of them would get transferred to England and I could take him out for a beer. Yes, I liked that idea a lot. I would definitely do that. As I walked to the taxi rank I allowed this thought to comfort me. It would be my way of saying thanks.

19

The Final Tackle

Leaving the Holy Land wasn't as easy as it might have been. Given that Israel is keen to boost its economy by encouraging tourism, the security policy at the airport constitutes something of a spectacular own goal. Before the traveller reaches the check-in desk, a heavily badged official takes each traveller aside to ask 'security questions'. These are not merely routine – these zealots give you a full twenty-minute grilling about your entire stay in Israel. When asked for the reason for my visit, I felt it wise not to mention that it had been to play and beat my eleventh and final Moldovan footballer. I may have been considered too dangerous to allow on to an aircraft. Instead I maintained that I'd been in the country for pleasure, and to meet with my Israeli publisher. As soon as I had done this, my interrogator asked me for Daniela's phone number so he could ring and have her verify my story.

'Are you suggesting that I'm lying to you?' I asked, patently riled.

'No sir. It's just that we have to be thorough.'

I gave him the number and he went off, made the call, and returned with the words 'That is OK.' But still further questions followed.

'Have you spoken to any Arabs while you have been here?'

This irritated me greatly.

'Can I ask you why you are asking me these questions?'

'You must understand that we have to be very strict with our security because of the sensitive political situation here.'

'That's as may be, but I'm trying to *leave* your country, not enter it. What is the point of asking me these questions now?'

'That is our business. Could you please tell me if you have spoken to any Arabs whilst you have been here.'

'And if I answer no – who are you going to call to verify that I'm telling the truth?'

The security man disappeared, presumably to ask how to deal with people who answer questions with questions. I hoped that the supervisor's answer would be 'How should I know?'

While I waited, I overheard the guy at the next desk being asked to produce hotel receipts which would verify his movements within Israel. A thorough search of his baggage then followed before he was finally thanked by the security officer and then wished a pleasant flight. The extraordinary thing was that throughout his entire interrogation there had been a magazine on the desk beside his bag which the security officer had failed to notice. I couldn't help thinking that it might have been worth a question or two, given that it was a magazine called *Handguns*.

After ten minutes of further questions by a different officer I was finally deemed safe enough to allow out of the country, and I boarded the plane with all the other disgruntled passengers, many of whom were so affronted by their treatment that they were swearing never to visit this country again. Israel has many things to put right, but perhaps they should start with the easy ones – like not causing people to leave with a nasty taste in the mouth.

I drank champagne on the plane and bored the American lady next to me with all the details of my heroic story.

'And will this guy Arthur really strip butt naked?' she enquired.

'He'd better.'

'What will you do if he doesn't?'

That was a point, I hadn't thought of that.

'He'll do it. I'm sure of it.'

'I hope you're right.'

I hoped I was too. I didn't want to have to go to the European Court of Human Rights.

2 March 1999 was the big night, and I'd booked The Bedford pub in Balham for the event. It would be one of the more unconventional evenings which its Function Room would host. Arthur was looking pretty smug when he arrived. Good. This meant that he had taken the bait. It would make for a more interesting evening.

On my return Arthur, naturally enough, had wanted to know the outcome of my Middle Eastern endeavours.

'So what happened then, Hawks?' he croaked down the phone, his vocal chords evident victims of recent excess.

'You'll have to wait until I present all my evidence in the pub,' I answered, unforthcomingly.

'Alright, I suppose that's fair,' he muttered with a pleasingly uncharacteristic insouciance.

Normally in a situation like this he would have kept on at me, desperately trying to discover the truth, but on this occasion he had no need since he already knew it. Or at least the *version* of the truth which I had wanted him to believe. Good old Johnny had kept schtum about what had really happened in Israel and Arthur had most probably been party to whispers among our mutual friends that my final match had provided something of an upset, since I'd provided the relevant information to a select few who could be relied upon to gossip.

'Can you keep a secret?' I had said, already knowing the answer.

'Yes.'

'Well, the last guy Spynu was really good and I went and bloody lost.'

'You're joking.'

'I'm not, but don't tell anyone yet will you?'

'No, of course not.'

Forty-eight hours later and that would have filtered its way back to Arthur, and everything would be in place for the denouement.

Despite being a miserable wet cold March night, the turn-out was pretty damn good. The promise in the invitation that 'At the end of the evening either Arthur or Tony will strip naked and sing the Moldovan National Anthem in Balham High Road' may have persuaded a few waverers to attend. One very special guest was Corina from the Journalism Centre in Chisinau who was studying for a few months in Oxford and had been able to make it down to London for the evening. It was wonderful to see her again, although she seemed smaller and quieter than I remembered her. Perhaps she was a little overawed by the raucous and boozy atmosphere of a Balham pub's back room. I could not imagine a more stark contrast to the world she knew in Moldova.

'I am looking forward to seeing how your little adventure ends,' she said as she arrived.

'I hope you brought a magnifying glass,' said a cheeky bystander, who thought he knew the outcome.

Corina smiled politely and took her seat with the rest of this specially invited and expectant audience. I felt strangely reassured having her here, delighted by the pleasing circular shape it brought to my journey. Corina had been one of the first people I had met in Moldova and now here she was six months later sitting a few feet from me at the finale of the whole ludicrous bet. Her physical presence in this pub somehow confirmed to me that the whole thing hadn't just been a bizarre dream. Corina was real. I really *had* done what I was about to recount to the assembled throng gathered before me.

Arthur kicked proceedings off, his many years of experience in hosting evenings of comedy cabaret meaning that there were few better able to perform such a task.

'Welcome to this evening's unusual entertainment,' he began, as at ease behind the microphone as most of us would be behind the wheel of a car or doing the washing up. 'My name is Arthur Smith, unless there is anyone here from Streatham Tax Office in which case my name is Daphne Fairfax.'

This prompted a huge cheer from a section of the audience whose love for this venerable old line had not diminished since they had first started listening to it fifteen years previously. After a brief bow which acknowledged the age of his opening gag, Arthur continued:

'Tonight, as a result of a bet which Tony Hawks and I made some eighteen months ago which I believe you all know about, one of us within the hour will be standing naked on Balham High Road, singing the Moldovan National Anthem.'

Big cheers. I looked at Corina who was both laughing and shaking her head incredulously. It was almost as if the whole time I'd been in Moldova she had never really believed that there were two people in England who were really foolish enough to see this thing through to its bear, naked, ballsy conclusion.

'Generally speaking,' continued Arthur, adopting a playfully deprecating tone, 'comedians like getting drunk, taking drugs and staying up late. Tony likes playing tennis. He is ranked 45th in Britain, which means he's at number 88 million in the world rankings – slightly below Cliff Richard. Anyway, the point is that, magnificently, he has spent the last six months chasing Moldovan footballers around the globe and he is now here to make a rather dull presentation of his evidence. I do not know who won this bet, in fact only Tony knows – so welcome him now so we can all find out – Tony Hawks.'

A confident-looking Arthur handed me the microphone and I began a talk about Moldova and outlined some of the difficulties that I had faced. The audience listened politely and attentively but I couldn't help thinking that a good proportion of them were keen for Arthur and me to get to what could be described as the 'meat of the evening'. For some tonight wasn't 'Playing the Moldovans at Tennis' – it was a show called 'Which Penis?'[6]

As I recounted my story I felt something of a glow of pride, for I had succeeded where, for a while at least, failure had seemed inevitable. When the moment arrived to present the video evidence of my tennis victories, I sat back in my chair and watched the events on the screen with a peculiar detachment. It seemed that time was allowing me an objectivity which meant that it was almost in disbelief that I watched myself vanquishing Moldovan footballer after Moldovan footballer on a tennis court in downtown Chisinau. Had I *really* done that?

The mood in the room changed when I began to show the footage of the phoney Marin Spynu. Gasps of horror. Mumbles of 'Blimey, he's a bit good isn't he?' Exactly the feelings I'd had at the time of the game. I felt them again now too, but they were easier to handle this time round, sharing them as I was with a roomful of people. And knowing the truth. Ah yes, the truth, the wonderful truth. I glanced at Arthur to gauge his reaction. He was smiling, as well he might.

[6]Surely it's only a question of time before the BBC runs a show along these lines. Well, I'd just like to state here and now that if they do, then I don't want to be the host.

Spynu struck his final backhand passing shot past me as I languished at the net, and the audience let out a big roar. No-one had expected this. Through a deluge of cheers and taunts I made my way forlornly to the microphone.

'So that is it. It was a case of so near and yet so far. Ten beaten but I'm afraid I fell at the last hurdle.'

'Aaahs' from the audience.

'In a moment I shall invite you to follow me outside where I will remove all my clothes and sing the Moldovan anthem, but for now I shall hand the microphone over to Arthur who may wish to say a few words in victory.'

Arthur strode proudly to the stage, the victor.

'There was a rather beautiful structure to that – Tony, smug throughout those first ten fixtures, easily beating footballers who had clearly never played tennis before in their lives. He met his match and he was beaten finally, so now it's time for him to take his clothes off. We know about Tony's tan – but is he tanned all over? Soon we will find out. All I'll say now is that after we have seen Tony naked and singing the Moldovan national anthem we will all re-adjourn here where I will have something further to say, germane to the subject. But do we want to see Tony with his kit off?'

Big cheers of approval. But I was about to play my trump card. I wrenched the microphone from Arthur's grasp.

'Before we all make our way outside, I just think you ought to know what happened immediately after I lost that match'

I now showed a final piece of film in which I had re-created my discovery of the real Spynu in the newspaper. The ever more vocal audience reacted noisily to this exposure of attempted sabotage, and I glanced at Arthur and saw him laughing sheepishly, like the naughty boy in the class who had been found out by teacher. On the screen, the story continued to unfold – my journey to Nazareth and subsequent location and defeat of the bona fide Marin Spynu. There was great excitement and expectation in the room now that all had been revealed. Well, not all, there was still the small matter of Arthur's penis, although he mightn't wish it to be described thus.

Arthur returned to the microphone to a chorus of both cheers and boos. Panto season had come early this year.

'It seems that Tony found out about my ringer,' he declared resignedly. 'I'm disappointed in a way because I thought they'd have been good, those footballers. They're young, they're fit, they're athletes – and yet they were all shit.'

Arthur looked at me, and I smiled back smugly. I was savouring my moment, and why not? I'd gone to quite a bit of trouble to get to this point, so I figured it was time to enjoy it. Unfortunately the expression on my face did not register with Arthur, who I noticed for the first time was now magnificently drunk. He had clearly accelerated his drinking during the presentation of my evidence and had arrived at a level of inebriation which would be distinctly advantageous given the nature of his imminent task. He wasn't dribbling, but he wasn't far off. 'I'm not afraid of what I've got to do,' he announced proudly without slurring, the power of coherent speech being the last of Arthur's faculties to surrender to drink. 'I've had some collagen implants put into my penis this morning and it's about forty-two inches long.'

We all giggled like schoolchildren. Corina included.

A bizarre spectacle followed in which a crowd of around eighty people spilled out on to the streets of Balham and marched up the pavement to a suitable location on Balham High Road. It was decided that the unveiling should take place outside Woolworths, and Arthur prepared himself. A megaphone was handed to him and he addressed the expectant gathering of voyeurs before him.

'Any women who see me naked singing this national anthem tonight and fancy a bit of slap and tickle, please form a queue to my left after the event.'

Cigarette in hand, he proceeded to strip to his underpants as cheers echoed down the High Road. Cries of 'Off! Off! Off!' ensued. Arthur then delivered a sentence which I feel will only ever be uttered once.

'I am an honest man and I am a just man, and when the music strikes up I will genuinely remove my pants.'

There's one for the century's book of best quotations.

I pressed play on the ghettoblaster, handed Arthur the Romanian words, and the dirty deed was done as, fag still in hand, he slid his pants over his ankles and held them aloft. The group who had previously been shouting 'Off! Off! Off!' immediately amended their chant to 'On! On! On!' but to no avail. Arthur stood before us all in his birthday suit. The great 'Tailor in the sky' had made better ones – but no matter, nudity was what this crowd had come for and nudity was what they had unequivocally got. The moment of revelation was greeted by a disordered mixture of cheers, gasps of disbelief, shrieks of horror and hysterical laughter. One only hopes this is not the reaction Arthur gets every time he undresses.

My reaction was different from everyone else's. For me, this larger than life comedy moment represented the end of a long journey which hadn't always been easy. The ludicrous sight before me filled me with a great sense of achievement causing my breast almost to puff up with pride. In fact it was a little worrying that the sight of another man's penis could mean so much to me.

Arthur, it has to be said, was a triumph. He battled gamely with the Romanian words which he sang with gusto through the megaphone, in spite of only being handed them only seconds earlier. For a full one minute thirty-five seconds, those gathered by this roadside in London SW12 were privy to a highly individual rendition of the Moldovan national anthem. Passers by looked on in amazement. A crowd quickly developed outside the pub opposite as the word went round that something most unusual was taking place over the road. Traffic slowed but a mass of bodies prevented drivers from seeing what we could all see only too clearly; a man stood stark naked in front of Woolworths singing the Moldovan national anthem through a megaphone.

One minute into the performance I noticed that people began pointing behind Arthur and into Woolworths itself, whereupon they burst into fresh fits of giggles. The reason became clear as I looked myself and saw that the Woolworths security cameras were recording the whole thing on a large TV screen inside the store. It presented the rear view of a bare arse, and beyond it a large crowd of people staring at a penis and laughing. It would make for some interesting conjecture from the security guards when they viewed the tapes in the morning.

'. . . I see what you're saying Bob, and that's a possible theory, but it still doesn't really explain the megaphone.'

As we walked back to the pub I sought out Corina. She was the only person who had been there at the very beginning and the very end of my story.

'Was that a moving experience for you?' I asked.

'It was funny,' she replied with a smile. 'Tony, I want to tell you that I am very happy for you. It is good that you won this bet and I think I know you better now.'

'Surely it's Arthur that you know better.'

'Yes, him also!' she laughed.

'Corina, can I ask you something in all seriousness?'

'OK.'

'Do you think this has all been a frivolous waste of time and money?'

She scratched her head, almost as if answering this was going to require all the brainpower at her disposal.

'Generally, all of us in Moldova were thinking that you were a little bit crazy when you arrived, but now I understand why you did it. In time I look at things differently, and maybe it is making sense to me now because I am seeing you in your own country.'

'Really? It still doesn't make any sense to me. I thought it would after tonight, but I'm still confused by it all.'

'That is because it is confusing. You have seen our country and all its problems – the transition to a system we don't know yet, poverty, and being ignored by the outer world. You have seen that we don't laugh as much as we should, I think. Maybe when people in Moldova will have everything they need, they will start doing these things like your bet, just to have fun.'

Of course, Corina hadn't really answered my original question.

But maybe all that mattered was that a certain family of four in Moldova might gain strength from the fact that Tony cel Mare had finally lived up to his name.

Epilogue

Two weeks later, a letter bearing Moldovan stamps dropped on to my doormat. It was from Adrian.

Congratulations Tony!

We are all so happy that you won the bet. Well done! Long live Tony cel Mare!

We all miss you and think of you often – you brought some real English spirit to our house. Things are the same in Moldova. We are having a really good, soft weather after a cold winter. (We had plenty of snow this year.) I finally finished my half year studies with really good grades. My sister has better marks since you visited her English class and she is really happy about that. My Dad is on a diet now and my mother is doing her best cooking dietetic meals. Elena and I made a bet not to watch T.V. for a week. This will be a hard one – nearly as hard as yours!

I am anxious to read your book about our country, so don't be lazy, and finish it as fast as possible. I also hope James Cameron or Steven Spielberg are ready to shoot the movie about your adventures in Moldova. (In that case I'll be able to see you at the next Oscar awards.)

You did the MOST IMPOSSIBLE THING, although it seemed as something that nobody could accomplish. That is a good lesson for me and from now on I'll try and follow your example in everything I do.

With Sincerity
Adrian

Now it all made a little more sense.